The Ultimate Band Saw Box Book

Donna LaChance Menke

Sterling Publishing Co., Inc.
New York

Photographs and drawings by the author.

LIBRARY OF CONGRESS CATALOGING-IN-PUBLICATION DATA
Menke, Donna LaChance.
  The ultimate band saw box book / Donna LaChance Menke.
     p. cm.
  Includes index.
  ISBN-13: 978-1-4027-2193-9
  ISBN-10: 1-4027-2193-5
  1. Woodwork. 2. Wooden boxes. 3. Band saws. I. Title.

TT200.M37 2006
684'.08--dc22

                                                                2006013636

10 9 8 7 6 5 4 3 2 1

Published by Sterling Publishing Co., Inc.
387 Park Avenue South, New York, NY 10016
©2006 by Donna LaChance Menke
Distributed in Canada by Sterling Publishing
$^{c}/_{o}$ Canadian Manda Group, 165 Dufferin Street
Toronto, Ontario, Canada M6K 3H6
Distributed in the United Kingdom by GMC Distribution Services
Castle Place, 166 High Street, Lewes, East Sussex, England BN7 1XU
Distributed in Australia by Capricorn Link (Australia) Pty. Ltd.
P.O. Box 704, Windsor, NSW 2756, Australia

Printed in China

Sterling ISBN-13: 978-1-4027-2193-9
        ISBN-10: 1-4027-2193-5

For information about custom editions, special sales, premium and
corporate purchases, please contact Sterling Special Sales
Department at 800-805-5489 or specialsales@sterlingpub.com.

Preface

As a child growing up in Massachusetts, I loved to play in the woodworking shops of my father and grandfather. They didn't mind if I played with the curls of wood off the plane. As my brother and I got older, they let us tear apart the pallets from which they got the wood that they used for most of their projects. I was a champ with a crowbar. Nothing was wasted; even the nails were straightened for reuse. My talented mother taught me to try everything; my father encouraged me to do the very best job possible; and they both showed me how important it was to have lots of patience.

My time in higher education was spent learning about art, science, English, engineering, and scientific illustration. At the age of 47 I was awarded a B.A. in art history, with honors, and a B.F.A. in studio art from the University of Texas at Austin. In addition to drawing and painting in various media, I have done pottery, stained glass, and illustration.

My first power tool was a 12" band saw, purchased in 1972. It is still my favorite tool. I had a great time making puzzles and ornaments over the years. I also took a few adult education courses where I made some furniture. Oiling my first piece, a maple-and-walnut cutting board, and watching the dull, dry wood pop into glorious color and depth, started my fascination with working wood.

I have been woodcarving since 1995, and I've enjoyed teaching others how to carve for the Texas Woodcarvers Guild and for other carving groups since 1996. Woodworking became a passion for me when I started to work for the Austin Texas Woodcraft store, where I taught "woodworking for women" classes. Constant contact with other woodworkers kept my interest high. In band saw boxes I found a technique that used all the interests I have had through the years. I carve on many of the boxes and use math and engineering for developing new ideas. Experience as a draftsman has helped me to draw plans and to illustrate the projects that I use when teaching classes.

These boxes are the ideal medium for artistic self-expression, and making them has been lots of fun. I know you will enjoy making these boxes as much as I did.

ACKNOWLEDGMENTS

I'd like to thank my husband, Raymond, for his support and encouragement during the process of making this book. To our grown children, Benjamin and Rebecca, who still seem to think that Mom can do anything, I thank you. My parents and grandparents taught by example that doing a good job was important and that being able to make things with your hands was an admirable quality. To my brother Mike, thanks for being there with advice and affection. To Tom Crabb, thanks for bringing the infinite possibilities of band saw boxes to my attention with your book. Thanks also to S. Gary Roberts, for aiming me in the right direction to make my dream come true. To Marnie Whillock, editor of *Carving Magazine*, thank you for allowing me to hone my communication skills by publishing my how-to articles in that magazine. To all the woodworking women and band saw box makers out there, thanks; I was encouraged by your enthusiasm for my project.

Contents

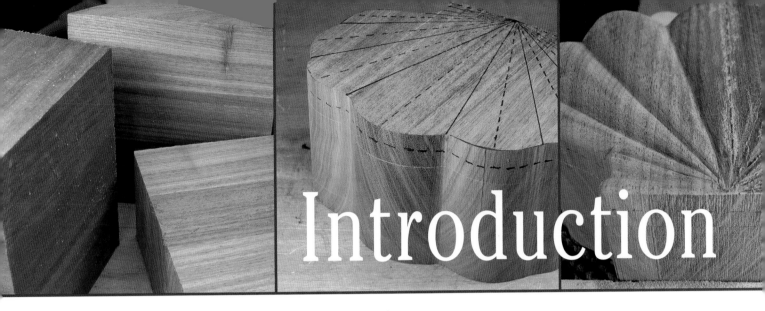

Introduction

I've always wanted to make wooden boxes, but until recently I had neither the tools nor skills required to make them. In 1998, while working at a store for woodworkers, I was excited to discover a technique of making wooden boxes that I could handle: band saw boxes. These boxes were beautiful and easy to make, and they used tools with which I was

comfortable: the band saw and the belt sander. I made many simple nesting oval boxes (Figs. 1 and 2) before looking for new techniques and styles. The books that were available did not answer the questions I had, so I researched all the books and magazine articles I could find to discover different ways of making band saw boxes.

As I accumulated a notebook full of design ideas, it became clear that I had the makings for a book on my favorite subject, band saw boxes. Such a book would cover band saw use and work safety, project design considerations, construction, and finishing techniques. It would include a series of projects using a wide variety of designs and construction techniques. I decided to write this book.

Since I began making boxes, I've acquired a full shop of wonderful tools that have enabled me to make boxes of every sort. But I still consider making boxes on the band saw the easiest, safest, and in many ways the best construction technique.

Band saw boxes don't require a shop full of expensive tools, they have unlimited design potential, and they are easy to make. Conventional boxes are usually rectangular and are made using a table saw and often a planer, joiner, and router. These tools require a considerable investment in both money and space. For those of us limited in one or both of these categories, a band saw and sander may be all we need to make beautiful boxes.

Band saws are inherently safer to use

FIG. I My first band saw box was an oval box made from lacewood. It wasn't difficult to make and it looked great to me.

FIG. 2 After flocking the interior, my lacewood box looked even better. What an accomplishment for a first try; I was ready for more.

than table saws. It is rare to get a dangerous kickback on the band saw because the blade is pushing the wood against the table, not toward the user. There are safety precautions that you need to follow, but serious accidents are easy to avoid.

Because a band saw uses a small, flexible blade that can cut curves in wood, your designs are not restricted to straight or flat planes. On the other hand, it is difficult to create straight and flat planes with a band saw. That is where the sander comes in handy to straighten out and square up the rough cuts generated by the band saw blade.

Then there is the *magic* of making boxes on the band saw. When the block of wood is cut apart and put back together again, you will have a guaranteed fit, because the reunited edges were cut by the same

blade at the same time. They are complementary parts and will fit back together like a key in a lock (Fig. 3). Unlike dovetail or miter joints, which are difficult to make perfect and to square up, a band-sawn joint works every time.

Band saw boxes in this book are defined as made from a block of wood, using just a band saw, a sander, and a drill. The block of wood may be cut from a log, purchased ready to use, or laminated using pieces of lumber.

A scroll saw could be used to make the smaller boxes, and the edges of the rough blocks could be squared with a table saw and jointer, but we will learn how to make do with our basic tool set. So, let's get to work!

FIG. 3 Edges that have been cut with the band saw fit back together like a key in a lock, making an invisible joint.

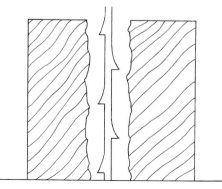

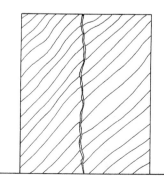

PART ONE

BASICS

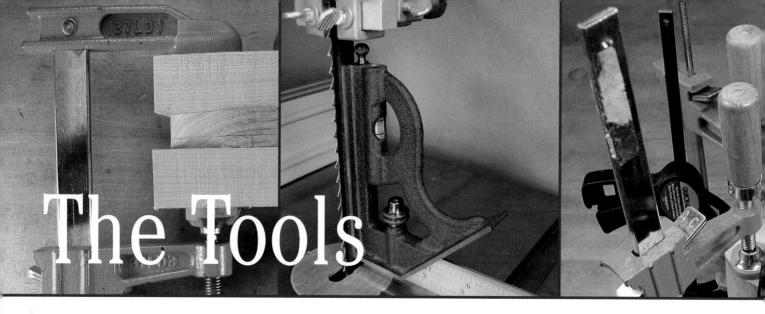

The Tools

Although some woodworkers are fortunate enough to have a complete shop with every tool ever made, there are many more aspiring woodworkers who would like to make something but have only a few tools. When I owned just a small band saw, sander, and drill press, I learned how to make band saw boxes. As long as I was just making small boxes I was satisfied; but

when I wanted to make bigger boxes, I burned up my stationary belt sander's drive belt and almost ruined the small band saw's motor. They were underpowered for big jobs, so I bought more powerful tools. I have gone from the have-not category to the got-everything-known-to-man category. Working at a woodworking supply store for six years was helpful. Now that I am well equipped, guess what I keep making: band saw boxes! You don't have to have a shop full of tools, but having better tools can enable you to make bigger boxes with less effort.

Here is some information about the tools used in making the boxes in this book, starting from the most important

and indispensable tools to the sure-would-be-nice-to-have tools.

Note: When you get to the projects, you will find that there is a specific materials list for each project, giving specific tools and supplies needed. Those lists assume that every shop includes a few basic items: a pencil, a fine-line permanent marker, a square, a straightedge, a ruler, screwdrivers, a hammer, double-sided adhesive tape, masking tape, clamps, sandpaper in 50 to 600 grits, wood glue, brushes, a knife, rags, paper towels, a dust mask; a band saw with $1/2"$ to $3/4"$ blade, fence, a miter gauge and feather boards; a belt sander with grits from 60 or 80 through 120 or 150 to 220; a drill; and a bench with a woodworking vise.

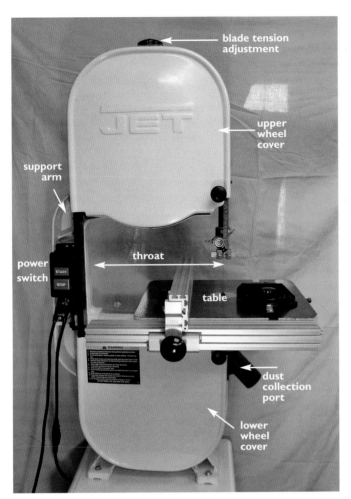

FIG. 1 A typical two-wheeled band saw. This model has been outfitted with an after-market fence and a miter gauge.

FIG. 2 Opening the wheel covers exposes the wheels, on which rubber tires are mounted. The blade rotates on the tires.

BAND SAWS

Band saws are my favorite tools in the shop. They are easy to use, not very dangerous, and very versatile. My first tool was a 12" band saw, bought new in 1972. I made puzzles for my children when they were small, cut out wood for carving projects, and made curved shapes for furniture. As my interest in band saw boxes grew, so did my list of tools. I added two more band saws, but I still have that old band saw, and I use it more than any other tool.

Anatomy of a Band Saw

The band saw derives its name from its cutting blade: a continuous band of steel that has downward-pointing cutting teeth on one side. This continuous blade runs around two (sometimes three) wheels on which rubber tires are mounted. As the wheels rotate (the lower wheel being driven by a motor), and with the proper tension between the wheels, the blade rotates around the wheels and through a slot in the table. Material to be cut is placed on the table and pushed through the moving blade by the operator. Figures 1 through 4 show some important features of the band saw.

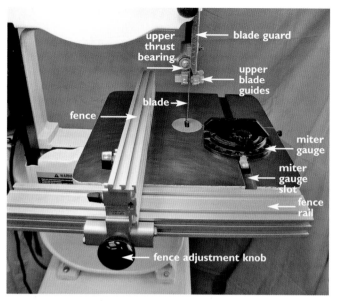

FIG. 3 A closeup of the band saw table shows the fence that helps to support and guide the wood for rip cuts. The miter gauge helps control and align pieces as they are pushed through the moving blade for cross cuts.

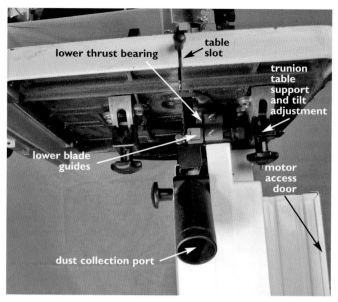

FIG. 4 A side view looking beneath the table shows the lower thrust bearing and lower blade guides. The trunion table support and tilt adjustment allow you to change the angle of the table to make angled cuts. Most band saws have a dust collection port to help carry away sawdust.

Choosing a Band Saw

Band saws with two wheels are categorized by the size of their wheels. This measurement determines the width of the throat, the distance between the blade and the support arm of the band saw, or its horizontal cutting capacity (Fig. 5). A 14" band saw has 14"-diameter wheels and is capable of cutting 13 3/4" between the supporting arm and the blade.

Three-wheeled band saws are exceptions to this rule. The 10" band saw shown in Figure 6, for example, has 6" wheels, a 3" cutting height, and 12" horizontal capacity. A band saw like this would be good for cutting shapes in plywood or for cutting small blocks, but the motor would not be powerful enough for deep cuts in hard wood.

FIG. 5 The size of a two-wheeled band saw is the same as the diameter of the wheels. This measurement is close to the cutting capacity between the supporting arm and the blade.

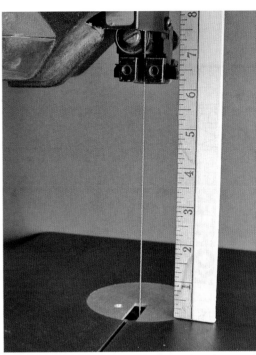

FIG. 6 On a three-wheeled band saw, the wheels are much smaller than its stated size, and the cutting area can be larger. This 10" band saw has three 6" wheels, 3" cutting depth, and a full 12" horizontal cutting capacity. It has a smaller motor, however, so it does not perform as well as a larger machine.

FIG. 7 The vertical cutting capability, the resaw capacity, of this 12" band saw is the same 6" as it is for a 14" machine.

Smaller band saws, such as an 8" unit, cost less, take up less shop space, and make less noise; but they are also more difficult to keep adjusted. They cannot cut larger pieces of wood, and they don't have enough power for many projects.

There are larger, 18" to 20" band saws with $1\frac{1}{2}$-HP to 2-HP motors that are great machines for resawing lumber (cutting vertically through the thickness of a board) and plowing through the toughest jobs in the shop; however, they take up more room, make a lot of noise, and cost twice as much as a good 14" machine. For the purposes of making boxes, a 12" to 14" band saw with a $1\frac{1}{2}$-HP to $1\frac{1}{4}$-HP motor is ideal.

Outfitting Your Band Saw

Some band saws are available with all the accessories you could need, but more often the tool comes without extras. Here are a few of the more common aftermarket accessories for 14" band saws.

Riser Block

A box generally cannot be made deeper or wider than the vertical distance from the blade guard to the table. This is referred to as the saw's resaw capacity. Although smaller band saws have smaller motors and are lighter in weight than their bigger counterparts, they can sometimes resaw the same 6" thickness of wood (Fig. 7). The biggest difference is that the smaller saw will cut slower because it has a smaller motor and less power.

Most 14" band saws can resaw 6". You can increase their resaw capacities by adding a riser block to the supporting arm. Riser blocks are 6" of cast iron, and they increase the saw's capacity to a full 12" (Fig. 8). It is very dangerous to have that much blade exposed. Riser block

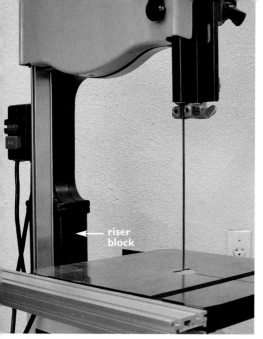

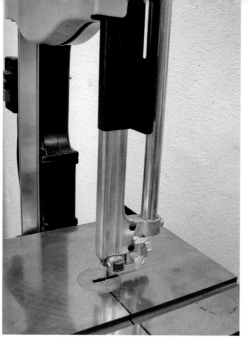

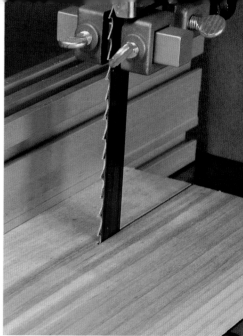

FIG. 8 This 14" machine has a riser block added to its vertical support arm. The 6" block of cast iron raises the top of the machine, enabling 12" resawing.

FIG. 9 With a riser block installed on this 14" band saw and so much blade potentially exposed, I am careful to keep the blade guard extension in the fully lowered position for safety.

FIG. 10 This after-market fence is easy to adjust, and it helps keep the wood feeding straight into the blade for precise rip cuts (with the grain). The blade guard has been raised for demonstration only. Always keep the guard as close to the wood as possible.

(or resaw) kits come with a blade guard extender that can be adjusted to completely cover the additional blade exposure (Fig. 9). Keep the blade guard as close to the wood as possible, and slow down the feed rate as you finish the cut.

Adding a riser block is usually a permanent change to a band saw; you will have to purchase longer blades for the now larger machine.

Fence and Miter Gauge

Some band saws come with a fence and miter gauge as standard equipment, and some require after-market models. The fence keeps the wood moving in a straight line so the resultant rip cut, with the grain, will be straight and even (Fig. 10).

Safety Note: In some of these photographs the blade guard has been raised dangerously high so you can better see the setup. In reality, the blade guard must be no more than ¼" above the wood whenever possible.

A good fence also will allow you to resaw boards into thinner pieces. You even can make your own veneers (Fig. 11). Keep your fingers out of the direct path of the blade when you are cutting thin pieces in case the blade should emerge through the wood. Figure 12 shows a thinly sawn piece of pine held up to the light to demonstrate the thin and even cut.

If you don't have a good fence, a piece of straight, smooth wood clamped to the table will work, but it is not as easy to set up or to return to the same place for a repeat cut. For many years when I made band saw boxes, I did not have a fence; that is why I made so many boxes with curved shapes.

Some fences can be outfitted with attachments like a micro-adjuster, a stop, and a resaw guide. The micro-adjuster allows the fence to be moved in exact, small increments, which is useful when resawing to make veneers or very thin stock. The stop attachment limits the length of the cut, allowing the user to make multiple identical cuts without having to measure every time. This comes in handy when making tenons (Fig. 13). Resaw guides allow pieces of wood to be fed into the blade vertically and at a consistent angle that is not parallel to the

FIG. 11 Resawing (cutting through the thickness of a board to make a board thinner) is made much easier with a good fence.

FIG. 12 Thin stock can be cut smoothly and evenly with a ¾", 4-TPI (tooth-per-inch) blade on a 14" band saw with a good fence, slow feed rate, and a steady hand.

fence. This is sometimes necessary to compensate for drift, the tendency of the blade to cut the wood at an angle. There will be more on drift in the section on adjusting your band saw.

Miter gauges slide in the miter slot and keep the wood perpendicular to the blade to make an accurate crosscut, across the grain (Fig. 14). When crosscutting, use a coarse, large blade for best results. You can also get good results by drawing a straight line on the wood with a combination square and cutting freehand.

FIG. 14 The miter gauge keeps the wood perpendicular to the blade for crosscuts (cuts across the grain). Band saws do not make the best crosscuts because of the tendency of the flexible blades to twist with the movement of the wood and wander off course (drift).

FIG. 13 A stop attachment allows you to make multiple cuts to the same length, as for the tenon cuts shown here.

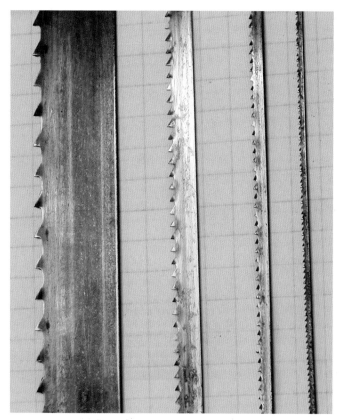

FIG. 15 For the box projects in the book, it is best to use ⅛" and ¾" blades, but a ¼" or ⅜" blade with 10 TPI should be able to make most of the cuts. Pictured here, left to right, are a ¾", 4-TPI blade; ¼", 10-TPI blade; ⅛", 14-TPI blade; and ¹⁄₁₆", 24-TPI blade.

Blades

One of the most important parts of your band saw is the blade. A good quality, sharp blade is necessary to do a good job on band saw boxes. Inexpensive blades usually are not a bargain because they do not last as long nor do they cut as well as more expensive blades. A worn blade will not cut true (straight), and it will leave a ragged edge on your wood. Carbide-tipped blades stay sharp for a long time, but they cost more than $100 each.

There are many different sizes of band saw blades, ranging from ¹⁄₁₆" wide to very wide blades used in sawmills. A ⅛" blade will cut a ³⁄₁₆" diameter circle, and a ¼" blade cuts a 1¼" diameter circle. Although some band saw boxes can be made using just one ⅜" blade, other designs in this book require tighter turns than that

blade could manage. It is also quicker and easier to make the larger squaring cuts and major through cuts with a larger blade, so I recommend a ⅛" blade for the curves and a ½" to ¾" blade for major straight cuts (Fig. 15). The more teeth per inch (TPI) on a blade, the smoother the resultant cut will be, but it will take longer to cut through the wood than a saw with fewer teeth. With a 3- or 4-TPI blade, the cut will go much faster, but the surface of the wood will be left with ridges from the teeth of the blade. A good compromise is to have a ⅛" blade with 14 TPI and a ½" to ¾" blade with 3 to 4 TPI. Of course, it then helps to have two band saws so the blades do not need to be changed frequently. If you have only one band saw in your shop, it would be wiser to use a ³⁄₁₆", 10-TPI blade as much as possible.

Push Sticks and Feather Boards

Push sticks and feather boards help support the wood as it goes through the band saw blade, keeping your fingers out of danger. Feather boards can be homemade, but store-bought feather boards are inexpensive and work very well (Fig. 16). They fit into the miter-gauge slot in the band saw table and are easily adjusted to hold your wood against the fence. Feather boards are especially useful when ripping veneer-thin pieces, when you don't want your fingers so close to the blade.

Push sticks can be used to hold the wood against the fence and to push it through the blade. As the blade is coming through the last of the cut, it is especially impor-

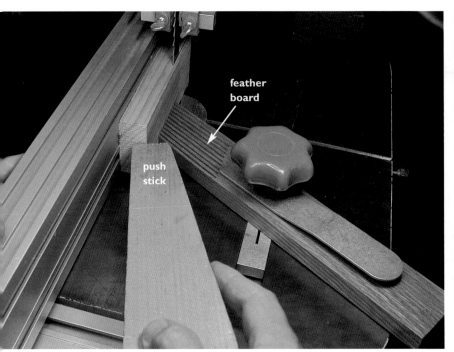

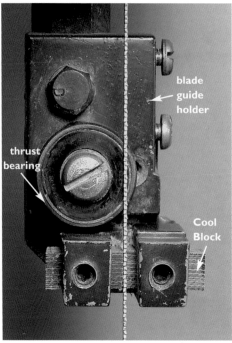

FIG. 16 Use a push stick and feather board to hold your wood in place, which keeps your hands well away from the blade.

FIG. 17 The three points of contact for the blade are the side guide blocks and the thrust bearing at the rear. In this case the side guides are Cool Blocks, a patented, lubricated fiber material. They reduce friction and will help to keep the blade running cooler, so it will last longer.

tant that your fingers be out of the danger zone. Use the push stick to complete the cut. Although store-bought push sticks are available, I've used pieces of scrap for push sticks for many years. Any similar soft wood scrap will do fine, and I believe it works better than a purchased plastic tool because the wood-to-wood contact is more secure.

Adjusting Your Band Saw

Now that the band saw is fully outfitted, the next step is to adjust the machine so it can cut your project wood as accurately as possible. Always make adjustments with the tool unplugged. Placing the cord on the table of the machine will remind you that it is unplugged, and it also will remind you that it needs to be plugged back in before you can get back to work. While you have the machine doors opened to make adjustments, clean the sawdust off the tires and vacuum the interior.

Installing the Blade

Installing a blade on a band saw is not difficult if you take the time to do it correctly and don't try to take short cuts. Too often we try to save a few minutes by skipping some steps and end up wasting time when the job has to be done over.

All band saws have six points of contact with the blade: three on top and a matching set of three beneath the table. There are two side guide blocks or bearings and a thrust bearing, all of which are supported by the guide holders (Fig. 17).

The side guide blocks help to keep the blade from twisting or wandering from the intended path as it cuts

FIG. 18 Roller guides offer excellent support because the rollers can be adjusted to lightly touch the blade without generating friction heat.

FIG. 19 This is how the blade should look when it is correctly centered on the wheel. Make sure it is centered on both wheels before turning on the machine.

through the wood. Some machines come with roller guides, which reduce friction with the blade and can be positioned lightly touching the blade. They also can be added after-market to some saws (Fig. 18). Side supports can be homemade from hard woods like maple.

Thrust bearings keep the blade from being pushed off the wheels by the force of the wood against the blade. These bearings should not rotate when the machine is turned on, but only when wood is pushed against the blade.

Here are the steps for installing a blade:

1 Loosen the locking mechanisms for the guide holders, side guides, and thrust bearings, and place them at least $^1/_4$" away from the blade area.

2 Release the tension in the upper wheel so the old blade slips off easily. Clean the tires of debris.

3 Center the new blade on the tires of the wheels, and increase tension until the blade is lightly secured. Twirl the wheel by hand to see if the tracking mechanism is adjusted

correctly. If it is correct, the blade will stay centered on the wheels and will not tend to wander forward or backward (Fig. 19). If it does wander, you'll have to turn the tracking knob in small increments one way or another until the blade stays centered. Make sure the blade is tracking in the center before you turn the machine on, or you may damage your blade.

Tensioning the Blade

After the band saw blade is in place on the wheels, it will need to be tensioned properly. Although each band saw has a gauge that indicates the recommended tension for each width of blade, there are different opinions about the best way to determine correct tensioning. Some blades are low-tension blades and come with a set of instructions indicating the process by which they should

FIG. 20 Pluck the blade between the wheels on the support-arm side of the machine to determine optimum tensioning by tone. Listen for the "twang."

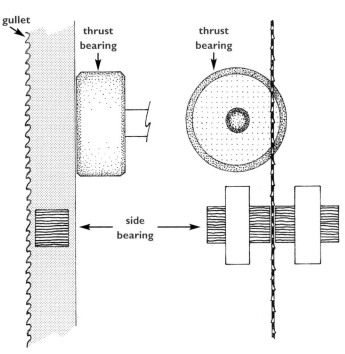

gullet

thrust bearing

thrust bearing

side bearing

FIG. 21 It is important that the blade guides be positioned correctly for maximum control of the blade. From the side view, you can see the narrow space between the back of the blade and the thrust bearing.

FIG. 22 In this front view, notice the slight distance between the sides of the blade and the side bearings.

be tensioned. Some woodworkers just crank on the tension until it won't easily tension any more. The best way is to listen to your saw blade. Tension it according to the gauge or directions that come with the blade; then, with the machine turned off and unplugged, open the top cover and pluck the blade on the supporting arm side of the machine. If it goes "ting," the blade is too tight and will likely break. If it goes "thunk," the tension is too loose, there will not be good control, and the blade may wander. The correct tension is signified by a melodious "twang" (Fig. 20).

Controlling the Blade

Now that the blade is tensioned, it is time to reposition the upper and lower blade guides.

1 First move the guide holder so that the front edge of the side bearing is located just behind the gullets of the teeth of the blade (Fig. 21).

2 Lock the guide holder in place, and then position the thrust bearing just behind, but not touching, the back of the blade. Adjust the side bearings so that they are almost, but not quite, touching the blade (Fig. 22). It is easy to judge the

proper spacing if a folded piece of writing paper is held between the blade and the guide during adjustment (Fig. 23).

3 Tighten all the locks on the side and thrust bearings.

4 Repeat these maneuvers on the matching blade guides located on the bottom side of the table.

5 Now rotate the wheels by hand to see if the thrust bearings move. If they move, relocate them further back.

6 If the blade is not binding against any of the guides and it is tracking true, it should be alright to close the doors and turn on the machine. Be sure to adjust your blade guard to just $1/4$" above the piece of wood to better control the blade and to protect your fingers (Fig. 24).

7 If there are any scraping or thunking noises, turn off the band saw and check to see what is causing the problem. There should be no sound other than the purr of the motor, at least until you start to cut some wood.

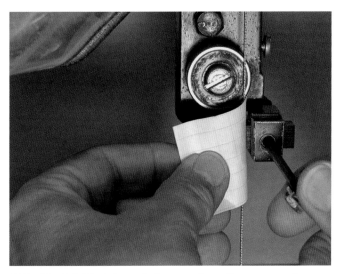

FIG. 23 A folded piece of paper works well as a spacer for setting the bearings.

FIG. 24 This is a good setting for the blade guard, just ¹/₄" above the wood.

Adjusting for Drift

It may be necessary to adjust the band saw fence to account for the tendency of the flexible band saw blade to cut at an angle (drift).

1 To see whether or not the blade is cutting true, draw a straight line lengthwise on the flat side of a squared piece of wood that is at least 3x12x¹/₂".

2 Without using a fence, follow the line as you cut through the wood. Stop the machine when it has cut 9" through the wood. Do not move the wood.

3 Draw a pencil line on the band saw table, using the side of the wood as your guide (Fig. 25).

4 Now move the fence over to the line and see if the fence and line are parallel (Fig. 26).

5 If they are not parallel, then the fence needs to be adjusted to match the required angle. If the angle is too great, a resaw guide can be used to keep the board upright while the board is fed freehand into the blade at the angle of the pencil line (Fig. 27).

Unfortunately, different blades and different types of wood have different degrees of drift. If your blade is sharp and you don't push the wood too fast through the blade, your normal fence setting should produce straight cuts.

Squaring the Blade to the Table

The trunion table support and tilting mechanism under the band saw's table allow the table to be tilted for angled cuts. Loosen the locking knobs, square the table to the blade with the aid of a square, and then tighten the knobs (Fig. 28).

Aligning the table to the blade in the front-to-back plane varies from tool to tool, so read your manual for those instructions.

SANDING TOOLS

Since prehistoric times, when cavemen used rocks to help smooth pieces of wood, people have been searching for better and easier ways to make wood beautiful and useful. One very effective way to eliminate irregularities in wood is to scrape it with a sharp piece of metal, either a scraper plane or a plain scraper blade. These tools have the advantage of shearing wood fibers without generating a lot of fine dust, which fills the wood's pores and gets into the air. Unfortunately, most of the time our band saw boxes are too small and complex to make use of these scraping tools.

Sandpaper is the method of choice for band saw box makers. It is flexible and can be shaped to fit into the oddest corners. Although we will be looking at many dif-

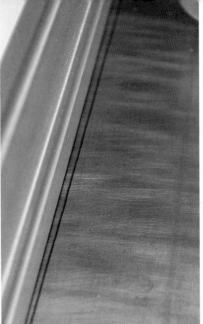

FIG. 25 Draw a line on the band saw table along the edge of the board after cutting partway through the board.

FIG. 26 Compare the edge of the fence to the drawn line to see the extent of drift with this blade on this piece of wood.

FIG. 27 Resawing and ripping with a resaw guide is one way of overcoming drift. The fence alone can also be adjusted to some extent to account for drift.

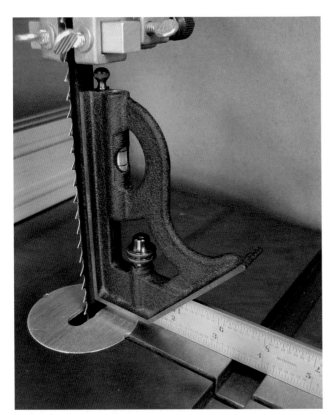

FIG. 28 Before cutting into your wood, check that the band saw table is adjusted square to the blade. Now you are ready to start making some sawdust.

ferent types of sanding tools, it is often one's fingers holding a piece of sandpaper that make the best tool.

First let me tell you a little about abrasive materials. They are composed of bits of grit, either sand or metal, glued to a paper or cloth backing. They generally are available from 24-grit to 600-grit for general woodworking. A 24-grit belt has fewer and larger pieces of abrasive; it is very coarse. A 400-grit belt has many tiny pieces of grit and is very fine. Most often, you will need an abrasive in the 60 to 220 range of grits, proceeding from 60-grit to remove and shape wood, to 120 to smooth out the ridges left by the 60-grit, and finally to 220-grit for a smooth surface ready for finishing.

Belt Sanders

Belt sanders are available in many sizes, ranging from small handheld models to huge industrial machines that can sand a full sheet of plywood in one pass. For the home craftsperson 4"- and 6"-wide belt sanders are most popular. Although a handheld belt sander can be used for some of the tasks, it does not have a

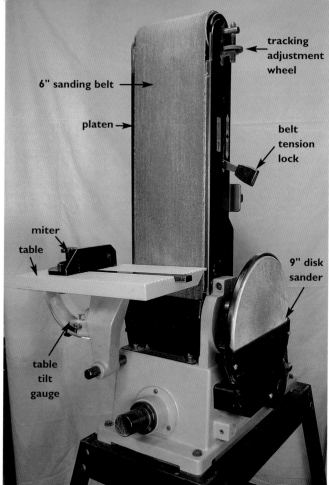

FIG. 29 This 6" belt sander ("Big Bertha"), seen from the left, gets more use than any other tool in my shop except the band saw. It has a 1-HP motor that is unstoppable, so watch your fingers!

FIG. 30 Belt sander, right view. The tracking adjustment wheel on a belt sander controls the tendency of the belt to drift. The tensioning lever loosens and tightens the sanding belts. Make sure the belt is in position and tight before turning on the power.

fence or table that would help you keep the wood square and true. If that is all you have, secure it in a vise or with strong clamps to a sturdy workbench. Having at least a small stationary belt sander is strongly recommended for making these boxes.

A 6" 1-HP stationary belt sander is my second most important tool (Fig. 29), the band saw being the first, of course. It uses 6×48" belts that slip on and off easily and are secured using the tightening lever, as shown in Figure 30. Sanding belts are directional, so make sure the arrow on the back side of the belt is pointing toward your table or fence. After you have changed the belt, secured it with the lever, and turned on the power, it is likely to

drift, or move across the end of the roller in either direction.

Drift is caused when the belt changes shape either during manufacture or over time in the shop. Use the tracking wheel (also shown on Figure 30) to correct for drift. It does not take much adjustment to make the necessary correction. Move it just a little, while the machine is running, and see how it affects the belt's path. When properly adjusted, the belt should hold steady at the center of the platen (the supporting surface) under the belt.

It is also important that the table be adjusted so it is as close as possible to the sanding belt while not actually touching the belt. This is necessary so your fingers or

FIG. 31 This 4" belt sander has been my best friend (second only to the old 12" band saw) for many years. It doesn't have the power of Big Bertha, but neither is it as noisy nor as dangerous. Note the low-tech dust collection system at left. It works quite well.

work does not get pulled between the sanding belt and the edge of the table. Notice that each time you change the angle of the table, the distance between it and the belt will change and will require a corresponding change in the position of the table.

"Big Bertha," the 6" sander, is better than a 4" belt sander (Fig. 31) because it has a larger sanding surface and bigger motor, both of which allow me to make bigger boxes faster. Just as important is the dust collection port (see Fig. 30). With my shop vacuum attached to this port, there is little sanding dust that escapes into the shop. Because this machine is used to shape wood, it generates a lot of very fine sawdust that needs to be collected at the source. The fourth benefit to having the larger machine is the great table (see Fig. 29). This table is much superior to the table on the 4" machine, which is smaller and has a flimsy miter gauge.

There are, however, a few advantages to owning the smaller machine. It is quieter, less intimidating, and doesn't cost as much. Having two belt sanders allows you to keep a different grit belt on each machine so that there are fewer sanding belt changes needed. Reducing setup time is always a good thing.

Drum Sanders

Drum sanders are the best tools to use for sanding curved interior surfaces (Fig. 32). They are available in an inexpensive hard rubber form that uses heavy cardboard tubing sleeves to hold the grit. They are designed to fit either in a drill press, handheld drill, or rotary power tool. They come in a variety of sizes from $1/2$" to 3" long and from $1/4$" to 2" in diameter. Figure 33 shows a hard rubber drum sander chucked into a drill press. It is helpful to place a piece of scrap lumber under the piece being sanded, as in Fig. 33. The scrap needs to be at least the same height as the piece being sanded. When this scrap piece is slipped out from under the work piece (Fig. 34), the work can be removed from the drill press without raising and lowering the spindle or table every time.

The biggest disadvantage to using a drum sander in

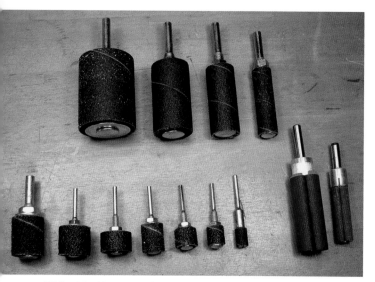

FIG. 32 Here is an assortment of sanding drums: The top row shows 4 diameters for 2" long drum sanders with ¹/₄" shafts. They can be used in drills, drill presses, and larger rotary power tools. The bottom row has 6 different diameters for shorter drum sanders that have ¹/₈" shafts, for use with smaller rotary power tools, like Dremel tools. The two larger sanders on the right bottom row are made of soft rubber and take small sheets of sandpaper instead of preformed drums. They work very well for sanding contours.

FIG. 33 Drum sanders, such as this 1¹/₂" diameter one chucked in the drill press, will work for sanding interior contours.

the drill press is that it creates parallel grooves in the wood, which must be removed by hand-sanding. The great advantage over using any handheld tool is that the table supports the piece, and the shaft of the machine is square to the table.

Drum sanders also are available as inflatable models with variable softness, depending on the amount of air that is put into them. Larger drums of this sort are available, up to 9" long and 4" in diameter; they can be powered by low-speed, chucked power tools, like a lathe, or by tools with power take-offs. These are handy for freehand contouring of wood, but not for control of regular forms.

Oscillating Spindle Sanders

The oscillating spindle sander solves many of the problems inherent in using drum sanders because the spindle moves in a vertical oscillation as well as rotating. This motion eliminates horizontal sanding grooves. It also is

available with a sanding length of up to 9", which allows you to make bigger boxes more easily. It is a single-purpose tool that does the job extraordinarily well.

Another advantage of this machine is that it has the power to use 3"-diameter spindles. This size is excellent for surfaces that are only slightly curved (Fig. 35). Spindles are available in variety of diameters down to ¹/₄".

Power Contour Sanders

Although sanding small contours with a power profile sander has a lot of appeal, I have found it difficult to control. It is easy to hold the tool in one place too long and reduce the wood too much. Hand-sanding usually is safer for these small projects.

Hand Sanders

Hand-sanding is one of the keys to producing quality boxes. A dedicated band saw box maker has very faint

FIG. 34 Pull the supporting block out of the way and the work piece can be easily slipped out from around the spindle, much easier than raising and lowering the spindle every time.

FIG. 35 An oscillating spindle sander is the best tool for sanding interior curves. Because the sanding drum moves up and down vertically, it does not make the horizontal scratches generated by a drum sander chucked in a drill press.

fingerprints because they have been worn away by hand-sanding. There are many tools that can assist your hands in doing a good job.

Sanding Boards

Sometimes you'll want to remove just a little corner of wood or make a slight correction to a bevel. Using the belt sander would be too dangerous. In that case, placing a nice new piece of sandpaper on a flat, smooth surface can work quite well. Draw the wood across the surface for excellent control of the amount of wood removed. You can go one step further and make sure that the sandpaper doesn't move and wrinkle by attaching it firmly to a piece of plywood with duct tape (Fig. 36). You'll probably want to make several of these surfaces using different grits of sandpaper. I find 120-grit and 220-grit to be the most useful.

Sanding Dowels

If you do not have any sort of drum sander, you may use a dowel of the correct diameter with a piece of sandpaper

FIG. 36 Make a couple of these sanding boards for controlled sanding of flat surfaces. Here I've used 12x12" squares of $^3/_8$" plywood and some duct tape.

FIG. 37 Profile sanders are available in many different shapes. The rounded shapes seem to be those I use most.

FIG. 38 Abrasive pads (scrubbies) range from very fine, the white pad, to very coarse, the green pad. Use them instead of sandpaper between coats of finish.

wrapped around it to shape inside curves. If it is a diameter used very frequently, you may want to glue the back of the sandpaper to the dowel.

Contour Pads

Many times, you'll find you have to smooth a groove. For this job rubber contour (or profile) sanding forms are great (Fig. 37). They are available in a variety of shapes and sizes to fit most profiles, and there is an area for your fingers to hold onto the sandpaper and the tool.

Flexible Abrasive Pads

Flexible abrasive pads are $1/4$"-thick sheets of mesh that work well to scuff coats between finishes. The green ones are for sale at the grocery store for scrubbing pots in the kitchen; so I call them "scrubbies." At woodworking supply stores you can get them in white (virtually no abrasive, for final rubout), gray (equivalent to 0000 steel wool), maroon (00 steel wool), and green (0 steel wool) (Fig. 38). These pads don't shed like steel wool and, unlike sandpaper, they are much less likely to abrade through the finish on corners.

Rasps

Rasps are useful for shaping and smoothing wood. They come in a vast array of sizes and shapes and range from inexpensive to very expensive. Their cuts vary from very coarse to quite fine (Figs. 39 and 40).

Sanding is one of the most important aspects of making boxes, and there is no getting away from the fact that elbow grease, or hard work, is necessary. It is worth it, though, when you complete a great box, step back, and admire the perfect finish.

OTHER TOOLS AND SHOP EQUIPMENT

Band saws and sanders are your most important tools for making band saw boxes, but there are other tools that are either required or very useful for your shop. Here are some of my favorites.

Double-Sided Tape

For woodworkers, heavy-duty, double-sided sticky tape is like baling wire for the farmer and duct tape for the householder. I use it throughout projects to keep two pieces of wood together so they can be machined at the same time or to attach a scrap piece of wood to serve as a stabilizer or handle. Get the heavy-duty variety used by wood turners. It is cloth-backed, cannot be torn by hand,

FIG. 39 Planing rasps leave a very smooth finish on the wood. From the left are small round, small square, large round, flat, and heavy duty planing rasps.

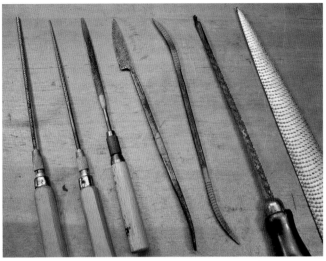

FIG. 40 Rasps come in hundreds of different shapes. Those with fine teeth will give a finer finish, and those with coarser teeth will remove wood faster.

and is thick enough to have gap-filling properties. It is also strong enough to hold an elephant in place. You may need to keep a wooden wedge around to pry the pieces apart when you are done. Do not reuse the tape. Wood fibers will become attached to the tape, preventing it from making good contact the second time.

Dust Collector

Making band saw boxes generates a lot of sanding dust. There are two ways of protecting yourself from this irritating and potentially dangerous dust. One way is to wear a dust mask, and the other way is to collect the dust where it is generated. For the sake of your safety and the cleanliness of your work environment, I recommend you use both methods. The dust collector can be as simple as a shop-vac that you run from tool to tool or as complex as a fully plumbed dust collection system having a large dust collector with outlets connected to each tool. I have a super shop-vac that is very quiet, has a long cord and hose, and is capable of reaching into every corner of my shop. It is connected to a remote control that allows me to control the vacuum from across the room. The hose has a small diameter and it is very flexible, which makes moving it from tool to tool very convenient (Fig. 41).

FIG. 41 This small shop vacuum is quiet and powerful, and has a long power cord and flexible hose.

Drills

Although you can make these boxes with just a hand drill, a drill press will help you to do a better job. Even a small drill press has a table that is square to the spindle shaft of the drill press, making it much easier to drill holes squarely. The other advantage to the drill press is the extra force that can be smoothly applied while drilling.

HELPFUL HINTS: JIGS AND SCRAP WOOD

■ There are store-bought and homemade jigs that can help you to do a better job with a hand-held drill. A simple aid is made by drilling a perpendicular hole, just slightly larger than the size hole you need for the project, into a piece of square hard wood stock. This block can then guide your drill bit squarely into the project wood.

■ When drilling all the way through a piece of wood, always use a piece of scrap wood under your project wood to help prevent tear-out, a ragged edge on the bottom side of the drilled hole.

FIG. 42 My workbench is one of the most used tools in my shop. I can store small tools in the shallow drawers, and the well-lighted surface is used for all layout and glue-up. Sanding and finishing are done on other benches.

Workbench

I became a genuine woodworker on the day that I bought a real workbench. There are places for all my small tools in the many shallow drawers in the cabinet beneath, and it has a flat surface top for assembling boxes. Wood vises are handy for holding wood while it is being cut, hand-planed, carved, power-sanded, or glued. My bench has overhead fluorescent lights and two swing-arm lamps attached to the bench top. You cannot do good work if you cannot see what you are doing (Fig. 42).

Squares

It is important that your blocks of wood be as square as possible. You will need a good square for checking your projects and for adjusting your tools' tables so they are square to their cutting edges. Even though the box's joints might fit together if they were cut at more or less than 90°, there would be problems going from one tool to another. For example, if you made an interior cut using the band saw offset at 91°, and then you tried to sand that cut with your drum sander set at 89°, the sander would not contact the wood for its entire length and your sanding job would be much more difficult.

FIG. 43 This square is not expensive, so I don't mind using it to check the square of the belt sander table to the rough surface of the sandpaper. It is also a good tool to carry around in an apron pocket because it is small and expendable.

The angle indicators on most power tools are not accurate enough for our purposes. Always use a square to confirm that your table or fence is square to your blade or sanding surface. Figure 43 shows a square that is one of my favorite shop tools. It is an inexpensive tool that is adequate for setting up all your shop tools, but not so precious that you worry about scratching its surface. Such a square is preferable to an inexpensive combination square because this simple tool cannot get out of square and will do everything you need for these projects.

Engineers' 90° squares are also accurate, inexpensive measuring tools. They measure only 90° or 45° and commonly are available with arms from 2" to 6" long.

Straightedge

If you are fortunate enough to own a good combination square or 90° square, the arms of either of those tools will work for testing that surfaces are flat. If you have just a very small square, you will also need a good quality straightedge. While making boxes, you will often need to determine the consistent flatness of a plane.

Clamps

They say that no one ever has enough clamps, but those of us who make band saw boxes can be satisfied with a few good clamps. I like the one-handed operation of quick-style clamps because they are so easy to use. I have a dozen 6" clamps and a couple each of the 12", 18", and 24" sizes that cover just about every clamping need (Fig. 44). One of the best qualities of these clamps is that they cannot be over-tightened. For our purposes gentle pressure is all that is usually necessary. Too much pressure

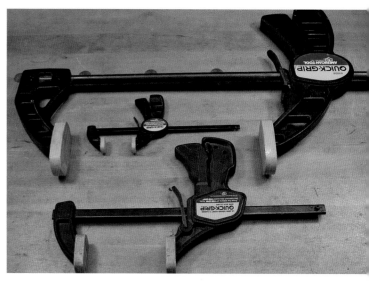

FIG. 44 One-handed clamps are quick and easy to use and they can apply enough pressure for most box-making purposes.

FIG. 45 Bar clamps (top) and hand-screw clamps (bottom) are very powerful and can crush small boxes if not used with great care. They also can bend a piece of wood into alignment during glue-up if that is what you need.

can squeeze out too much glue, and the joint will be weak. Sometimes the boxes are so delicate that a stronger clamp, applied with too much pressure, could crush the wood. In some projects, however, more pressure is necessary to coerce the wood into place. For that purpose I have a dozen 8" clamps with screw action, and a couple of really big clamps that could crush a brick (Fig. 45).

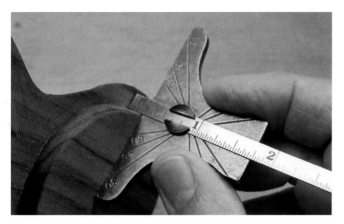

FIG. 46 This inexpensive depth gauge is useful when making band saw boxes. Here I'm using it to measure the thickness of the lid liner of a box.

FIG. 47 A few drafting tools come in handy for creating new patterns or for modifying those in this book.

Depth Gauge

The depth gauge is another inexpensive tool that will be a big help in making boxes (Fig. 46). Not only can you use it to measure the depth of holes and saw cuts, but it is a handy reference for angles as well. When the bar has been set to an angle, it is easy to transfer that angle to either another part of the project or to a protractor for measurement.

Drafting Tools

In some of the projects in this book I've given instructions on how to draw the plans, as well as giving you the plans themselves. This is so that you can learn how to vary any given plan to fit the wood you want to use or to the size box you want to make. There are a few tools that can help you in drawing plans and in transferring the plans to your piece of wood (Fig. 47).

■ **Graph paper** has regularly spaced lines printed on it that allow you to sketch and draw your plans without using drafting tools. It is often essential to see on paper how things will fit and look.

■ **Layout paper** is a thin sheet of white paper that has very light blue lines printed on it. The blue lines are nonreproducible and will not show up on copies of the plans.

■ **5 mm mechanical pencil and eraser** are invaluable tools in the shop, not only for working on plans, but also for making marks on your wood. Most pencil lead is too wide to make a fine mark unless it is kept very sharp. The 5 mm lead is always fine and leaves a clear mark. A mechanical eraser is great for when you mark lines incorrectly. These erasers are made of white rubber that does not leave a colored mark, and they will clean up smudges too.

■ **Rulers** are very important. Different styles are useful in different ways. A good quality 12" to 18" stainless steel ruler with a nonslip cork backing is necessary for making long straight lines. A 6" plastic ruler is great for drawing in small details. A flexible ruler is a great aid when drawing on a curved surface.

■ **Protractor** measures angles. To measure angles accurately you need to extend the lines beyond the small dimensions with which we usually work. You cannot measure an angle accurately if the arms are just ¹/₂" long. Extend the arms to 6", and then use the protractor to measure the included angle between these arms.

■ **Ruling compass** lets you draw an arc and circle of any radius, up to the limits of the compass you have. Get one that adjusts with a thumbscrew so that it will not move during use. If you don't have a compass, you can use the bottoms of cans, glasses, saucers, or bowls as templates for circles.

■ **Templates of large and small circles and ovals, and French curves** will help with drawing curves and arcs.

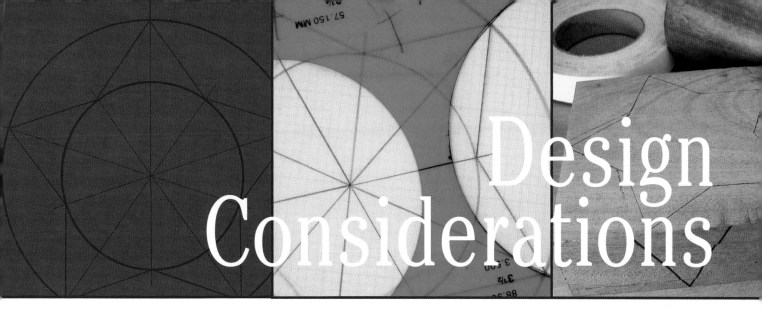

Design Considerations

One of the most fascinating properties of band saw boxes is that they can be made in almost any form you can imagine. Unlike boxes constructed from boards, which generally result in boxes with flat sides and square corners, band saw boxes are cut out from a block of wood and therefore can be cut into almost any shape. With a little imagination and a bit of forethought, there is no limit to the design potential for band saw boxes.

Communicating can be confusing when referring to the parts of a box and the surfaces of the box, or to the faces of a block of wood. To make it easier, I've drawn a reference box with the surfaces and directions labeled (Fig. 1). This way I won't confuse you with such references as the "top of the box's bottom."

DESIGN BASICS

Sometimes you will have a design for which you are seeking a suitable piece of wood; at other times you will already have a piece of wood and will be looking for a pattern. Either way, it is a challenge to match the design with the wood. If the design is simple, the wood should be interesting. If the design is complex, keep the wood simple. If you are planning to carve the piece, choose a softer wood, which will be easier to carve.

Secrets of Design Success

As you start to design a box, there are some fundamental properties of boxes that you should consider. Here are some things to think about that will contribute to your design success.

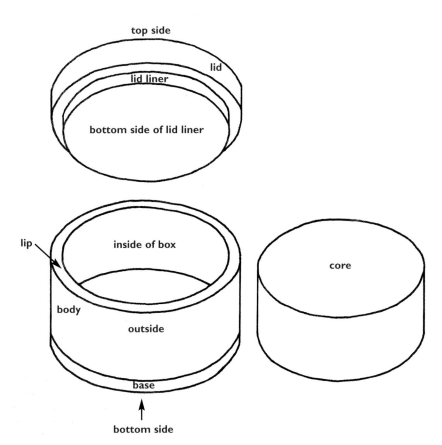

top side

lid

lid liner

bottom side of lid liner

lip

inside of box

body

outside

core

base

bottom side

FIG. 1 Some basic directional references for boxes, to avoid confusing directional and positional terminology.

■ **Size.** The size of your box is limited by the capacity of your machinery. This is not such a disadvantage. My favorite boxes fit into the palm of my hand. If you make smaller boxes, you can make more boxes out of a piece of wood and making a box out of an exotic, expensive piece of wood is possible. With smaller boxes there is less sanding work involved, and anything that cuts down on hand-sanding is a good thing. The problem with smaller boxes is that they do not have much interior space and won't hold much.

■ **Interior space.** Keep in mind that for many of the designs in this book there is an additional piece of wood attached to the inside of the lid, the lid liner; this reduces the space inside by at least 1/4". Personally, I consider these boxes to be works of art, and if they have a practical use it is a secondary consideration (Fig. 2).

■ **Wood thickness.** The dimensions of the sides, base, and lids are flexible. The wood needs to be thick enough so that you can glue it and it will hold together, but thin enough so the box does not look awkward. Bigger boxes require thicker

sides; 3/8" is a good average dimension. The smallest boxes sometimes have sides just 1/8" thick.

■ **Lid.** To make your box useful, you need to plan ahead when it comes to the lid. If you want the box to be easy to open, the lid can fit very loosely. If the lid needs to be tight, however, you may need to cut the lid liner out of another piece of wood. This technique will be covered in the Man in the Moon Box project.

■ **Saw kerf.** Remember that although some wood is lost in the saw kerf when cutting out the interior of the body, some bulk will be added when the finish is applied, if you use a surface finish.

■ **Handles and knobs.** Consider whether or not to add a handle to your box. Sometimes, as with the Muscle Fiber Box (Figs. 3 and 4), where the drawers open from either side, a handle would be superfluous. For other boxes, it is easy to lift the lid with just a finger groove for access, as with the hidden hinge box in Fig. 5. Sometimes a handle can act

FIG. 2 Consider whether you're making something for its design and looks alone or if interior space is a requirement. For example, these Tea Boxes can be sized to hold tea bags or loose tea.

FIGS. 3 AND 4 My daughter works in the field of physical therapy. She wanted to make a box that reflected her occupation, so she developed her own design. The drawers on Rebecca's Muscle Fiber Box can be pushed open from either side so they don't need handles.

FIG. 5 This hidden hinge box has a simple finger groove in the body that allows the lid to be lifted easily. Such a design element is both elegant and effective.

FIG. 6 Our friend Leo's original design for his Infinity Box has nicely turned handles that complement the overall design.

as a beneficial design element, as with the turned handles shown in Figure 6.

- **Rounded forms.** It will be easier to make a smooth band saw cut for rounded forms if you leave at least 1/8" between the edges of the pattern and the edges of your block of wood. If the blade comes out of the wood on a curve, it is always hard to get it started in the block again.

- **Finessing.** Sometimes a design that may seem impossible to make just needs a bit of finesse. Figure 7 shows such an example. As first conceived, the hinge end would not fit under the blade guard of a 14" band saw; by reorienting it 90°, it fit nicely.

- **Long cross-grain pieces.** For practical reasons of durability and stability, it is good to avoid factors in your design that would require long, thin pieces of wood that are oriented across the grain. Wood is very strong and flexible along the length of its fibers, but once the fibers are cut short, wood loses strength and can be broken easily (Fig. 8). If it is necessary to have a long, thin piece of wood as part of your design, as in the Armadillo Box's tail, make sure that the length runs parallel to the grain of the wood.

- **Planning.** Work out your designs on paper first. It is much easier to erase a pencil line than it is to change a cut in a block of wood.

Mix and Match Your Designs

The designs in this book should be just a starting point for you. I hope that after making some of these designs you will be ready to come up with variations of your own. Even when you are using these plans, you should feel free to mix and match plans, designs, and finishing techniques. Maybe you think it would be better to make the Yin Yang Box with a lift-off lid, or make the Butterfly Box into a Ladybug Box. Many of the techniques shown for one box can be used for any of the other designs.

CHOOSE YOUR WOOD

Choosing wood for your project is an important task that will contribute to the success of your project. The whole character of the box may be affected by your choice of wood. You should choose a hard wood, unless you are going to carve it. Look for wood that is free of defects, unless they are part of the design. Dense or hard woods have a solid feel to them and make a satisfying clink when the lid is closed or the drawer is shut. They also are less likely to dent.

Choose wood without figure and character for designs that are complex, like the Celtic Knot Box. Look for stock that has interesting aspects when the design will show

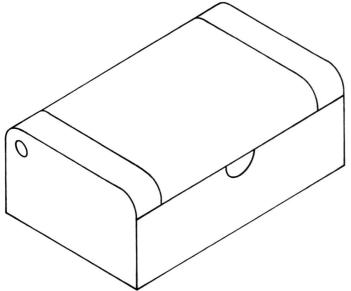

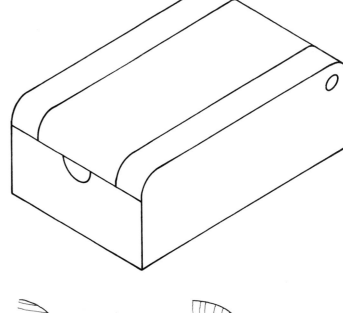

FIG. 7 A design is influenced by the limits of your tools. With the block oriented as in the left drawing and the long side at 8", the hinge would be impossible to cut with a band saw that has just 6" clearance under the blade guard. In the right drawing, the 5" (short) side has the hinge (circle); the long side is 8". This is the way the box would have to be oriented.

FIG. 8 Long, thin wooden parts like this Armadillo Box's tail must be oriented along the wood's grain direction for strength (left). Cross-grain thin pieces (right) will break off too easily.

FIG. 9 The natural coloration of this piece of box elder was not evident in the raw block of wood. I had planned to use it for the Man in the Moon Box (page 93), but it looks good without coloring as a Hurricane Box.

them off. For example, when looking for wood to make the Man in the Moon Box, I originally had chosen a piece of box elder, a variety of maple. The figure and color of the wood became apparent as I started to make the box. It was fantastic, and I couldn't see any benefit to adding any detail to the box. The box was finished with clear coats and retitled The Hurricane Box (Fig. 9). I subsequently used a simpler piece of wood to make the Man in the Moon Box (Fig. 10).

Then there are pieces of wood that you choose because of their character. Spalting, for example, is a fungal infestation that results in black lines and interesting coloration. Using spalted wood can result in a spectacular box. Similarly, a knot or a wormhole can add interest to your box. Figure 11 shows a box in ambrosia maple, a wood with natural color and a pattern that turns a simply designed box into a work of art. The box will need to be

FIG. 10 It is hard to believe that the piece of wood used for the Man in the Moon Box was cut off the same block of wood as the Hurricane Box, but it was.

FIG. 11 The natural spalting, wormholes, and coloration of ambrosia maple, used for this box, are caused by an infestation of the ambrosia beetle. This is a perfect example of nature improving upon the natural state.

FIG. 12 When you use firewood as a source for your boxes there will be some surprises. The knothole on this armadillo's mouth does not add to her good looks.

planned carefully so the defect does not interfere with the function of the box. A line of spalting that has gone too far can crack the wood and make it unsuitable for a box. The knot on the Armadillo Box (Fig. 12) was a surprise and was not beneficial to the looks of the box. The box is made out of mesquite, a wood that has lots of character and character defects.

Less dense types of wood, like basswood, cherry, and walnut, are good candidates for boxes that will be carved. Exotics and very hard domestic woods like oak and maple will make carving very difficult and time-consuming.

Free Wood

For beginning projects and practice pieces, it is practical to use inexpensive scraps of wood. Housing construction projects often have scraps cut off from wood used in rafters and joists. Explore businesses that mill lumber for

FIG. 13 The weathered and discarded cedar cut-off looked dry and dull in the stack of scraps. There was such a difference when I cut into the wood and exposed the color and grain of the natural cedar. Can you believe it became the Infinity Box in Figure 14?

FIG. 14 The Infinity Box (page 208).

doors and windows. They will have cut-offs that are of no use to them. Be sure to ask first before helping yourself to this free wood.

In my area there is a company that makes cedar timber-frame structures. They were more than happy to let me take whatever I needed from their scrap pile (Fig. 13). This wood was used to make the Infinity Box (Fig. 14).

Another source of free wood is the firewood pile. Here in south central Texas, mesquite and post-oak wood are found in abundance, and they are often used for firewood. Both of these woods are excellent for making boxes, but it will often take a lot of time and energy to fix inherent defects. Mesquite has very little clear wood. It splits, cracks, and has knots aplenty. It also may include fence staples, nails, and even lead from bullets hidden inside the wood. Always check this kind of found wood for metal inclusions using a metal detector before you cut into it with your expensive band saw blade.

In other areas, you will find types of wood that are abundant and considered ordinary, which are prized in other parts of the world. Koa, for example, is common in Hawaii, but it is a very expensive wood when purchased elsewhere.

Finally, just about any wood that grows in your area can be used for making boxes. If a neighbor is cutting down a tree, or if a large tree limb breaks off, or a tree is uprooted due to natural causes, you could make use of that otherwise wasted wood.

Drying Wood

Wood must be dry to be used for boxes. If the wood is not dry when you make the box, it will dry later and warp out of shape. Drawers will not slide, and tops will no longer match with bottoms.

How can you tell if a piece of wood is dry enough to use? One way is to make a fresh cut through the wood and hold it to your cheek. If it feels cool, it may still hold too much moisture. If you are not sure if a piece of wood is dry enough, cut it to slightly larger than the required size and put it on a paper towel in the microwave oven.

Run the oven on high for a minute. If the paper towel is moist under the wood, the wood probably is not dry enough.

One way to speed the drying process is to use a microwave oven to cook out the moisture. If you repeatedly heat it for a minute, cool it for an hour, and change the paper towel between cycles, the wood will dry out. A safe way to monitor this drying process is to weigh the piece of wood first and then again after each heating and cooling cycle. If the wood loses weight during a cycle, it is still losing water; if it stays the same, you need to stop before it becomes too dry. Ideally, moisture content should be around 13% for best results. This process may also be done with a conventional oven set at 120°F for many hours. Be sure to keep checking every couple of hours to monitor the weight of the piece of wood so it doesn't become too dry and brittle.

The safest way to dry wood, however, is to coat the ends of the block or boards with a nonporous material like wax or paint; then let it sit in a protected, well-ventilated area until it has dried naturally. Unfortunately, that can take a year or more per inch of wood thickness, depending on the density of the wood.

Buying Wood

If you have no ready supply of free wood, you will have to purchase your project wood. The benefits of purchased wood are that you will know for sure what kind of wood it is and that it usually is already kiln-dried to the proper working moisture content.

You'll often have a choice between buying lumber to laminate into a block and buying a block of wood from a wood specialty store. If you are tempted to buy lumber, be aware that no piece of wood is either straight or flat when you buy it. It may have been flat immediately after it was milled, but storage and the effects of changing humidity levels have warped it out of true.

You will have to mill the wood before you can laminate the pieces together. Milling wood is made much easier with a planer and either a jointer or a table saw. Because we are working under the restrictions of a shop with lim-

ited resources, we will not go into that process in detail. If you already have these tools, however, it is an easy task to run the lumber through the planer to smooth the surfaces, cut the boards to approximate length, and glue them together with pressure from clamps or weight. After the glue dries, the block can be squared up with either the jointer or the table saw.

Ash is an inexpensive wood that is available in large blocks, and it has an interesting, if not exciting, grain pattern. It is a hard wood that makes good boxes. After some practice, though, you will want to try some of the more exotic woods that are alive with natural color and chatoyancy. Chatoyancy is an optical reflectance that some wood grains (and other substances) have. The grain shimmers like a cat's eye, due to irregular grain patterns.

Buying blocks of wood can be expensive, but the variety and beauty of some of the more exotic woods can be worth every penny. There are many types of wood that are usually only available in blocks because of their rarity, expense, or workability. Ebony, for example, is quite brittle and is seldom available in pieces more than 3" inches thick or wide. Although boxes could be made out of ebony, it would be very costly, so it is more often used for accents like drawer pulls or inlays.

You will find that planning what kind of wood to use and what style of box to make out of a piece of wood is almost as much fun as making the box. Consider all the possibilities, and then try to make the most beautiful, unusual, clever, and fascinating box that you can imagine.

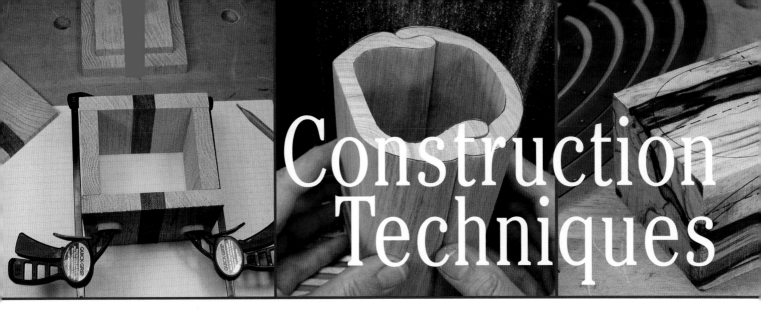

Construction Techniques

Band saw boxes have some unique properties that distinguish them from every other type of box. They are constructed from a single piece of wood that has been cut apart and reassembled, usually keeping the same directional grain orientation. The result of this technique is that the grain of the block of wood remains consistent, and the joints fit automatically. Unlike dovetail, rabbeted, or mortised joints, which are made from different pieces of wood and require exacting measurements and careful fitting, band saw box joints will always fit, even if your technique is less than perfect.

There are a few techniques, however, that will help you make the best boxes with the least effort. There is often more than one way to accomplish a task, but there is usually one way that is better than the others. I will give you my favorite techniques. First, here are some basic reminders about safety.

SAFETY IS NO ACCIDENT

Our goal is to make beautiful band saw boxes without danger to life and limb. With a few safety rules in mind, we can keep ourselves safe in the shop.

1 The most important rule is to never use a band saw, or any power tool, when you are tired, upset, in a rush, or when you have been using drugs, medications that make you drowsy or uncoordinated, or alcohol.

2 I always keep some part of my hands or arms in contact with the power tool as I am using it. This simple act helps me to orient my body to the tool. Perhaps that is why all my body parts are still firmly attached to me.

3 Do not adjust your power tool setup, other than adjusting for drift on the belt sander, while the machine is running. Stop the machine before moving the fence, table, or any other accessory. There is too

FIG. 1 Looking at your project under straking light, that is, light coming at an acute angle to the wood, will show any defects.

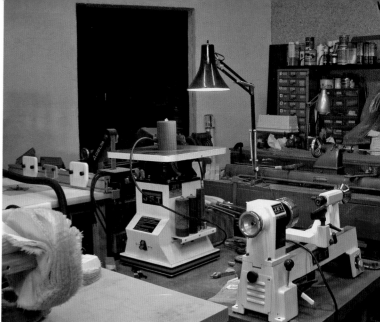

FIG. 2 Because of its central location, I can use this swing-arm light to illuminate any of four different tools.

great a chance that some moving part will come in contact with a stationary part and cause damage to either the machine, the box, or to you.

Lighting

You need to be able to see what you are doing at all times. This means evenly distributed overhead lighting and task lighting at every tool. You will also need to look often at your work under straking light, light coming from an acute angle, to see if there are any defects (Fig. 1).

Figure 2 shows my arrangement, which allows one light to be used for any one of four different tools. By swinging it around I can use it for either of two lathes, the router table, or the oscillating spindle sander.

HELPFUL HINT: USE A FLASHLIGHT

Keep a flashlight handy for seeing under your power tools to make adjustments and for finding that tiny handle that slipped out of your fingers and is now somewhere in the dark, with the spiders, under your workbench.

Environment

Although many woodworkers successfully make wonderful projects in a corner of their garage, it is great to have a space dedicated to woodworking. In either case, have your tools arranged in a way that allows you to safely go from task to task. Keep work surfaces uncluttered so that tools that aren't in use don't get pushed onto the floor. Keep the floor clear so you don't slip on wood chips or trip on electrical cords. Keep your power tool tables clean. An errant chip of wood left on the tool's table can tilt your wood and make the cut crooked.

Hearing Protection

Wear hearing protection whenever you are working around noisy machinery. Ears are delicate instruments that are damaged by loud and continuous noise. A simple pair of earmuffs is all that is needed to prevent hearing loss. You also can get earplugs that fit into the outer ear canal to block sound waves (Fig. 3). If you want to get fancy and expensive, there are earmuffs that have electronic noise-canceling properties and headsets that contain radios.

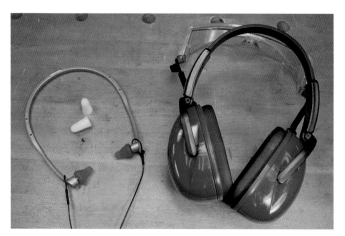

FIG. 3 There are many different ways to protect your hearing. On the left are band-type, in-the-ear hearing protectors. Inside them you see a couple of yellow ear canal, form-fitting plugs. My favorite earmuffs have protective glasses attached.

FIG. 4 Three different types of eye protection. On the left are inexpensive goggles that will do the job, but are not very comfortable. In the middle, a full-face mask that will protect your facial bones as well as your eyes. On the right, safety glasses that are comfortable to wear; some even fit over your glasses.

Eye Protection

Our sense of sight is very precious. Wear eye protection whenever you work with machinery capable of sending your project flying. You may not think that the band saw and sander will do this, but it has happened to me with both tools. The least expensive safety goggles offer sufficient protection, although they are not very comfortable. Safety glasses are much more comfortable, and are available in styles that slip over your regular glasses. For some work where kickbacks and fly-offs are more common, like using the table saw, router, and lathe, I use a full-face mask. With a full-face mask, the force of a shooting piece of wood is dissipated over a larger area of your face; it will not only protect your eyes, but also your nose, teeth, and facial bones (Fig. 4).

Dust Control

Your lungs are very sensitive to wood dust. Some people are extra sensitive and have an allergic reaction to some types of wood dust. Use dust collection where the dust is generated, and use a dust mask to keep stray dust out of your airways. I find that a dust mask made of cloth is preferable to any other type. They last for years and are easy to hand-wash. The best thing about them is that they don't fog your glasses or impede your breathing. I

FIG. 5 Dust masks. Clockwise from left: A disposable surgical mask that attaches over the ears; a nuisance dust mask with replaceable filters; an inexpensive, disposable, but uncomfortable paper filter mask; and my personal favorite, the cloth filter that I can wear all day in comfort.

can keep mine on all day long (Fig. 5). Use at least a paper filter mask whenever sanding.

Wear a respirator whenever you are using solvent-based finishes (Fig. 6). Many finishes are toxic and should

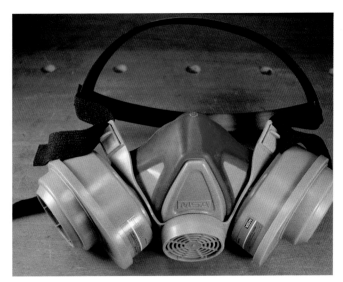

FIG. 6 You will need a respirator if you are going to be using solvent-based finishes. They are not comfortable, but they effectively protect your lungs and brain cells from harmful fumes.

FIG. 7 This outfit may not look fashionable, but that isn't as important as your health.

only be used in well-ventilated areas and while you are wearing a respirator. You may look like a creature from outer space, but you will be protecting the only body you have (Fig. 7).

Clothing

Wear a shop apron to protect your clothing and to give you a place to keep a few tools. It is very important that there are no loose ends about your clothing or hair. They could be caught up in the machinery and pull your body parts into harm's way. Tuck in your shirttails if they are floppy, and make sure that there are no loose shirtsleeves that can get in your way. You don't want your sleeve to get hung up on a corner of the band saw table, for example, preventing smooth feeding of the wood into the blade.

Other Factors

Above all, tell your shopmates or housefellows to be sure they let you know they are present when they come into your workspace while you are running power tools. Accidents can occur when someone startles a person who is using a power tool. There is always a lot of noise, and usually you are wearing earmuffs, and have total concentration on the job at hand. A sudden distraction can lead to a disastrous accident.

When I worked at a woodworkers supply store, I often asked customers for details about their worst accidents. Invariably, they responded that they knew they were doing something stupid. They were in a rush and didn't want to waste time in changing the machine's setup; or they knew it would be better to do the job differently, but just this once they would do it this way; or they were tired and knew they should quit, but just one more operation would finish the job. Quit when you are tired or when things just don't seem to be going right. Taking a break or coming back to the project tomorrow is often the best way to solve the problem. Safety is no accident.

CUTTING: START SMART

The band saw is your friend. Treat it right, and it can do almost anything you want it to do. Here is some good advice to make your relationship thrive.

FIG. 8 Here the blade guard is positioned correctly, just above the wood. In some of the pictures in this book the blade guard has been raised to make it easier for you to see the setup; but the blade guard is always just above the wood when I am cutting with the band saw.

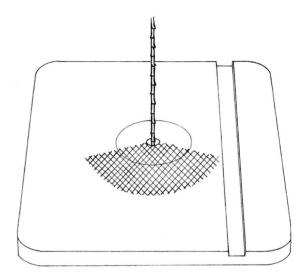

FIG. 9 The danger zone (gray area) is primarily at the front of the blade, extending out for 3" in an arc to the sides. Locate your fingers behind or off to the sides of the blade.

- **Don't be pushy.** While making most cuts, briefly stop pushing the wood every couple of inches to let the blade settle into the wood you are cutting. The blade is flexible and will tend to wander off course. By giving it a few seconds to reestablish its correct bearings, you will prevent it from veering further off course and cutting crooked, or possibly breaking.

- **Be a good listener.** Listen to the motor as you are cutting through a thick piece of wood. If the sound changes pitch and it sounds like the motor is straining, you need to back off a little on the feed rate so the motor can get back up to speed.

- **Leave a trail, like a good scout.** The best advice I can give to you is to use registration marks to keep your pieces in the correct order from the beginning of the project to the end. By clearly and consistently marking the wood in its relationship to neighboring pieces before you make your cuts, you will avoid the agony of cutting or gluing the wrong pieces and wasting a valuable block of wood.

Safe Cutting

Using the band saw is not as dangerous as using some other shop power tools, but keep in mind that the butcher uses a band saw very like yours to cut through your steaks. To live long and prosper, always follow these safety procedures.

- **Use your blade guard wisely.** Position the blade guard as close to your wood as possible without getting in the way of seeing the cutting line, usually $1/4$" above your work (Fig. 8). Don't forget that the blade guard will have to be repositioned whenever a piece of wood of a different thickness is being cut. Whenever the blade is left exposed, your hands are in danger.

- **Protect your hands and fingers.** Push sticks allow your hands to stay out of the danger zone. The danger zone is that area in front of the blade and within 3" of the teeth (Fig. 9). When you come to the end of a cut, you are pushing against the wood while the blade is cutting through. As the blade finishes the cut, resistance stops, and the pressure you are exerting against the wood can carry your fingers into the path of the blade. Slow your feed rate and position your fingers so they stay out of the danger zone. If you need to apply

FIG. 10 Use a sacrificial push stick for the last push through a piece of wood. It is better to have a chewed-up, battle-scarred piece of scrap wood hit the blade than to take a chance of cutting your fingers.

FIG. 11 On very deep cuts the blade is hidden until it emerges from the block. Keep your hands out of the danger zone, and use your push stick whenever possible.

pressure near the exit point of the blade, use a piece of wood as a push stick to push it through (Fig. 10). The greatest danger is when you are cutting a thick piece of wood and must have the blade guard raised. When making such a cut, you must be careful, use push sticks if possible, and slow your feed rate down to a crawl at the end of the cut so your momentum does not push your hands into the blade (Fig. 11).

Cutting Small or Rounded Pieces

An important technique in handling small pieces of wood when using power tools is to attach the smaller piece to a larger piece of scrap wood to stabilize it. This provides a larger holding surface. A piece of heavy-duty, double-sided tape will hold pieces together well. Make your stabilizing block of wood smooth and square so the tape will stick to it well and so it will support your block correctly (Fig. 12).

Another dangerous maneuver is cutting wood that is rounded. When the blade first contacts the wood, there is nothing under the wood to support the pressure of the

blade pushing down, and the piece of wood will fly out of control. When this first happened to me, I was cutting a log, a big log, and it made a terrible noise as it flipped off the band saw table and went careening around the shop. After catching my breath, I looked down and carefully counted my fingers to make sure they were still there. They were, and now I make sure my wood is supported before I make every cut.

For smaller rounded pieces, a stabilizing block like that used to stabilize the smaller pieces of wood will do fine (Fig. 13). If you want to stabilize a larger, irregular cylinder, like a log, it may be necessary to nail a larger stabilizing block to the log to keep it from rolling (Figs. 14 and 15).

Squaring Up Blocks

Many of the boxes in this book require that you start with a perfectly squared block of wood. Wood seldom comes square from your source. If the block is slightly out of

FIG. 12 It would be dangerous and almost impossible to cut this tiny piece on the left without using a stabilizer. With a piece of larger, square wood firmly attached with double-sided tape there is more to hold onto, your fingers are safely out of the way of the blade, and the work is held perpendicular to the table.

FIG. 13 To attach a stabilizing block to a small or odd-shaped piece to be cut, use cloth-backed, double-sided tape. Thick cloth-backed tape will bridge gaps between pieces of wood better than thin tape. Attach the two pieces while they are both resting on a flat surface so they will act as one unit as they go through the band saw blade.

FIG. 14 Working with something as irregular as a log requires a stabilizing piece to be nailed to the log.

FIG. 15 The stabilizer can rest on the fence to allow you to get a straight cut, or you can use your miter gauge to keep the wood square to the blade. Make sure you do not cut into the nails. Band saw blades are not very useful after they try to cut steel.

FIG. 16 While squaring up a block, use your combination square to determine which of the two sides of the block is closest to square with the top. In this case, this is not it; there is a large gap between the combination square and the side of the wood.

FIG. 17 This side of the block is almost square to start with, so this is the side to mark. This marked side goes against the fence, and the top of the block is positioned on the table as the side opposite the marked side is cut square to the top.

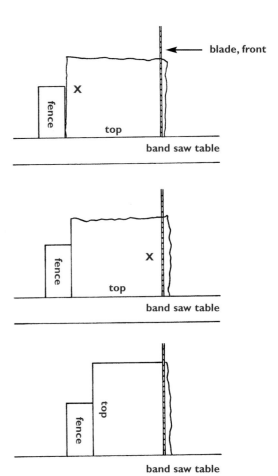

FIG. 18 Squaring up a block of wood. Top: Place the best side of the piece, marked TOP, on the band saw table and the X side against the fence. Cut off the opposite side. Middle: Keeping the top on the table, turn the wood 180°. Place the newly cut side of wood against the fence, and cut the X side smooth. Bottom: Cut the fourth side smooth and flat. Next, use the miter gauge or belt sander to square the ends (not shown).

square, you may choose to correct it using the belt sander. If it is off square by 1/8" or more, however, the band saw is the tool of choice. (Note: If you are laminating lumber to make a block, see the section on gluing. Once the glue has dried, you have a block, and can follow the directions for squaring.) Here are the steps for squaring up:

1 Smooth the best face with your belt sander first to provide a suitable reference plane. Mark this surface TOP.

2 Look at the top of the block in relation to one of the long sides, to determine which side is closest to being square to the top (Figs. 16 and 17), and make an X on this side so you don't use the wrong side in the next step.

3 Place the smoothed "top" face-down on the band saw table with the X-marked side of the block against the fence. Cut as much as necessary off the opposite side to result in a flat surface (upper drawing in Fig. 18).

4 For the second cut, turn off the band saw, keep the "top" surface on the table, and place the newly cut side against the fence. Move the fence over so the entire X side will be cut flat (middle drawing in Fig. 18).

5 Now you have three surfaces that are square to one

MAKE AN AUXILIARY MITER GAUGE FENCE

It's easy to make an auxiliary fence for your miter gauge. All you need is a piece of straight lumber or plywood about 3x18x³/₄" and a couple of bolts with nuts (Figs. 19 and 20). Drill the bigger holes first, wide enough to hold the bolt heads and the tool to tighten them and deep enough to cover the heads of the bolts. (If you are using machine screws instead of carriage bolts, you can counter-sink the heads instead.) The second hole needs to be the size of the shank of your bolt, and it goes all the way through the board.

Attach the auxiliary fence to your miter gauge, and you are ready to go to work. The dimensions of an auxiliary fence are not critical, and sizing can vary with the type of miter gauge you have. Some miter gauges come with sliding extensions, but a higher fence like this one gives you a place to attach clamps. You will need an auxiliary fence like this one for making the Double-Cross Box.

FIG. 19 Supplies for an auxiliary miter gauge fence.

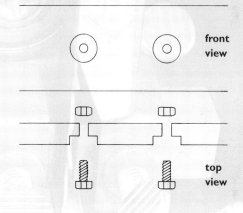

front view

top view

FIG. 20 Plans for the auxiliary miter gauge fence. Above: Front view. Below: Top view showing bolt holes.

another, and the fourth side can be cut square (bottom drawing in Fig. 18).

6. To square the ends you may use your miter gauge or follow a line, depending on the proportions of the block of wood. It may be necessary to add an extension or auxiliary fence to your miter gauge to support the wood near the blade.

Exterior Cuts

Exterior cuts that include tight curves require relief cuts. Relief cuts are made from the edge of the block to the outline to be cut. In this way, as pieces are cut off there is more room for the blade to make the curve cut (Fig. 21).

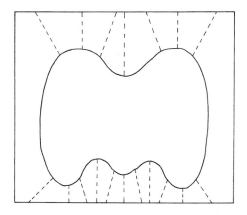

FIG. 21 Relief cuts (dashed lines) keep the blade from being pinched in a tight curve by allowing waste pieces to fall away and the blade to straighten out.

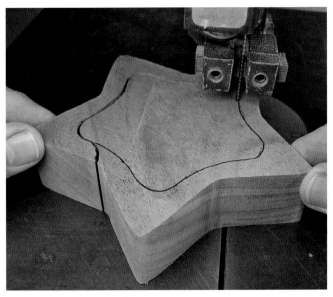

FIG. 22 Making inside cuts is not difficult if you take your time and are careful. Your first attempts may not be perfect, but you will get better as you practice. Notice here I've cut to the inside of the line, so afterward I can sand up to the middle of the line and end up with the exact configuration I need.

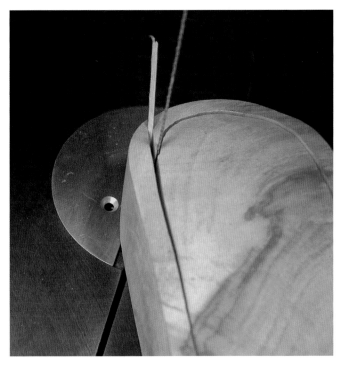

FIG. 23 A small chip of wood or a toothpick can be used to keep the kerf open so the blade has a void to enter without making an unwanted cut in the box. Turn off the band saw before inserting the small piece of wood, because you would otherwise have to get your fingers too close to the moving blade.

Interior Cuts

By far the easiest interior cuts are straight cuts made using the fence as a guide. On curved interior cuts that start and finish at the same point outside the block, gently guide the block so the blade cuts cleanly to the waste side of the line (Fig. 22). Keep your eyes focused a little ahead of the cutting teeth of the blade as you guide the wood. If you are cutting an arc in the wood, there is no time when the wood should be directed in a straight line.

Beginners often push their wood straight at some point in a curved cut. Imagine that you are pivoting the wood around a given radius, with your arm acting like the sweep second hand on a clock. Turn, turn, turn, and don't stop turning until you have completed the curved cut.

Many of the cuts required for these projects will be made within the block of wood and will require an entrance cut, a cut from the outside to the inside. You'll want to make this cut as unobtrusive as possible, unless it is part of the design to emphasize this feature. Make

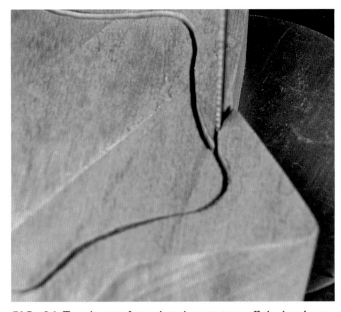

FIG. 24 To exit out of your interior cut, turn off the band saw and carefully back the blade out through the entrance kerf.

this cut through the end grain to help disguise the area where the wood was removed by the blade. The width of the saw cut is known as the kerf. Keep in mind that you will need to clamp this cut shut for gluing, so plan its placement accordingly.

As you get to the end of the cut, slow down. If tension in the wood causes the kerf to close up as you come around, stop the machine and place a sliver of wood or a toothpick in the kerf to keep it open (Fig. 23). This will keep the blade from damaging the wood. Run the blade right past the entrance cut and into the previously cut kerf. Turn off the power and wait until the blade has stopped moving (you'll know it has stopped when you can count the blade's teeth), before backing out through your entrance kerf (Fig. 24).

Angled Cuts

Sometimes, angled cuts can be made with the block of wood held so that the blade cuts diagonally through the piece (Fig. 25). If the cut is in a plane that is longer than the resaw capacity of your machine, you will have to cut the angle using another technique.

You may change the angle of your band saw table and use the fence on the downside of the wood to hold it in place as you rip the required angle. Another way is to support the block of wood with another piece of wood that you have cut to the complementary angle. Cut a piece of scrap wood to the angle required, and temporarily attach it to the block you want to cut (Fig. 26).

FIG. 26 If the piece of wood is too long to fit under the blade guard, you can hold it at the required angle with a scrap piece of wood cut to the proper angle. This angle is 90° minus the required angle. For example, if we wanted to cut a 60° angle, we would support it with a 30° block.

FIG. 25 Making an angled cut is easy and safe as long as the piece fits under the blade guard.

SANDING: THE PATH TO PERFECTION

Now that you have cut your block into pieces, the next step to perfection will be to sand the project to get it ready for assembly. Making band saw boxes requires a lot of sanding. They get sanded to shape, usually using power tools, and they get sanded to final smoothness with a lot of muscle power. The same general guidelines apply to both types of sanding.

- **Coarse to fine.** Always work your way from the coarsest grit necessary to remove the current blemishes up to the finest grit you need for the type of wood you are using and the finish you are planning to use. Do not make more than a 100-grit jump between steps. For example, on a really rough job you would start with a 60-grit belt, then move to a 120 grit, and probably end with a 220. Then switch to hand-sanding for a 320-grit finish, and even 400 and 600 for very dense woods that are going to be finished with oil and wax.

- **Direction.** Always sand with the grain for the final step of each grit. I like to sand across the grain as the first step for each grit so I can see when I've removed all the scratches from the previous grit. Then, I often will sand in a circular motion (if sanding by hand) before finishing by sanding with the grain.

- **Keep things clean.** Always clean off your piece and the work space beneath the piece between grits. This will keep the old bits of grits from contaminating the new sandpaper and getting errant scratches back into the nicely smoothed wood.

Power-Sanding

Power-sanding with a belt sander is a fast and easy way to remove a lot of wood quickly. It is also noisy, dusty, and can allow the operator to make mistakes very quickly. I doubt that anyone has ever had a major accident from working on a belt sander, but that does not mean that these machines are without danger. You can get a finger pinched between the table and moving belt, lose some skin while holding a small piece of wood on the belt, and you can be hit with a block of wood that has been thrown off when grabbed by the belt. This section will not only teach you how to get the best results from your sander, but how to keep yourself safe as well.

FIG. 27 **Always check the belt/platen to table/fence for square before each day's work. Shop gremlins come in during the night and reset your tools out of square. That is their job.**

FIG. 28 **The miter gauge on your sander needs to be square to the belt if your blocks and boxes are to come out square.**

- The first step in power-sanding, as with using all the tools, is to make sure that everything on the tool is square. Check that the belt is square to the table or fence (Fig. 27) and that the miter gauge is square to the belt (Fig. 28).

- There is a fine line between holding the wood firmly and holding it too tight. You need to hold it firmly enough so you have control of it, but not so tightly that your fingers will be forced into the belt if the wood shifts.

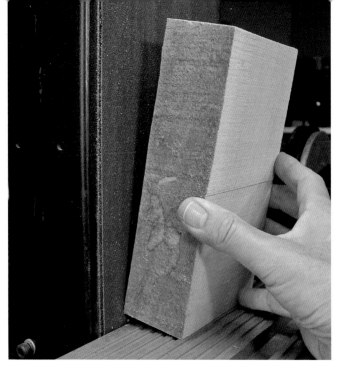

FIG. 29 To avoid accidents at the belt sander, it is important to have the piece of wood supported by the fence or table. Touch the end closest to the support first, and then immediately tip it flat onto the belt.

FIG. 30 When using the sanding belt in its horizontal position, it is easy to forget the proper sequence for sanding the block. Remember that the end closer to the fence stop touches the belt first.

■ The edge of the block closest to the table/fence needs to touch the belt first (Figs. 29 and 30), Then quickly lay the other side against the belt. This is most important for your safety. The workpiece needs to be supported by the table or the piece may slam down against the table or fly across the room. This is not good for either the project or the operator.

■ Once the wood is flat against the table and flat against the platen, you should apply pressure as evenly as you can (Figs. 31 and 32). Look at the wood block in relation to the grooves on the table so you do not sand too much on one side, making your piece crooked. Keep the wood moving back and forth across the moving belt so you use the entire width; this will help the belt to wear evenly.

FIG. 31 Sanding the edge of a block squarely is easier when there is a nice big table on which you can rest the block.

FIG. 32 When flattening a large surface, keep pressure evenly distributed across the block and watch your fingertips! Your touch needs to be firm, yet gentle. If you press too hard, you may take off more wood than you want.

FIG. 33 If you need to sand a curved piece over the rollers, hold onto the wood firmly, but apply very little pressure to the sander.

FIG. 34 Keeping your belts clean of sawdust will greatly extend their effectiveness and their lifespan. Sanding dust does not make a very good sander, and you may stress your sander motor unnecessarily trying to sand with a sawdust-filled belt. Use a rubber sanding cleaning stick regularly.

■ For some maneuvers, you need to hold the wood freehand against the platen or end of the belt where it goes over the rollers (Fig. 33). Pressure needs to be very gentle when doing this work. Any heavy-handed pushing against the sanding belt may cause the force of the sanding belt to rip the piece out of your hands. This is the voice of experience speaking.

■ If the piece is larger than the width of your belt, you will have to move it slowly to the right and the left so the entire surface is sanded evenly.

■ If the piece to be sanded is very small, you need to have another way to keep it under your control and keep your fingers out of harm's way. A good way to accomplish this is to use your cloth-backed, double-sided tape to attach the piece to another, larger piece of scrap wood that will be easier to hold.

■ Keep your sanding belts clean. Use an abrasive belt cleaning stick made of crepe rubber as often as necessary so you are not trying to sand with sawdust (Fig. 34).

■ Always use the correct grit for the job at hand. If you need to remove a lot of wood and you use a 220-grit belt, you will waste a lot of time, wear out the belt quicker, and strain the motor. It only takes a minute to change the belts, and the project will turn out better if you use the right tool.

■ One of the most important secrets to success in using the belt sander is to constantly check your progress. You should be looking at the piece every 5 seconds or so to make sure you are getting the results you want.

■ You can use the belt sander to square your block of wood if it is not too far out of square. Smooth the top of the block first, and then place that side on the belt sander table. With a 60-grit belt, sand the next best side until it is square to the top. Spin the block around, keeping the top on the table, and sand the opposite side until it is square to the top and parallel to the opposite side. Use the miter gauge on these sides to sand the other sides true. If your sander table has grooves, you can use them to keep the block square to the sanding belt. If you don't have a good table, use your square to draw guidelines on the block of wood and sand to the lines.

Hand-Sanding

Hand-sanding is labor intensive and time-consuming, but nothing is more important for the quality of your box than a great sanding job. Hand-sanding gives you much greater control over the finished product. I like to think of

FIG. 35 Use a rubber nonslip mat to keep the piece from sliding around as you work. A soft mat not only protects your box, but also keeps the workbench from getting scratched.

FIG. 36 With strong side-directional lighting, or straking light, you can see the slightest imperfections in your sanded surface. For this Star Box interior, I left the edges untouched so the bottom seam will be invisible.

handwork as the Zen of sanding. Here are tips to achieve that Zen.

- I always sand the surfaces in a certain order. That way I neither forget to sand a surface before going on to the next grit, nor do I keep sanding the same surfaces over and over again. I like to do the interior of the body first, doing the inside of the base, the sides, and then the lip. Then I do the outside of the sides and finally the bottom of the base. I do the lid in the same relative order: inside of lid, lip, finishing with the sides and top of the lid.

- I hand-sand for all the grits from 220 to 600 so that I can feel for smoothness as well as see it.

- Work on a smooth, clean surface (like a rubber mat, designed to keep rugs from slipping) to keep the smoothed wood from developing new scratches (Fig. 35). The mat also will help keep the piece from slipping out of your hands.

- There are many instances when hand-sanding is the best technique to use. You need to hand-sand any time you need to smooth just a portion of a surface. Sometimes you will want to leave the areas that will be glued back together rough, and just smooth the surfaces that will be left exposed.

- Keep an adjustable light nearby so that you can hold the piece at an acute angle to the light, a straking light, to show up any defects (Fig. 36).

- You should hand-sand between coats of finish, because power sanders would remove too much finish, too quickly.

FIG. 37 Grabbing the wrong grit of sandpaper can waste your time and scratch your work, so keeping the paper organized is a smart thing to do. This old desk organizer does the job just fine.

Be careful in sanding the edges of your block between coats of finish. It is easy to cut through to the lower layers and leave your final finish uneven. Use scrubbies for the best results between coats of finishes.

- Organize your sandpaper. A handy way to organize the sandpaper you are currently using is to keep the sheets in an office desktop file organizer on your workbench (Fig. 37).

FIG. 38 My supply of well-used sandpaper in its usual condition.

This way you can see at a glance what you have ready and where it is. Unfortunately, due to my waste-not, want-not motto, my supply of sandpaper that is "too good to throw out yet" often overpowers my sense of order, and the result is a disaster (Fig. 38). Don't let this happen to you.

GLUING, CLAMPING, AND REPAIRS

Gluing is a critical part of constructing band saw boxes. There is no fancy joinery like dovetails or pinned mortises that can hold the joints without glue. There are no screws or nails, only butt joints, without fasteners of any sort. This is the good news; because it's so simple, it's hard to mess up construction of a band saw box. My wood-burning stove, however, can attest to the fact that it is possible to make mistakes. The best way to keep your project out of the fire is to use registration marks to keep all the pieces in correct relative order so you don't glue the wrong pieces together.

Gluing actually has two components: gluing and clamping. Wood absorbs glue into its pores, creating a physical bond between the two wood surfaces. Clamping is necessary to hold the pieces firmly in position until the glue sets up. We'll also learn a few tricks of the trade for using glue to repair mistakes and natural defects in the wood.

Gluing

There are three different types of glue that are used on projects in this book: wood glue, epoxy, and instant or super glue (cyanoacrylate). Epoxy and super glue have very specialized applications, but wood glue is the best glue for most wood-to-wood contact.

Wood Glue

Wood glue comes in various formulations. Some are water-resistant, one is darker for use on darker woods, some set up slowly to allow more time for positioning. However, the one I use most of the time is ordinary yellow carpenter's glue. It dries fast enough, but it also allows enough time to position and reposition the joining pieces before clamping, referred to as "open time." Best of all, it is not a dangerous substance, it is not expensive, its bond is stronger than the wood fibers, and it cleans up with water. It is amazing that such an effective glue is so easy to use.

The best way to avoid problems in your glue-up is to always do a dry run with clamps so you have everything ready before you apply glue and you learn where to apply pressure (Fig. 39).

Knowing how much glue to use is a matter of experience. Keep a rag around to wipe any excess off your fingers or wood. Paper towels will shred and get stuck to your fingers and your project. Because yellow carpenter's glue is nontoxic, it is safe to use your fingers to spread it around. I use my little finger to spread and even out the glue so the rest of my fingers are clean to handle the wood and clamps.

If you need just a very small amount of glue, pour a couple of drops onto a nonabsorbent surface and dip a toothpick into the glue puddle to use as an applicator.

Getting excess glue squeeze-out on the outside of the box is not too much of a problem with band saw boxes. If there is a lot of glue, it can be scraped off, and the rest will be removed when the box is belt-sanded to shape. Squeeze-out inside the box, on the other hand, is very difficult to remove. Try to spread the glue so there is only

FIG. 39 Doing a dry run will keep you from putting glued surfaces together and then realizing that the clamps are too short and the ones you need are located at the other end of the shop.

FIG. 40 Using your little finger to spread wood glue is not very high-tech, but it works well. You can precisely place the glue, as here, to keep squeeze-out toward the exterior edge of a box.

a fine skin of glue left on the inner side of the surface to be glued (Fig. 40).

You have a minute or two to position your pieces and get them clamped before the glue sets. Align your edges and registration marks before the glue sets up. Breaking the bond, repositioning, and clamping after more than a couple minutes will result in a weak joint. The joint will be set within 10 minutes, and after an hour it will be stronger than the wood itself.

Epoxy

Epoxy is a two-part adhesive that is very strong. It is good for attaching metal to wood, and as a filler. It is messy, smelly, and difficult to clean up, however. Epoxies are resins to which some people develop an allergic reaction. Use disposable gloves, and work in a well-ventilated area. We'll use epoxy to glue the brass hinge pins and handles into the lids of some boxes. You also could use it to attach metal that is being used as an accent strip on a box.

Always mix up a little more epoxy than you think you will need. You don't want to have a project that is half-

assembled and run out of mixed epoxy. It is important that epoxy be well-mixed. Use a flat piece of nonabsorbent material for your mixing surface. It will be ruined, so choose something disposable. Shiny cardboard, such as that used for cereal boxes, works well.

You will need a disposable mixing and applicator stick. I find that half of a tongue depressor, a craft stick, or a toothpick does the job. Pour out equal amounts of each of the components so they are not touching, but are close together. Look at the puddles to be sure they are equal, and then stir them together thoroughly. Every drop on the mixing surface and stick must be mixed. Unmixed

HELPFUL HINT: GLUING

Don't try to do too many joints at once or the glue may set up before you get a chance to get them all clamped. It is much less stressful, and ultimately is time-saving, to do less extensive gluing operations.

FIG. 41 If you don't have enough clamps, a few will do. Use pieces of scrap wood to distribute their pressure evenly on your project.

epoxy components will never set up. Apply the mixture thinly and clamp until set, usually 5 minutes. There are also epoxies available that set up over 8 hours.

Cyanoacrylate Glue

Cyanoacrylate glue, or super glue, is very fast-acting, and it can glue your fingers to the project or to each other. Its action is accelerated by moisture, so it is critical to protect your eyes from contact with even a tiny drop of this adhesive.

Instant glue can be used when clamping is impossible. It also can make very quick repairs to your project so you can keep working without waiting for the glues to dry. It comes in different consistencies and setting times. The fastest is also the thinnest. It is water-thin and sets up in 3 to 5 seconds. It will move by capillary action between surfaces that are touching. This means that you can apply a few drops of this glue around the perimeter of two relatively nonporous, flat pieces of wood and the glue will move between them to secure the entire piece.

Thicker formulations come in handy if you need to attach a piece that cannot be clamped. You could apply glue to one of the pieces of wood, like a small handle, and quickly position it where you want it. Don't take too long though because these glues set up in 10 to 50 seconds.

Clamping

If you have lots of clamps, clamping is just a matter of positioning them evenly on the wood so that the surfaces

FIG. 42 You can use one-handed quick-type clamps to align your pieces to be glued and then add screw-type clamps for more pressure, if necessary.

FIG. 43 Oops! My edge-sanding must have been crooked, and now the corners don't meet squarely. When filled with a wood glue and sanding dust mixture and then sanded flat, the repair will be invisible.

FIG. 44 I keep some extra sanding dust in small containers like this condiment cup and film canister. That way I have a supply ready to use for a quick fill. Add the wood dust to the drop of glue until you have the consistency of toothpaste. Use it quickly, before it dries.

to be joined are held together firmly. If, however, you are short on clamps, there are still ways to secure your piece. By using a piece or two of scrap wood you can distribute the pressure from just a few clamps to the entire surface (Fig. 41).

Another technique would be to put a heavy weight on top of the piece. The problem with weights, however, is that the two joining surfaces may slip out of position, and if the weight is large, it may be difficult to see the movement.

Glue acts as a lubricant between the two pieces of wood; they will tend to slide as pressure is applied. I use a couple of the one-handed quick clamps to align the wood pieces, and then use the heavier-duty screw clamps to apply more pressure (Fig. 42).

A clamp can be a clothespin, a rubber band, pieces of cut-up inner tube, masking tape, duct tape, or a vise. Sometimes you will need to improvise to get the job done.

Repairs

Unless you have been very lucky, there are probably some things that don't fit quite right or some dents or gaps that need to be repaired (Fig. 43). Fix these problems now so that future sanding can smooth out irregularities. Wood glue can be mixed with sanding dust to make a very effective wood filler (Fig. 44). This is a good application for the darker type of wood glue, used if your project is made with a dark wood like mahogany, mesquite, or walnut.

For surface blemishes, mix a bit of fine sanding dust from the project with some wood glue to make a paste that you can force into the cut or dent. If you use the dust from the same piece of wood, it will always be a close match. You can generate some dust by sanding a scrap of the wood with 120-grit sandpaper. Keep some of the excess dust in small containers to save time when you need to quickly fill a small area. Overfill the void to allow for glue shrinkage as it dries. Allow the glue to dry completely, and then sand using sandpaper wrapped around a piece of wood, cork, or rubber to keep the repaired area flat to the project's surface.

FIG. 45 When using epoxy to make a repair, mix the wood dust with one of the components first; then add the second component and mix thoroughly.

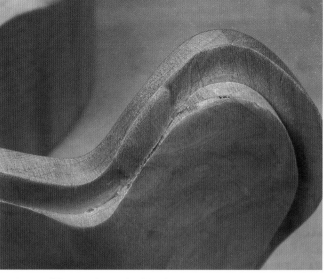

FIG. 46 The repair to the lid of the Nested Hearts Box.

If you are in a rush, you can mix the sanding dust with epoxy to get the same effect (Fig. 45). For emergencies, sanding dust may be forced into a crack and thin cyanoacrylate glue dropped onto the dust. None of the glued repairs will accept penetrating finishes, stains, or dyes as well as bare wood does.

For deeper holes or major errors, it is better to cut a piece of wood that matches as well as possible and glue it into place. Then use the techniques just covered for filling in the resulting small gaps. I used this technique to repair the lid of a Nested Hearts Box, shown in Figure 46. I wasn't paying attention when power-sanding and sanded halfway through the lid and liner. With lots of trial and error and much sanding, I cut a new piece to fit the error, glued it in place, and then carefully power-sanded it to the proper contour. The edge voids were filled with the sawdust and wood glue mixture, and then the piece was hand-sanded to blend in the edges.

Sometimes the lid liner becomes too small to make a good fit with the body. This happens when the lid is circular because wood is removed with the kerf on all sides. An easy way to fix this is simply to cut a different lid liner from the same type of wood instead of from the core cut

FIG. 47 Making a different lid liner is one way to get a tight-fitting lid when working with round, flat lids. Don't forget to use registration marks so you know how everything fits back together during glue-up.

out of the body. Place the glued and sanded body over a piece of wood of the correct thickness, and trace around the inside of the body onto the wood (Fig. 47). Cut out this new lid liner and glue it to the inside of the lid.

Another way to correct a bad fit is to glue wood strips to the perimeter of the lid liner that you cut from the

FIG. 48 This box had a badly fitting lid that was not apparent until after glue-up. The wood was too beautiful to use to feed the fire, so I had to come up with a way to fix the fit.

FIG. 49 I ripped about every $^1/_{16}$" into the end grain of a $^1/_2$" block of tupelo wood, which is very soft and flexible, yet strong, wood. You could also use basswood.

body core. The box shown in Figure 48 was glued up before I noticed the fit of the lid was too sloppy. It is necessary to use a soft and flexible wood to make the strips to go around the liner. In this case, I used tupelo. The strips of wood must be thin and cross-grained so they will flex around the curves (Figs. 49 and 50). The pieces may be held securely with a rubber band or a hose clamp (Fig. 51). The fix, in this case, is obvious, but it almost

FIG. 50 I then crosscut the pieces from the main block of wood, just above the rip cuts.

FIG. 51 It may take more than one strip to go around the lid liner. Glue one strip at a time and your job will be a lot easier. Trying to keep more than one piece of slippery wood in place while you apply the rubber bands is nearly impossible.

FIG. 52 The finished lid fits firmly into place, and the repair looks mighty good after careful sanding and a surface finish.

FIG. 53 For a poor fit on a curved lid, you can add epoxy around the lip. When set up, you can sand and shape it. The box will have to be finished with a surface finish.

looks as though it had been planned to look that way (Fig. 52).

If the lid is curved, as it is on the Nested Oval Box in Fig. 53, none of the previous techniques will work. If you have a wonderful piece of wood like this box elder burl and you don't want to waste the box, you can use epoxy for an effective fix. Apply epoxy to the perimeter of the lid liner (Fig. 53). After the epoxy has set up, test the box lid for a tight fit. You may need to sand a bit to smooth the epoxy, or even use a sharp knife to remove any epoxy that is in the wrong place or messy looking. When used with a surface finish like the lacquer used on this box, this technique can yield acceptable results (Fig. 54).

FIG. 54 The final lid looks good, and the fit is much improved.

Finishing

When a box is put together and sanded smooth, it is time for the finish. This can be as simple as brushing on a coat of varnish, or it can be a complicated process of exotic surface treatments and protective coatings. Each of the projects in this book will introduce techniques you can use to make your boxes unique.

SURFACE TREATMENTS

Sanding until the wood is smooth is one of the easiest treatments; and it is the one you want to use to showcase exceptional grain, color, or pattern on beautiful woods. When the wood is not exciting, carving, texturing, or other surface treatments will make your box more interesting.

Carving

Some of the projects in this book reflect my experience with carving, but every box design will look good even if it is not carved. Carving requires the use of gouges; three of the most helpful include a #11 sweep, $1/8$" wide; a #7 sweep, $3/8$" wide; and a #3 veiner, $1/2$" wide. It is important that gouges be kept razor sharp if you are to

enjoy carving. Use a safety glove whenever the wood is not held in a vise. Figure 1 shows some basic carving tools.

Texturing

Texturing can be applied to the surface of the wood with a shallow carving gouge. The wood does not have to be sanded beyond 80-grit as long as the shape is correct and there are no irregularities in the surface. In the peanut-shaped box shown on page 62, for example, the entire surface was textured using a #3 gouge to make the box look like a peanut shell. The cuts are shallow, slicing cuts that remove just a sliver of wood (Fig. 2). The cuts can be made deeper for a more heavily textured look, or a gouge with a different curve

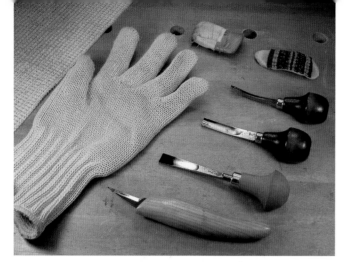

FIG. 1 Basic carving tools sufficient for many of the carving projects in this book. From the top left: nonslip rubber mat; Kevlar safety glove for hand-holding wood; finger and thumb protection for the hand-holding knife, and gouges. From the bottom: carving knife; #3 sweep, $^1/_2$" wide; #7 sweep, $^3/_8$" wide; #11 veiner, $^1/_8$" wide. Add a couple of chisels and you are set.

FIG. 2 Overlapping shallow slicing cuts produce a pleasing overall texture on this Peanut Box.

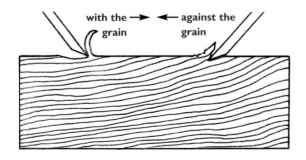

FIG. 3 If your tool digs in (right) instead of cutting off a piece of wood and slicing smoothly (left), you are going against the grain and have lost control of your cut.

FIG. 4 The petals on the Flower Box are appliqués that were made from yellowheart wood.

could be used to produce different effects. Each cut must be made "with the grain," in the direction that the wood fibers lie (Fig. 3). If your gouge digs into the grain of the wood, you are going against the grain. You should be able to slice into and out of the wood in one smooth movement.

Texturing also may be done on softer woods with various stamping tools. These tools may be purchased at leather-working supply outlets or hobby stores. You also can find stamping tools in your shop. Look around for common tools, such as different-sized nail sets, screwdrivers, and the head of a nail or screw. Staining will emphasize the texturing on a textured project.

Appliqués

You can add other materials to your box to give it more interest. You can add pieces of wood with other colors or patterns, as I did with the Flower Box (Fig. 4). A thin sheet of yellowheart wood was cut into petal shapes, sanded

FIG. 5 Figured maple strips are inlaid into the surface of this mahogany box using just the band saw for all the cuts.

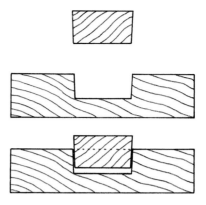

FIG. 6 Cross-section of inlay and inlaid strip.

smooth on the back, rounded on the front, and then glued to the box lid, providing exciting contrast with the red bloodwood box. These additions are called appliqués because they are applied to the surface of the project.

Inlays

Another surface technique is inlay. To inlay, you create a void in the wood to accept another piece of wood or another material, like metal, which is then laid in place. An example of inlay can be seen in the Double-Cross Box (Fig. 5). The pattern was made by cutting $3/16$" into the wood surface with the band saw blade, gluing in $1/4$" strips of contrasting wood, and then sanding the surface smooth (Fig. 6).

Wood-Burning

Wood-burning is an easy way to add color, texture, and designs to wood. I have found that variable-temperature models of wood burners that have interchangeable hand pieces do a good job. The Celtic Knot Box has a design on the lid that is a simple stippled drawing done by wood-burning (Fig. 7). It isn't too difficult to trace a pattern onto a piece of wood and go over the lines with the wood burner. The Bamboo Box project uses a writing tip to

FIG. 7 A wood-burning tool can be used to create designs on your boxes to give them more interest.

draw the bamboo pattern (Fig. 8). Always use the wood burner before you apply the finish.

I like to sign my boxes with the wood burner, because it is permanent and looks professional. Unlike a branding iron, with a wood burner I can change the information

FIG. 8 If you can trace a pattern onto your wood, you can decorate your box with the design. This bamboo wood-burning took a long time, but not much skill (Bamboo Boxes, page 111).

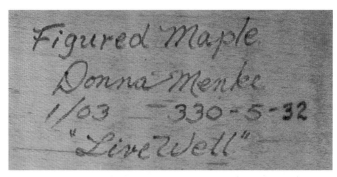

FIG. 9 Identify your finished box with your name and the name of the wood used. You can add a personal note or any other information you want.

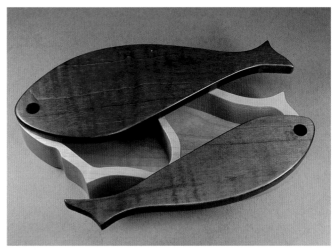

FIG. 10 The Guppy Box's intense color is the result of using a couple of coats of dye (page 151). The color is a mixture of blue dye and a little yellow. Experiment first on scrap to see how the color will look when dry on that particular wood species.

for every box. It is nice to write the type of wood used in the project so the recipient of the box has that information, and I sometimes write a little message to personalize the box (Fig. 9).

With a little imagination, there is no limit to the surface decoration you can use to vary your boxes.

COLORANTS

There are three main classifications of colorants for wood: stains, dyes, and paints. For the most part, we will focus on the first two because painting obliterates the wood grain. Both stains and dyes change the natural color of the wood, but in different ways.

Stains

Stains are available in colors that imitate species of wood and in various basic colors. If you need to use an ordinary wood, but want it to look like a more exotic wood, stains are what you want to use. When you apply stains, they are absorbed only slightly into the pores of the wood. The pigment particles remain for the most part on the surface of the wood. If there is figure in the wood, it may be partially obscured by these particles. Stains are easy to use, however, and so are the method of choice for beginners.

If you use a soft wood like pine, the stain will sink more into the end grain and look much darker than it does on the rest of the piece. Use a sanding sealer before staining soft wood to even out the color.

Dyes

Dyes are not as easy to control as stains, but the effects you can achieve with dyes are wonderful. The dye solution is absorbed deeply into the pores of the wood and enhances the depth of figure instead of hiding it. Dyes need to be flooded across the surface of the wood to avoid a bad, blotchy, uneven coverage (Fig. 10).

For all but a couple of the projects in this book, I worked with beautiful pieces of wood that did not need, and would not benefit from, either dyes or stains. If all you have is pine or fir to work with, you may want to experiment with colorants to jazz up your projects.

TOPCOATS

Clear coatings perform two basic functions for your project: They protect the wood, and they add to the beauty of your piece. Knowing which finish to use for each type of wood and for each box is a challenge. There are entire books that deal with just that subject. I have picked up a few pointers through the years, and I've experimented on the boxes I've made; so I will share with you the techniques that I like.

■ Make sure the surface of the box is clean of dust and dry. You can blow off or vacuum up most of the excess dust. Then wipe it with a tack cloth or a rag dampened with mineral spirits.

■ For some of these finishes, the first coat should be thinned 50/50 with the appropriate solvent. Cleanup is also done with the same solvent.

■ For all finishes that are available in gloss, semigloss, satin, or matte, I use gloss for all but the last coat. The dulling agents that are in the less glossy varnishes take away from the clear effect of any finish you used. Many layers of these finishes could make your wood look muddy and dull. If you want a less glossy finish, just apply one of the nongloss finishes as the last coat.

■ Plan to do either the inside or the outside surface at any one time. That way you will have something to hold onto while you take care of the other side, and it will give you a place on which to lay the piece down while it dries.

Your main choices for finishes are penetrating finishes, like oil, and surface finishes like varnish. We'll talk about those finishes below, but first let me pass on a few thoughts about finishing safety.

Finishing Safety

Read the directions for all finishes, and dispose of your rags or paper towels properly. Solvent-soaked rags or paper towels can combust spontaneously and start a fire. Place them in a tightly covered metal container or spread them out and allow them to dry, preferably outside, and then put them in a trashcan.

Always work in a well-ventilated area when working with finishes. Most finishes have strong odors and fumes that are dangerous to your health. Use the proper respirator for the finish. We need to keep all the brain cells we have to figure out how to make more and better band saw boxes.

Penetrating Finishes

Penetrating finishes are usually oil-based. Some formulations, like Danish oil, have additions of driers or colorants. The main advantage to using these finishes is that they soak into the wood and emphasize the wood's chatoyancy. Another benefit is that oil is easy to apply. A rag soaked in oil makes an excellent applicator, and a dry rag will remove any excess. You do not have to be concerned about dust settling on, and getting trapped in, the finish; that makes it easy to use.

Some Danish oils, such as Watco oil, will not build up on the previous coat, and that thin film does not offer much protection. The finish also will be dull, or matte, unless it is buffed with wax (Fig. 11). Tung oil, however, will improve the finish with succeeding coats, giving the box more protection and a lovely satin sheen. The Double-Cross Box (Fig. 5) was finished with coats of tung oil.

Varnishes and lacquers may be used over a fully cured oil finish for more protection. Some products contain com-

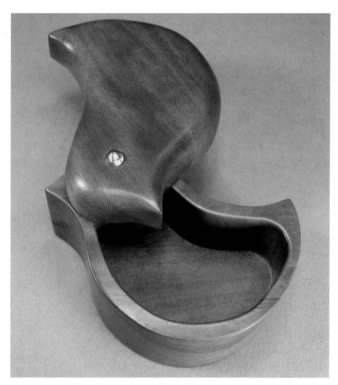

FIG. 11 Danish oil makes a good clear coat for a box project on which you are going to use buffed wax, as shown on the Chickie Box (page 142).

FIG. 12 This mesquite wood Texas Box (page 88) was finished with Danish oil and buffed with wax.

binations of oils and varnishes. The oil component is absorbed into the wood to bring out the color and figure, and the varnish component sets up on the surface of the wood to protect it and add varying degrees of luster. Lately I have been using a semigloss topcoat that is a combination of tung oil and urethane (Arm-R-Seal by General Finishes), which is easy to use and yields good results.

Wax is a good final coat for oil finishes. I used it in the Texas Box shown in Figure 12. There are systems available that use cloth buffing wheels on low-speed grinders or lathes. One such system, the Beall Wood Buff System, uses two buffing compounds, a tripoli and a white diamond. Then a final buffing with a carnauba wax imparts a wonderful shine to your project. I used that technique for all of my first boxes, and I still use it for many of my smaller boxes that are made with hard woods. You also can apply and buff wax by hand instead.

Surface Finishes

Varnish is a generic term that describes any clear surface finish that is put on wood to protect and beautify the item. There are both water-based and oil-based varnishes. However, because water-based finishes tend to obscure rather than illuminate the wood's character, I use only solvent-based finishes on natural wood. There are acetone-based, alcohol-based, and mineral spirit-based solvent varnishes. All solvent-based finishes, either penetrating or surface finishes, will yellow over time. The ambering effect imparts a warm look to the piece. If it is important that the finish have no color, however, a water-based varnish would be your best choice.

Sanding Sealers

Sanding sealers are available in each of the solvent categories. Their purpose is to seal the surface of the project so succeeding layers of finish are not absorbed unevenly. End grain wood absorbs stain like a sponge; more stain gets into the wood, and the resulting color is much darker. Most of the time this is not what we intend for a project, so an application of sanding sealer will fill the pores and keep the color even.

Sanding sealers are easy to sand, and leave a nice surface after sanding. Because sanding sealers are not very hard finishes, they require additional layers of more durable finishes over them.

Lacquers

Lacquers are acetone-based finishes. They are available in either brushing or spraying consistencies. Both types of lacquer dry very quickly, which is both the good news and the bad news. The good news is that because it dries quickly, there is little time for dust to settle on it. You can also recoat quickly to build up many thin layers in a short period of time. The bad news is that it is easy to overwork the application and cause streaking in the finish; too thick an application will result in unsightly runs or drips in the finish. Sanding between lacquer coats is not recommended. Spraying lacquer for these small projects is easily purchased in aerosol cans. I used it on the Sea Shell Box (Fig. 13).

Lacquer finishes are improved by "rubbing out" the surface if there are imperfections. This can be accomplished by using a medium-coarse nylon abrasive pad to remove surface irregularities, and then smoothing out those scratches with progressively finer pads, finishing with the white pad. Buffing and a final coat of wax complete this fine finish.

Shellac

Shellac is an old-fashioned, alcohol-based finish. I remember my grandfather using shellac to finish all his projects, some of which are still in use 50 years later; their finish still looks good.

It is easy to use shellac if you know a few tricks. For the first coat, apply shellac that has been thinned 50/50 with denatured alcohol or shellac thinner. Apply the mixture with a rag. Succeeding coats also should be applied with a rag. It will dry quickly. Shellac makes an excellent sanding sealer, as well as being a good topcoat. Shellac is available in different shades and in either flakes or pre-

FIG. 13 The Sea Shell Box (page 162) was coated with varnish; lacquer applied with a spray can gave the box its final lustrous coat.

mixed. The flakes keep for many years, and you can mix the flakes with denatured alcohol as you need it. But the easiest way to use shellac is to buy a premixed can in the shade you prefer, even though it has a shelf life of just three years.

Varnish

Mineral spirit-based finishes are what are commonly called "varnish." There are many different formulations of varnishes, including gels, tabletop, and polyurethane. They are all very durable finishes that are best applied in thin coats with a rag. A sponge brush works well too (Fig. 14). The first coats of all but gel varnish should be diluted to a 50/50 mixture with mineral spirits. Varnish takes a long time to dry, and it attracts dust like a magnet. You need to apply varnish in a clean environment. Before you varnish, let the dust settle after cleaning so airborne dust particles don't float down onto your finish. If you apply varnish with a brush, you will have a thick coat that

FIG. 14 Tea Boxes, drying between coats of varnish. Seal your brush or rag in a plastic bag so you don't have to clean it between coats.

FIG. 15 Flocking is best done in a large, plastic-bag-lined cardboard box. Supplies include adhesive, an old brush, flocking fibers in bright red, and a cardboard flocking poofer.

can take 12 or more hours to dry. Cover the item with a clean, dry cover so dust will not land on the wet/tacky surface. I use a plastic shoebox supported on some scrap pieces of wood. Not a high-tech solution, but effective.

FLOCKING

Flocking is a system for putting a feltlike coating on the interior surfaces of boxes and drawers. It has two components: colored adhesive and flocking fibers to match.

First you have to have a finish of some sort on the surface of the wood so the adhesive does not sink into the wood and dry too quickly. Brush on the adhesive, which is like a thick, sticky paint. Before the adhesive dries, you must "poof" on a good coat of fibers using a mini-flocker fiber poofer. It is nothing more than two cylindrical cardboard containers that fit into one another (Fig. 15). There is a hole at one end, and when you pump the flocker, the fibers get all excited, jump around, and get poofed out the hole to cover the box area evenly. The fibers stick to the adhesive and make a fuzzy, attractive surface. The main benefit to band saw box makers is that it works very well on irregular surfaces and on small items like these boxes (Fig. 16).

FIG. 16 These finished boxes look great with their bright red flocked lining. It would have been nearly impossible to line these irregular shapes with felt or other material. Flocking is the perfect solution for interior finishes of many small boxes.

After flocking, let the box sit for a day or two without disturbing it, and then pour the excess fibers back into their bag. A little goes a long way, and you will want more colors, so buy small quantities.

PART TWO

PROJECTS

W ith so many possibilities and with our mix-and-match concept of design, you should now be ready to make an unlimited number of unique boxes. The following projects, divided into six sections, provide some examples and show you how different types of boxes are constructed.

At the beginning of each project section there is a quick reference list of the main steps in the construction process for that type of box. Each project offers insight into the type of wood used, design choices, specific instructions for making that box, and an introduction to a new technique or two.

The plans in this book are flexible. The plan drawings shown intentionally do not include dimensions. Your block of wood may start out at a different size or proportion, and it will change as you work with it. If you follow the relative dimensions, listed as final dimensions and given in the Materials list, your box will look similar to mine. When you find that perfect piece of wood for a project, just enlarge the plans on a photocopier to the appropriate size to fit the wood you've selected. Remember that you will need to resize the recommended dimensions for lids and sides accordingly.

Basic Boxes

We'll start out with some basic boxes that have simple planes and then go on to some exciting shapes. If you learn to make basic boxes like these, you'll be well on your way to designing and making more complicated band saw boxes. This section includes the Basic Bangle Box, Star Box, Texas Box, and Man in the Moon Box.

OVERVIEW OF BASIC BOXES

These projects are designed to teach you the basic concepts: cutting the body and lid parts, making sure you mark parts to keep them in order for reassembly, gluing and clamping procedures, and basic finishing techniques. The eight projects in this section use the following basic work plan:

1. Square the block using a band saw or sander.

2. Cut off the top and bottom using your largest, coarsest blade. Keep the same side against the fence for both cuts.

3. Reassemble the pieces and cut the outline; or, for rectilinear boxes, cut off the sides.

4. Remove the core of the body with one cut, and cut off the top of the core for the lid liner. Stabilize rounded and small pieces with a block of squared scrap before cutting.

5. Glue the body back together after sanding the insides of the slab sides. On boxes with interior cutouts, always sand after gluing the body together.

6. Glue the lid liner to the inside of the lid. Align the liner piece on the lid through the box body opening. Match up the saw marks unless the mating edges have been sanded.

7. Sand the inside surfaces of the box and make

adjustments, if necessary, for a good fit. You can sand just where there will be no glue if you want a great fit, but this is more time-consuming.

8. Glue the body to the base; try to avoid getting extra glue on the inside edges. Place clamps evenly all around the box assembly.

9. Assemble lid to body and sand the box to shape using a belt sander. Use sanding grits starting with coarse and ending with fine. Keep the assembly square during the sanding process.

10. Hand-sand to relieve the sharp edges. End each grit in the direction of the grain.

11. Apply a surface treatment if desired. Decorate plain wood, but leave interesting woods alone.

12. Apply finish to the box in a well-ventilated and clean area.

Basic Bangle Box

We begin with one of the easier, no-fail, band saw box designs. All the cuts for this box are straight and can be made with one blade. A simple

design like this will be more successful if you use a highly figured piece of wood. Figured maple, used here, usually comes from a silver maple tree, which most commonly grows on low ground in the eastern part of the United States. It is considered a "soft" maple, but it is hard enough to make a substantial box.

This box is square, so it can hold a collection of bangle bracelets. By changing the dimensions, however, it could become a box for holding playing cards, jewelry, or any other item that needs to have its pieces corraled in one place.

Level of difficulty: Easy

MATERIALS

4x4x2¹/₂" figured maple, or other interesting wood

³/₄x1x2" scrap wood

Graph paper

Brushing lacquer, semigloss

Acetone or lacquer thinner

Spray lacquer, semigloss

top

front

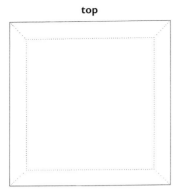

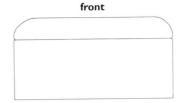

PLAN A Top and front views of the Basic Bangle Box.

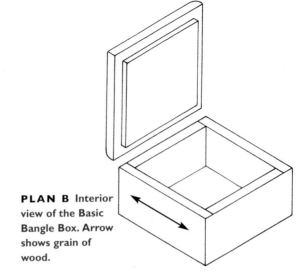

PLAN B Interior view of the Basic Bangle Box. Arrow shows grain of wood.

MAKING THE BOX

1 Plans A and B show the basic configuration and assembly of the box. Choose a wood with an interesting grain, color, or pattern.

2 Check all your tools for square, and then square your block to size before doing anything else. In this case the block was nearly square, so it was sanded to make it completely square and smooth.

3 Take a good look at both faces of your sanded block to determine which is the best surface to be the top of the box lid. Mark this surface TOP with pencil. This piece of maple had much better chatoyancy on one face than the other, so the more chatoyant side became the top of the box.

4 On one side of the block mark a large V so the block will be easy to realign after it is cut apart. Registration marks save a lot of time throughout the project, helping you to fit the pieces back together to keep the grain orientation consistent (Fig. 1).

5 Place the top of the block against the band saw fence, and cut off $^1/_4$" for the base. Then keep the block's top against the fence to cut off the lid $^1/_2$" from the top of the block. Set the lid and base pieces aside for now.

6 Make registration marks on the top of the body on all four sides, marking from 1 to 4 clockwise, to make it easier to reassemble them later. Now set the fence $^3/_8$" from the blade, cut off the two body side pieces that run with the grain, and then cut off the two that run across the grain (Fig. 2).

7 Take the core that is left after the sides are removed and sand the top of it to 220-grit with the belt sander. At the same time, sand the bottom of the lid. Then slice $^1/_4$" off the top of the core to make the lid liner. Lightly sand the edges of this piece while keeping it square. Glue the sanded lid liner in place, centered on the inside of the sanded lid and matching the grain pattern and orientation. When the glue is dry, sand the inside of the lid liner to 220-grit.

FIG. 1 Registration marks will help when you reassemble the pieces for gluing after cutting the block into the box parts.

FIG. 2 This is how the body should look after the sides have been cut off. Notice how the registration marks help keep everything in order.

FIG. 3 Sanding freehand will not give you the square ends you need for the short sides of the body because you can easily create an angled gap between the wood and the belt (exaggerated here for the example).

FIG. 4 Here is a simple jig you can put together in less than a minute. Clamp a squared piece of wood to the stop/fence with small clamps. Use your square to check that the setup is square to the belt.

8 The trick to making a good band saw box is to make the lid so it fits well with the body. We cut the block with a blade that removes quite a bit of wood in the kerf, making most lids too loose. So, we have to cheat a little. For this box we will make the sides fit snugly to the lid by building the body around the lid liner. Sand the inside surfaces of the four body pieces to 220-grit. Sand the ends of the two shorter body pieces so they are the same length as their matching sides of the lid liner. Remember that these are the end grain body pieces, so measure them on the end grain sides of the lid liner. It is not easy to get these small pieces sanded smooth and still keep them square (Fig. 3). A simple jig is helpful if you don't have a table and miter gauge setup (Fig. 4). Just attach a small, squared block of wood to your fence with a couple of clamps. Check it with a square. Now there is a second reference surface to help you square the ends (Fig. 5).

FIG. 5 Here the jig is being used to keep one of the short sides square during sanding. Be careful of your fingertips when sanding these small parts.

FIG. 6 Always do a dry run with clamps before gluing to check your fit and to make sure that the choice of clamps is correct for the job. Here the assembly has been moved to a piece of lined paper, the lines of which help to keep the assembly square. The paper also keeps glue drips off the workbench.

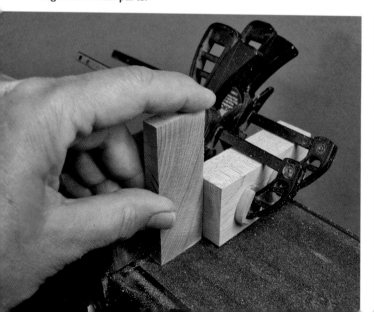

FIG. 7 My box would not win any beauty contests at this point in its construction. There are uneven edges and glue squeeze-out all over, but wait, it will get better soon.

9   Take the two longer body pieces and position them against the short sides to complete the body. There will be a small amount of extra wood on the ends of these longer sides. Make this amount the same on each corner. Trial-fit with clamps to check that the edges all meet and the assembly fits firmly to the lid liner. When the fit is good, remove the setup from the lid and put it on a piece of grid paper on the workbench. The lines on the grid paper will help you to keep the assembly square while resetting the clamps (Fig. 6).

10 Glue the body pieces together, and apply the clamps. Use a square to make sure the body pieces are glued together perpendicular to the table. When the glue is dry, sand the top and bottom of the body and the top of the base with 120-grit sandpaper. Glue the base and body together.

11 Your box looks really bad at this point (Fig. 7). Don't despair; you are about to transform your ugly duckling box into a swan. All that's needed is a little sanding power. This is where a belt sander is necessary. Keep the box together, and with the bottom of the box on the table, sand with a 60-grit belt on the sides of the box until the wood is even. Continue with 120-grit on all six exterior surfaces until the box is smooth. Brush off the dust, and take a good look at your box before proceeding. Check it over to see if there are any cracks in the joints that need to be filled, and do that first before going any further.

12 Decide how you want this box to look. Where will the curves start? Where will they end? Will you curve the bottom edges, and if you do, by how much? Do you want curves at all or would a chamfer, an angled edge, look better? When you have made these decisions, you're ready to refine your box. For this box, with its superb figure, rounded edges seemed right.

FIG. 8 It takes a little practice to use your fingers as a mark-ing gauge. By spacing the pencil mark with your fingers against the piece of wood, you will save tedious measuring time. Use this technique especially when making measurements in from the edge of a complex, curvy shape.

FIG. 9 Make the pencil lines on both the top and sides of the lid. It is your choice how far over you want the curve to go, from just a little on the edge to all the way to the middle of the lid.

13 Mark the top and side limits of the round-over with a pen-cil, using your fingers as a guide (Figs. 8 and 9).

14 Hold the lid edge lengthwise against the moving sanding belt, using a 60-grit belt. Move the lid in an arc to generate the curve in the wood (Fig. 10). Check your progress often, and keep the wood moving until you have the appropriate curve. Continue on the other three sides. Your aim is to end the sanding halfway through the pencil lines so all four corners look the same. Change to a 120-grit belt, and smooth out the marks from the coarser belt; then move onto 220-grit, sanding all the outside surfaces of the box.

15 Now the box is looking quite a bit better, but still not very impressive (Fig. 11). This is where muscle and sandpaper come into play. Sand by hand over the entire box with 220-grit sandpaper, first across the grain and then with the grain, until it is smooth. Use this paper to generate a slight rounding of the edges where the lid meets the body and the bottom edge of the base. The belt-sanded edges can be dangerously sharp. Clean off the wood and workspace, and then sand with 320-grit sandpaper inside and outside the box. Finish all over with 400-grit sandpaper, and then 600-grit if you have a great hard wood like this one. Softer woods will not benefit from sanding beyond 220-grit.

FIG. 10 Hold the wood so it meets the belt evenly, and keep it on the table as you move it smoothly from pencil line to pencil line until you have generated a pleasing curve. Sand just to the center of the pencil line so the remaining half line can continue to act as a guide as you change to finer grits.

FIG. 11 Rough sanding is complete to 220–grit, and the box has a pleasing shape. But it still needs lots of work to make it special.

FIG. 12 The Bangle Box was finished with lacquer.

FINISHING

1 I wanted a glassy smooth finish to emphasize the chatoyancy in the figured maple, so I decided to use lacquer. Lacquer dries quickly, but it still needs to be protected from falling dust. Have a covered area ready to slip the box pieces into as soon as they have been coated.

2 The first coat was brushing lacquer thinned 50/50 with acetone or lacquer thinner. The thinned lacquer is absorbed more deeply into the pores of the wood.

3 The second lacquer coating was applied full strength after the first coat was thoroughly dry. Try to make the coat as thin as possible to avoid runs, and work quickly. If you are brushing when the lacquer starts to dry, you will make streaks in the finish.

4 The final coat of lacquer was applied with a spray can so there would be no chance of drips or brush marks.

5 Figures 12 and 13 show that the results were worth the effort. That unimpressive block of wood has been transformed into a lovely box that is fine enough to hold the Crown Jewels, or at least my costume jewelry.

FIG. 13 The finished Bangle Box. Figured maple, $3^7/8$x$3^3/4$x$1^3/4$".

Star Box

The basic Star Box is not difficult to make. If you want to make the star pattern three-dimensional, however, it will take more time and consid-

erably more effort. I'll show you how to carve it, but remember that you also could make a variation by texturing part of the lid; painting it; or cutting out an appliqué of a smaller star in a different colored, thin piece of wood and attaching it to the lid.

One of the skills I want you to learn from this book is how to design your own boxes. I'm going to go into some detail about how to divide a block into segments. You may decide you want to make a seven-pointed star instead of a five-pointed one. Later in the projects, you may want to increase or decrease the number of petals on the Flower Box. This little lesson will show you how.

Level of difficulty: Easy. Moderate if carving the top

MATERIALS

$5^1/_2$x$5^1/_2$x$2^1/_2$" mahogany or other easily carved wood

$^1/_8$" band saw blade

Drum or spindle sander

Double-sided adhesive tape

Carving chisel, 1", full-sized tool (if carving the top)

Tung oil

Mineral spirits

Beall Wood Buff System, or wax applied and buffed by hand

Measuring tools for design construction (optional): Ruling compass, protractor, large circle template, small circle template, carbon or graphite paper, thin cardboard or plastic

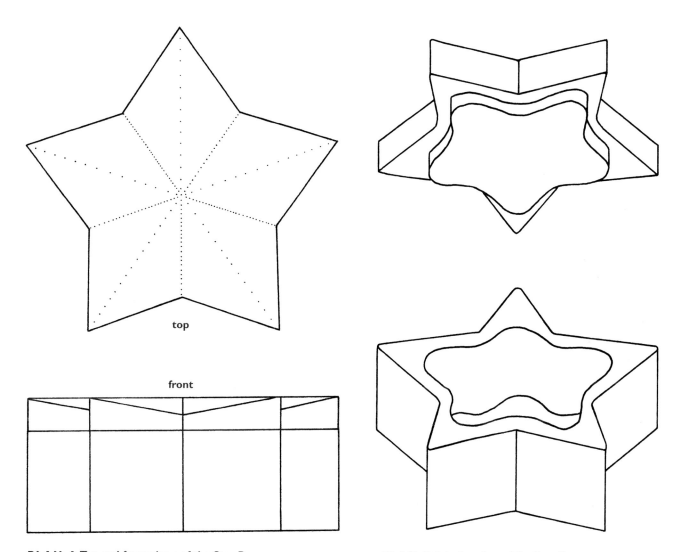

top

front

PLAN A Top and front views of the Star Box.

PLAN B Interior view of the Star Box.

MAKING THE BOX

1 Plans A and B show the basic configuration and assembly of the box.

   NOTE: If you are not going to carve the top of your box, go on to Step 8. You could enlarge the plan in Fig. 4 to get the star pattern. If you want to create your own star plan, proceed with Steps 2 to 5.

2 The first step in drawing the pattern for your star is to define the limits of your box. In this case, we have a block of wood slightly larger than 5" square. The star can be 5" across, so by using a compass to draw a circle with a $2^{1}/_{2}$" radius (half the width of the star), the outside limits of the points of the star are set. To maximize space inside the

box, and yet keep it looking like a star, 3" will be the inside limits. Draw another circle, using the same center, with a $1^{1}/_{2}$" radius (Fig. 1).

3 The next step requires a little math, but not too much. Because every circle has 360°, we can segment any circle by dividing the number of segments desired into 360°. In this case, 360° divided by 5 equals 72°. This tells us that the points of the star will fit equally along the perimeter of the circle when placed every 72°. Use a protractor to mark the larger circle every 72° (Fig. 2). Draw straight lines from the center of the circles through the perimeter at these marks.

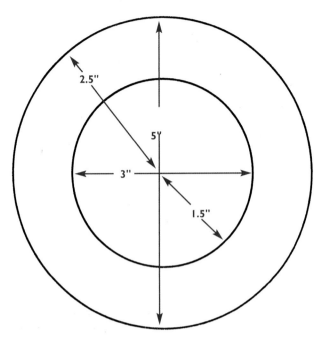

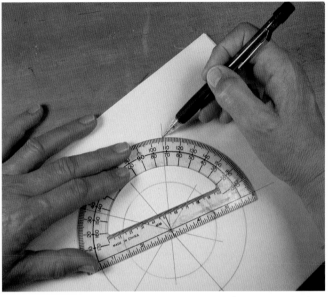

FIG. I To design the box, you need to first define the perimeter and interior dimensions of the star: 5" and 3" circles.

FIG. 2 Lines drawn through the center at 36° intervals divide the circle into 10 sections: five for the exterior points and five for the interior points.

4 We also need to know where on the inside perimeter to locate the inner points of the star on the inner circle. We could measure 36° around the circle from an outer point, but if we just extend the lines already drawn across the circle, they will nicely bisect the opposite segment (Fig. 3). This trick only works for odd-numbered segments.

5 Connect the points of contact along the circles to get the outside dimensions of your star (Fig. 4).

6 The sides of this box will need to be at least ¹/₄" thick, so use a ruler to lightly draw lines ¹/₄" inside the outer star. Because we want to cut the interior of the box with one cut, we will need to round all the corners. Use a large circle template to draw an arc from the tip of one point to the other point, staying ¹/₄" inside the inner corner (Fig. 5). Then use the small circle template to draw a smaller arc within each tip of the star (Fig. 6). The result should be a gently curved interior that will be easy to cut with your ¹/₈" blade (Fig. 7). You will have a nice leftover piece to make into another, smaller box.

7 Go over the lines for the final shape, and you are ready to transfer the pattern to the wood.

8 You can transfer the pattern with carbon or graphite paper, or you can cut out a pattern template from thin cardboard or plastic (Fig. 8). The benefit of making a template is that you can shift the pattern around on your block to find the best grain direction and any desirable color or pattern on the wood. Also, it's handy to keep these patterns for future boxes. Make the cutting lines on your block with a thin-line black marker, because pencil lines are hard to see, especially on darker woods.

9 It is not necessary to have all six sides of the block square for this piece because we will be cutting the star shape out of the block without reference to the sides. It is only important that the top and bottom of the block are parallel to each other and smooth, and that one of the sides is square to these faces. Mark that side with an X.

10 At this point you have two choices: Either cut out the out-

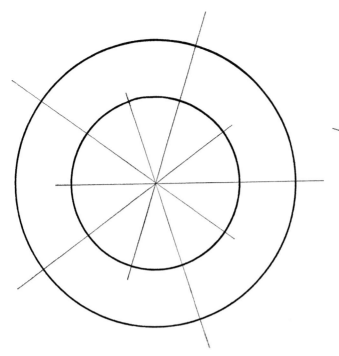

FIG. 3 Connect the points of intersection with the circles to make the five-pointed star.

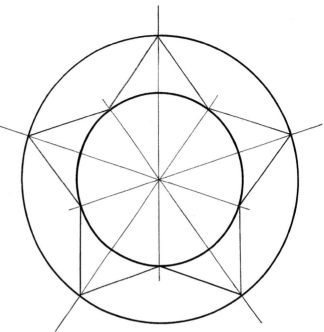

FIG. 4 Now you have a perfect 5-pointed star pattern. This technique will allow you to make any number of divisions for your boxes.

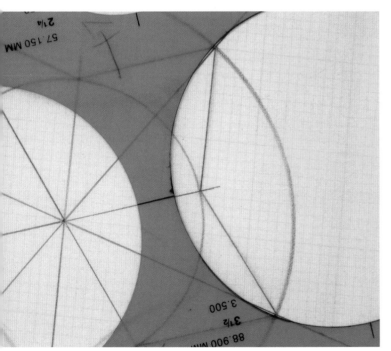

FIG. 5 A large circle template is helpful when drawing smooth curved lines. Here, it is used to define the inner curve for the walls of the box.

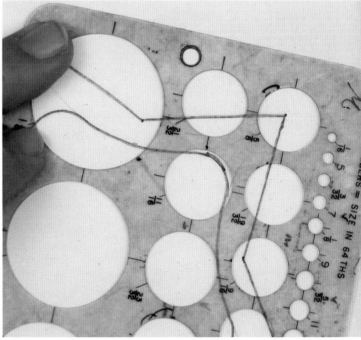

FIG. 6 Use a smaller circle template to draw a smaller radius curve at the tips of the star so the interior can be cut out with a ¹/₈" band saw blade.

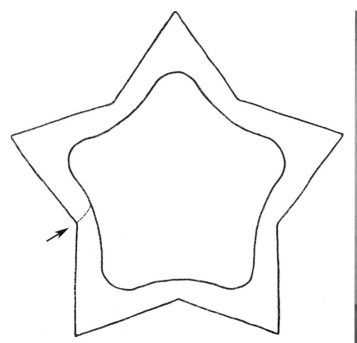

FIG. 7 Rounding the interior wall lines makes it possible to cut out the core easily in a single cut. Dashed line is entrance cut kerf.

FIG. 8 If you transfer the pattern to lightweight cardboard, such as that used for cereal boxes, you will be able to use the pattern template many times.

line, and then cut off the top and bottom, or cut off the top and bottom, reassemble the three pieces, and then cut out the outline. Due to the irregular nature of this design, it is safer to keep it as a block while doing the major cutting.

11 Make a large V registration mark on one side of the block. With the "X" side on the table and the top of the block against the band saw fence, cut $1/4$" off the bottom of the block. Stop the machine, move the fence over, and cut the body off at $1/2$" from the top of the block.

12 Brush off any sawdust that would prevent the double-sided tape from making a good bond, and then reassemble the three sections according to the registration mark, using tape (Fig. 9). Tap it firmly with a mallet or put the assembly on the floor and press on it with your foot to make sure the pieces are stuck together tightly.

13 With the band saw, cut out the outlined piece (Fig. 10). If you use a wide blade, as shown in the photograph, you will have very straight sides that will need very little sanding. But if you use a narrow blade, such an $1/8$" blade, you will

FIG. 9 The block has been reassembled, using the registration marks, with cloth-backed, double-sided tape.

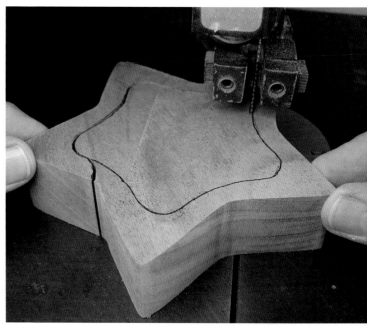

FIG. 10 The exterior was cut with a ³/₄" blade, which made nice, straight sides and a sharp angle where the points met. It proved difficult to sand the inner corners of the star, and I ended up using the ³/₄" spindle sander and rounding the inner corners. It would have been better to cut the inner corners slightly rounded at the outset, using a ¹/₈" blade, unless the sharp angle was something for which I was willing to work hard. Notice how the push stick supports the block in line with the blade, keeping my fingers safely out of the way.

FIG. 11 Mark and cut out the interior of the box body. Notice how my fingers are well away from the path of the blade.

be able to make the inner corners slightly rounded, which will make sanding easier.

14 Using a ¹/₈" blade, make the entrance cut (Fig. 11), and continue smoothly around the interior of the block. When you get back to the entrance kerf, keep the blade aimed along the cutting line and just barely cut through the last fibers of wood. Turn off the band saw, wait until the blade stops (remember to count the teeth of the blade), and then back the blade out through the entrance kerf (Fig. 12). This way, the teeth of the blade will not disturb the wood and the entrance cut will be nearly invisible after gluing.

15 The body may need to be cross-clamped, as shown in Figure 13, for gluing the body together.

16 Cut the lid liner ¹/₄" from the top of the core. Sand the

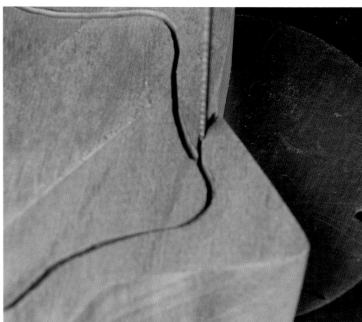

FIG. 12 After you have cut around the interior, turn off the band saw and back out through the entrance kerf. If you try to do this with the machine running, you'll likely cut into the box sides, making an invisible joint impossible.

FIG. 13 Use two clamps to hold the body joint together: one to hold the sides in alignment and one to close up the kerf. Light-duty clamps are best for these jobs, where too much pressure could break the wood.

FIG. 14 Join the liner and lid firmly so there is no unsightly gap between them. Use as many clamps as necessary. Check the position of the lid liner before finally tightening the clamps.

edges only enough to remove the saw marks, or else cut a new lid liner from another piece of wood, as shown for the Man in the Moon Box.

17 Glue the lid liner to the interior of the lid, being careful to keep the saw marks lined up and the liner piece centered on the lid (Fig. 14).

18 For this box, the interior of the base was sanded smooth only in the exposed areas and not where the bottom of the body joins the base. Mark lightly with pencil on the base to indicate where the base will be visible after gluing. Sand the center area until smooth, being careful to leave undisturbed the area that will be glued. Use a straking light to highlight any missed areas.

19 Sand the interior of the body. Remove as little wood as possible so the lid will fit as tightly as possible (Fig. 15).

20 Glue the body to the base. Assemble the box and sand all of the exterior surfaces smooth. If the box will be carved, do not sand finer than 120-grit.

21 If you want to carve the lid into a three-dimensional star, you need to have a sharp chisel. Carving can be done with ordinary chisels, but it is a lot easier to do with properly ground and sharpened carving tools. The essential differ-

FIG. 15 An oscillating spindle sander makes light work of sanding the interior. This job also can be accomplished with a drum sander, or by hand. Always sand the interior before assembly.

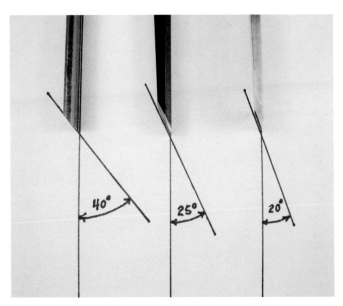

FIG. 16 Carving chisels are ground to angles sharper than those used for general carpentry. From the left: An ordinary carpenter's chisel, with a 40° angle, is designed to be forced into wood with a hammer to remove chunks of wood. A Japanese woodworker's chisel, ground at 25°, is much easier to push or tap to slice into wood. The sharper angle of the carving chisel, ground at 20°, allows it to slice into the wood more easily, but it also makes the edge more likely to break if misused.

FIG. 17 The top of the box is ready to be carved. This box would look nice just as it is, after the finish is applied, but carving the top adds another dimension to the design. The carving marks were made with a pen for clarity of our presentation; it would be better to use a pencil on your project.

ence between a common carpenter's chisel, a more refined Japanese chisel, and a carving chisel is in the angle of their bevels (Fig. 16). If you are going to use a carpenter's chisel to carve the star, grind it to a more acute angle so the chisel can slice into the wood. Note: If you are not going to carve the top of the box, go to Step 27.

22 Mark the star pattern on the lid from the center of the lid to the interior and exterior points. Measure down 1/4" on the side of the lid at the inside points, and connect these marks to the top of the lid at the tips of the star (Fig. 17).

23 Secure the block in a vise or with clamps to your bench. The first carving step is to make vertical cuts straight into the lid at the inside points of the star. These are called stop cuts, and they will keep the chisel from going too far during the next cuts. Make them deeper at the outside edge, and taper them up to the surface at the center. Hold the chisel straight up, on the line, and tap firmly with a mallet. If you are not sure how deep to make them, make them shallow; you can always make them deeper.

FIG. 18 First, make stop cuts straight into the wood at the inner corners of the star. Then make slicing cuts up to those stop cuts. Work from the top of the star points down to the low points between them.

FIG. 19 Carving is almost always a gradual slicing away of wood. In that way you have control over the depth and extent of your cut. If you try to remove too much wood at once, you likely will remove a point from your star.

FIG. 20 You need a lot of control to keep your blade from cutting into the wood on the opposite point. Work slowly and carefully.

24 Next, take very light, shaving cuts from the lines that mark the top points of the star down to the stop cuts (Fig. 18). Near the center of the star, the cuts will be shallow; but at the outside edge they can be deeper. The aim is to generate planes that start at the lines connecting the points of the star to the center and end in the troughs between the points. The safest way to accomplish this is to make gradually deeper cuts by carefully paring away layers of wood (Fig. 19). If you try to remove too much wood with one stroke of the chisel, you are likely to cut into wood that you don't want to cut. (See more on carving in the Sea Shell Box project.)

25 After generating one side of the star's point, make a matching plane on the other side (Fig. 20). Continue around until all the points are finished (Fig. 21). If you slip and make a cut too deep, just make all the star's points match the error, and nobody will ever detect your design variation.

26 Use a block to hand-sand the planes of the lid so oversanding does not round the edges.

27 Sand the exterior of the box to 320-grit, by hand. Relieve all the edges.

FIG. 21 The box has been sanded to 220-grit. Start with coarse, 80-grit sandpaper to get the carving marks out, and then move to 120-grit before finishing with 220-grit. Wrap the sandpaper around a flat block so the sides of the star's points remain flat.

FIG. 22 The Star Box was finished with tung oil and then buffed with the Beall Wood Buff System.

FINISHING

1 This box was finished with tung oil and wax. The first coat of oil was thinned 50/50 with mineral spirits, applied liberally with a rag and then wiped away.

2 When the first coat of oil was dry, after a few days, a full-strength coat was applied and then wiped off.

3 After the tung oil dried, I used the Beall Wood Buff System to give the box its final sheen.

4 Figures 22 and 23 show the finished Star Box.

FIG. 23 The finished Star Box. Mahogany, 5x5$^{1}/_{2}$x2$^{1}/_{4}$".

Texas Box

The Texas Box was made from mesquite, a tree native to Texas and the Southwest United States. Although ranchers have long cursed mesquite's

ability to invade pastures, suck up all available moisture, and puncture tractor tires with 2" long thorns, mesquite is now recognized as a beautiful wood with characteristics that make it suitable for woodworking. The wood is dimensionally stable, so it will not change shape over time. It is a hard wood that resists denting and wear, and it is available from many suppliers. If you live in the South, your supply may be as close as the nearest firewood pile.

Texas mesquite wood often has interesting inclusions and defects. Because it was often used as a living fence post, there are frequently nails and barbed wire in the wood. I've even seen a piece of fence post with a Civil War era lead ball embedded in the wood. Check carefully with a metal detector for metal debris in found wood like old fence posts.

Many states and countries have pleasing shapes that could be used to make boxes. You could make a box in the shape of Massachusetts, of Italy, or of the United

States. In my case, I took the liberty of modifying the shape of Texas to make it easier to create a box. By cutting around a copy of a map of the state with scissors, I eliminated sharp angles and some details.

The construction of the Texas Box is the same as that of the Star Box. Instead of carving the lid, however, we will be texturing the entire upper surface. We'll also discover techniques for fixing damaged wood.

Level of difficulty: Easy

MAKING THE BOX

Plans A, B, and C show the basic configuration and assembly of the box.

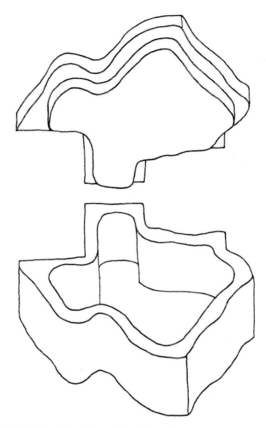

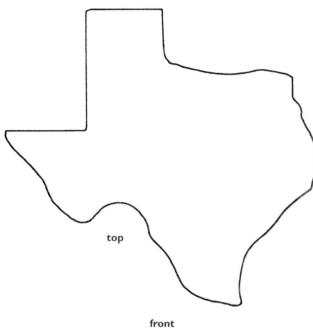

top

front

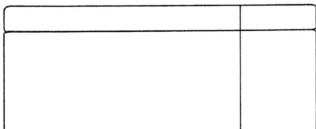

PLAN A Top and front views of the Texas Box.

PLAN B Interior view of the Texas Box.

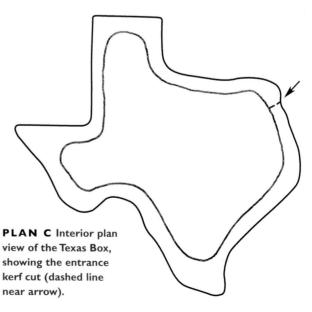

PLAN C Interior plan view of the Texas Box, showing the entrance kerf cut (dashed line near arrow).

FIG. 1 Mesquite is prone to a beetle infestation that leaves holes in the wood. These holes can be filled with black-tinted epoxy or with colored bits like turquoise or brass mixed into the epoxy. For a rustic-looking project, the holes can be left just as they are found.

FIG. 2 Other voids in the wood, like these shakes, can be treated as decorative or filled.

2   The mesquite beetle enjoys boring into mesquite, leaving behind nice, round holes (Fig. 1). In this piece of wood, the tree had developed "shakes" when it was blown about in high winds (Fig. 2). These voids in the wood were not apparent until the wood was cut to shape. Although sometimes these defects can add to the appeal of the finished piece, in this case I needed to make them disappear.

3   The first step in filling a void is to determine where the good wood starts. Punky, or soft, wood can be dug out with a dull knife until only solid wood is left (Fig. 3). Because there is some black in the mesquite wood, black epoxy makes a good filler for the gaps.

FIG. 3 Punky wood can be dug out with a screwdriver or similar tool. You need to remove all but the hard, undamaged wood.

4   When mixing the epoxy for this messy job, place newspapers on the work surface and use disposable gloves (Fig. 4). Thoroughly mix a small amount of black colorant with one of the epoxy components before adding the second epoxy component. If you are using a quick-setting epoxy, you will have to mix up succeeding batches to fill all the holes. There are epoxies that have a 25-minute working (open) time, but they take overnight to set up.

5   Force the epoxy mixture into the voids with a stick; leave it a little over-filled to allow for settling and shrinkage.

6   Let it set up until it no longer feels sticky, and then scrape off any excess with a cabinet scraper (Fig. 5). If you don't have a cabinet scraper, a large kitchen knife held perpendicular to the wood is a good substitute (Fig. 6). The process may have to be repeated if there are still voids to be filled.

7   Figure 7 shows that the repair on the bottom of the box is practically invisible. When finished it looked like a natu-

FIG. 4 Filling voids is a messy job, but it may be the only way to salvage your box. Put down newspaper, and use gloves and a disposable applicator.

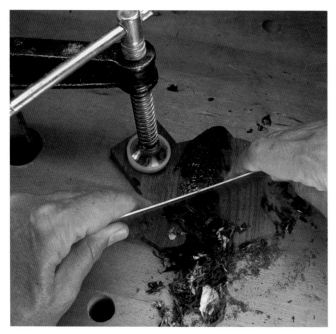

FIG. 5 Sanding thick epoxy will fill up your sanding belt with a gummy mess and ruin it. Use a scraper to remove the epoxy on the surface of the wood, and then finish with the belt sander and hand-sanding.

FIG. 6 If you substitute a large, sharp kitchen knife for a cabinet scraper, be careful. Keep your fingers across the top of the blade, not underneath it.

ral part of the mesquite wood. The lid liner had a very crumbly edge that was potholed with voids. The only way to fix it was with black epoxy, which was used to fill the holes and form new sides. The lid was sanded to shape and the new edges smoothed. It is now as good as new (Fig. 8).

8 The surface of the Texas Box was textured with a shallow #3, $^1/_2$" wide carving gouge, which was used to make shallow overlapping grooves all over the top and sides of the box.

FIG. 7 Repairing this large shake crack on the bottom of the box was not difficult, and the results are pleasing. After the finish was applied, it was impossible to discern that a repair had been made.

FIG. 8 This repair on the inside of the lid was tricky. It required several separate applications of epoxy over a few days' time until the surface was built out, and then it was shaped with a knife and sandpaper.

FIG. 9 The
Texas Box was
finished with
Danish oil and
the Beall Wood
Buff System.

FINISHING

1 Mesquite is a hard, dense wood that looks good with an oil finish and wax. First, I applied a coat of Danish oil.

2 When the oil was dry, the box was buffed with the Beall Wood Buff System (Fig. 9). Alternatively, wax may be applied and buffed by hand.

3 Figure 10 shows the completed Texas Box.

FIG. 10 The finished
Texas Box. Mesquite,
$5^{1}/_{4}$x$5^{1}/_{4}$x2".

Man in the Moon Box

Here's an example of how to turn an uninteresting, featureless piece of wood into a beautiful box. The lid decoration technique is called

segmentation because the piece is cut apart, contoured, and then glued back together. Segmentation is related to the woodworking technique called intarsia, but in intarsia the sections are cut from different types of wood and then fitted together like a puzzle.

We will be covering the wood with dye

and design, so if the wood has any unique features, they will be wasted. In this project we will be using a wood burner. If you don't have one, you can draw the design with an indelible marker or with paint. You can paint the box if you don't have dyes.

Level of difficulty: Moderate

MATERIALS

4x4x2$^1/_8$" box elder

$^1/_8$" band saw blade

Coping saw or scroll saw

Drum or spindle sander

Wood burner with writing tip (or indelible marker or paint)

Graphite paper

Blue dye or thinned blue paint

Yellow dye or thinned yellow paint

Varnish sanding sealer

Spray lacquer, semigloss

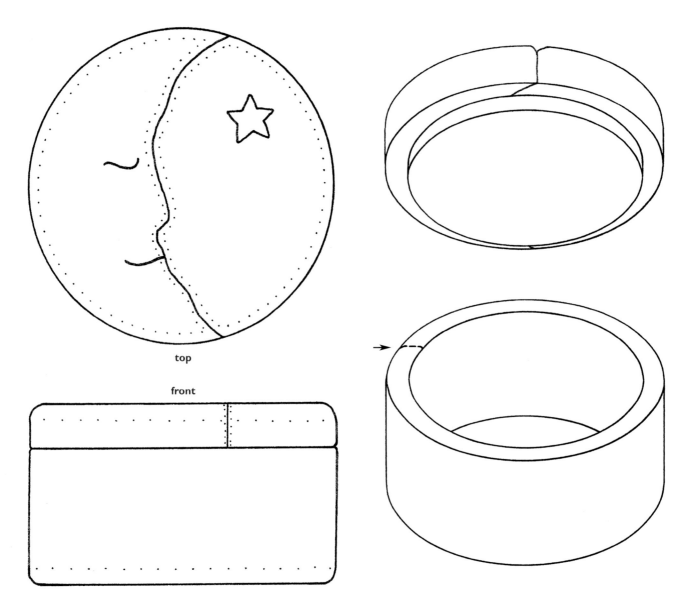

top

front

PLAN A Top and front views of the Man in the Moon Box.

PLAN B Interior view of the Man in the Moon Box. Dashed line is entrance cut kerf.

MAKING THE BOX

1   Plans A and B show the basic configuration and assembly of the box.

2   This box is made like the previous boxes, except that the lid design is different. We will cut out a separate, fitted lid liner and experiment with using dyes to add color to our projects.

3   Make a photocopy of Plan A at the appropriate percentage,

cut out the pattern, and lay it on the block of wood so you can position it to make best use of the wood's grain and to avoid defects (Fig. 1). In this case, the block was large enough to reposition the pattern off center and still keep enough extra wood around the pattern so the band saw blade would remain in the block for the initial cut. (Once the blade escapes from the block, it is difficult to resume a smooth cutting line.)

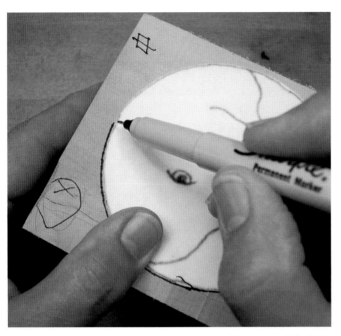

FIG. 1 By cutting out a copy of the plan, it is easy to shift the pattern around to avoid blemishes in the wood.

FIG. 2 When you need to remove just a little wood, as in the slight rounding where the two lid pieces meet, you don't want to use power. Power tools are great time- and energy-savers, but you'll have better control under your own power for delicate jobs like this.

4 Cut the lid into two sections, as indicated on Plan A. Although a fine band saw blade will work for this job, the finer kerf left by a scroll saw blade is better.

5 Sand the top edges of the lid just enough to round them to shape (Fig. 2). Then glue the two lid pieces together, using a flat work surface and clamps to keep them aligned (Fig. 3).

6 Circular boxes result in lid liners that are too loose, so we will make a new liner for this box. After the body has been glued together and sanded on the interior, use it as a template to make a perfectly fitting lid liner. Use a sharp pencil to trace around the interior of the body onto a ³/₈"-thick piece of the same wood as the rest of the box. Because we are not working with a perfect circle, make registration marks so you will be able to get the liner in the same position when you glue it to the lid. Cut out this new liner, following the outside of the line. Sand the liner to halfway through the line, and you should have a perfect fit.

7 Put the liner in place in the body and line up the body and lid registration marks so the liner will be glued in the right

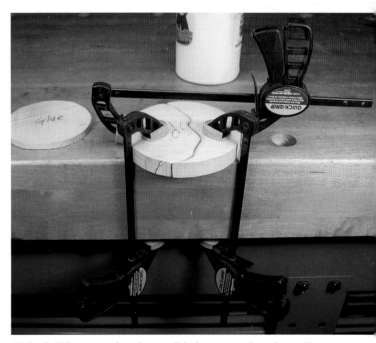

FIG. 3 When you glue the two lid pieces together, they will want to pop up at their joining edges. Avoid that problem by holding the pieces down on a flat surface with clamps during glue-up.

Man in the Moon Box **95**

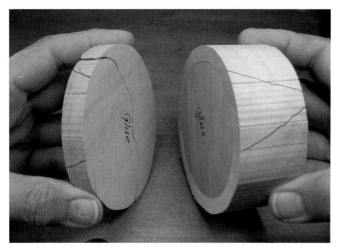

FIG. 4 Registration marks and notes on the mating surfaces will help you to keep the pieces in the right order. With this technique the lid and body will fit together well.

location (Fig. 4). Carefully remove the body, and mark the lid and liner positions. Glue the liner to the lid, and you will have a nicely fitting lid liner that also reinforces the joined lid pieces.

8 Glue the sanded base and body together, using as many clamps as necessary to effect a good joint (Fig. 5), and then finish sanding.

FIG. 5 You will want a lot of pressure when gluing the body to the base. The light-duty quick clamps were positioned first, and then the heavy-duty screw clamps were set in between them.

FINISHING

1 We'll put details on the box with a wood burner, using the writing (ballpoint) tip. First, transfer the designs to the wood with graphite paper.

2 My wood-burning unit has a temperature control. I usually practice a little on a piece of wood of the same species as the wood I'm about to burn to get the correct temperature (Fig. 6). You don't want smoke or fire, but a nice dark line will look good. Try to get it right the first time because if you go over your lines, you'll often wind up with double lines. You can always sand the burn marks away and start anew.

3 The burned box looked good, and I could have finished it with a clear coat, but I wanted to give it some color (Fig. 7).

4 Working with dye is tricky because it tends to run with the grain (bleed) and not stay where it is put. You could use thinned acrylic paints to get a similar effect, but dye

FIG. 6 A wood burner with a temperature control will make your job a lot easier and will make the project look better. If all you have is an inexpensive, stick-type burner, however, it probably will handle most of the projects in this book that call for wood-burning.

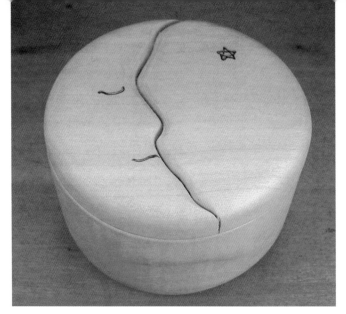

FIG. 7 Wood-burned details add character to this box. If you don't have a wood burner, paint the designs, draw them on with a permanent marker, or carve them.

FIG. 8 Here is the setup for dying. On the left is a practice piece for testing dye concentrations. Use small containers of diluted dye, and test on the same type of wood as your project.

has its own translucent and grain-enhancing qualities that make working with it worthwhile.

5 Wood dye comes in concentrated powder or liquid forms. The dye can be thinned with water or acetone. I mixed up solutions of small quantities of water with just a couple of drops of dye. Figure 8 shows the trials I made on a similar piece of wood to test the intensity of the colors.

6 You may want to try placing a piece of thin plastic or paper between the two sections of the lid to keep the colors separate. Apply the darker color first; if there is much bleeding into the wrong areas, you will be able to sand away the error. When the first color has dried, apply the second color.

7 The clear protective coat on this box was an initial coat of varnish sanding sealer, which was followed with semigloss spray lacquer (Fig. 9).

8 Figure 10 shows the completed Man in the Moon Box.

FIG. 10 The finished Man in the Moon Box. Box elder, $3^3/_4$ x $3^3/_4$ x 2".

FIG. 9 The Man in the Moon Box was finished with varnish sanding sealer and semigloss spray lacquer.

Nesting Boxes

Nesting boxes are a great way to completely use a piece of wood. The inner box is made out of the core or scrap from the larger box. Making nested boxes is not much more difficult than making basic boxes, but tolerances are tighter, especially if you want to make three boxes out of a 2×2×4" block of wood. That is a real challenge. Give a little forethought in your design to how many boxes you want to cut out of one block of wood.

OVERVIEW OF NESTING BOXES

Construction procedures don't vary much for nested boxes versus the basic boxes of the previous section. It's just a matter of repeating all the steps on each new nested box, making sure that each time you start out with a newly squared block. All the projects in this section follow the work plan outlined below:

1. Square the block.
2. Either cut off the lid and base pieces, or cut out the outline, depending on the shape of the box. Then do the other maneuver. (See individual project for details.)
3. Cut out the interior of the body.
4. Cut the lid liner from the top of the core.
5. Square the remaining core.
6. Keep making more boxes in the same way until the remaining block is too small to safely handle.
7. Glue the lid liners to the lids.
8. Glue the bodies together.
9. Sand all the interior surfaces, and then glue the body to the base.
10. Sand the lids and bodies to fit.
11. Sand the exteriors to form.
12. Sand all surfaces to finish.

Tea Boxes

These boxes are called Tea Boxes because they are cubes, like tea boxes, and the lids are tight-fitting enough to keep tea fresh. To give these plain-shaped boxes more interest we will laminate two different types of wood. Because both of these boxes are cut from the same laminated block, the design is the same on both of them. Choose wood species that have different colors to create contrast. If you want to laminate more than three pieces of wood, do only three at a time or the glue will dry before you can get all the pieces clamped together.

Level of difficulty: Moderate

MATERIALS

4x4x1³/₄" red oak, two pieces

4x4x³/₄" purpleheart

Planer or belt sander

Large parallel-jawed clamps

Graph paper

Wood burner with writing tip (or indelible marker or paint)

Varnish sanding sealer

Gel varnish, satin

Gray scrubby pad

Newspaper or waxed paper

Carpenter's yellow glue

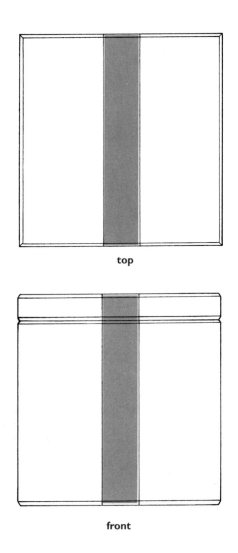

top

front

PLAN A Top and front views of the
largest Tea Box.

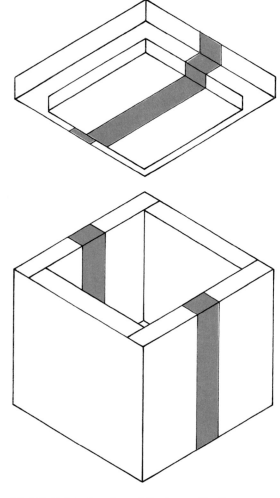

PLAN B Interior view of the largest Tea Box.

top view

front view

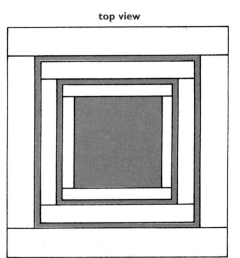

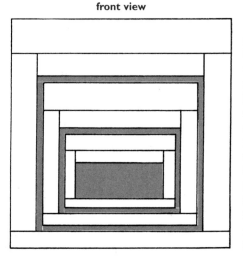

PLAN C Top and
front cross-sectional
views of the **Tea Boxes**
show how three nesting
boxes look. The far left
drawing shows three
nesting boxes, without
lids, viewed from the
top. The near left draw-
ing is a cross-section
through the boxes, seen
from the front, to show
how the boxes are
made from the core of
the previous box.

FIG. 1 Choose lumber with a straight grain and good contrast between the different pieces. Wood seldom comes from the mill in good enough shape to laminate, so you'll have to plane or sand it flat and smooth.

MAKING THE BOX

1 Plans A, B, and C show the basic configuration and assembly of the boxes.

2 To get a good fit between the laminations, a planer was used to make the pieces of wood perfectly flat. If you are using a planer, leave the boards long and cut them to length afterward (Fig. 1). If you don't have a planer, cut the boards to length first, and then sand them flat and smooth for gluing.

3 Fit the sections together to see how they look (Fig. 2). Look at the orientation of the grain on the top of the block, and alternate the curve of the end grain to compensate for possible later warping of the pieces. At this point it is easy to change the design. For example, a thin piece of ebony on either side of the purpleheart would be striking.

4 Glue-up will be messy because you will be using sufficient glue to make sure there is a good bond between the pieces of wood. Put newspapers or waxed paper on the work surface to keep it clean. Put waxed paper around the clamps to protect them. Don't worry about squeeze-out because the edges will be trimmed off later. Notice that big screw-type clamps were used for this job (Fig. 3). It takes a lot of pressure to hold these big blocks together while the glue dries. Wait until the next day to remove them, giving the glue all the time it needs to bind the wood together.

FIG. 2 After they are milled with the planer or sander, the pieces are ready for lamination. They need to fit together without gaps to make a workable block for your boxes.

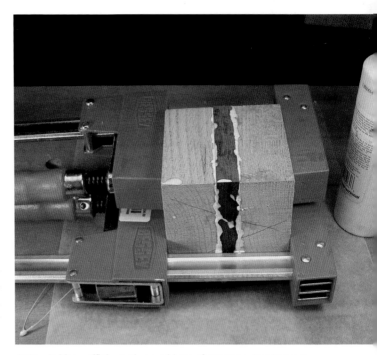

FIG. 3 Use sufficient glue and lots of pressure to assure a good lamination. Here I've used the big guns, screw-type clamps, for maximum power.

FIG. 4 During your dry-fit test, draw lines on the sheet of paper inside the pieces to make it easier to realign the sides when doing the actual gluing. Draw lines on the inside of the body sides to indicate where the corners overlap to help you to keep the pieces square during clamping. Note: Make your notations lightly with pencil.

FIG. 5 With everything laid out and clearly marked, there is less chance of gluing the wrong sides together.

5 More than likely there will have been some slippage between the pieces of wood, so the blocks will need to be squared up again. Use the band saw for squaring so you don't ruin your sanding belts with a glaze of glue residue.

6 Make registration marks so you will know how everything fits back together. Following the same procedure as for the Basic Box (page 71), slice the lid off at $5/8$", the base at $3/8$", and sides off at $1/2$". This is one of the rare instances when setting the fence $1/2$" away from the blade allows you to safely cut all four sides without turning off the power to reset the fence. Cut the front and back first, then the two sides.

7 Sand the top of the core; then cut $3/8$" off the top of the core for the lid liner.

8 Dry-fitting the box on graph paper will help you to keep the assembly square during gluing and clamping (Fig. 4). Now you know where to put the glue and how to position the pieces for gluing (Fig. 5). After the clamps are tight-

FIG. 6 The sides moved during glue-up, and the lid liner no longer fit. Sand the lid liner with sandpaper wrapped around a block of sharp-edged wood to keep the edges flat and square. Work to keep the stripes in alignment as you remove wood.

FIG. 7 With a wood as coarse-grained as red oak, the glue-line practically disappears with a good joint. This is a side with three joints, but they are almost invisible.

FIG. 8 The alignment of the laminations between the lid and body is less than perfect, as you can see in this straight-on view.

FIG. 9 Chamfers at the meeting of lid and body effectively disguise the alignment error. Chamfers make the box easy to open and look good.

ened, double-check that the sides are still perpendicular to the work surface. The glue will set up quickly, so work fast.

9 If you have to adjust the lid for fit on the body, make sure your sanding won't disturb the continuity of the stripe. Sand in a way that makes the stripe as unbroken as possible (Fig. 6). After sanding the exterior, it is amazing to see that the side joints are practically invisible. The red oak's coarse grain pattern has disguised the glue joint (Fig. 7).

10 Sand a chamfer (beveled edge) at the meeting edges of the lid and body to hide any imperfections in the stripe and to provide a better grasp when removing the lid. See Fig. 11, page 158, for one way of sanding a chamfer, by tilting the band saw table. When you look at the box straight on, the error in the stripe is visible (Fig. 8), but when viewed at any other angle, the chamfer disguises the defect (Fig. 9). Matching 30° chamfers were also made around the top and bottom edges of the box.

11 To make succeeding boxes from this laminated block, sand the core to the proper shape, and then proceed to follow the instructions for the Basic Box. As the block of wood gets ever smaller, be sure to use a stabilizing block to keep your fingers away from the band saw blade and the sanding belt. Sand the core smooth, cut the top at $1/2$", base at $1/4$", sides at $3/8$", and lid liner at $5/16$". Construction is the same as for the big box.

FIG. 10 It's easy to forget which end is up on a box like this. I was getting ready to apply finish to the smaller box when I noticed a small problem: I'd wood-burned on the top of the box instead of the bottom. I made a trip to the belt sander and the top became a little thinner, but it looked as good as new.

FIG. 11 The bottom of the smaller box was so porous that light shone through. A sanding sealer and heavy-bodied surface finish were necessary seal the pores to make a tight box.

FINISHING

1   The first thing I always do when the box is ready for finishing is to wood-burn information on the bottom of the box (Fig. 10). What's wrong with this picture?

2   Of even more concern was the porosity of the red oak. A very graphic example of that can be seen on the bottom of the small box. At a little under ¼" thick, it was so porous that light was visible through the wood (Fig. 11). This is a perfect illustration of the analogy of wood fibers to a bunch of straws, except that most woods have a much tighter structure than red oak (Fig. 12). Notice how tight the grain of the purpleheart is in comparison to the open grain of the red oak. Because of this porosity, a varnish sanding sealer was used for the first coat. With its thickness and filling characteristics, the sanding sealer fills the wood pores so subsequent coats of finish will be smoother and no longer will be absorbed by the wood.

3   The final finish was done with two coats of gel varnish,

lightly sanding with a gray scrubby pad between coats. To give yourself something to hold onto while finishing the boxes, do the interiors first (Fig. 13) and the exteriors later. In that way there is always a dry surface for you to handle and one on which you can set the box down.

4   Figures 14 and 15 show the finished boxes.

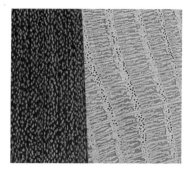

FIG. 12 Notice how open the grain is on the red oak side, and how closed it is on the purpleheart side. Red oak shows the "bundle of straws" structure of wood very well.

FIG. 13 When you have to put on many coats of surface finish, you can seal your brush or rag in a plastic bag so it doesn't dry out and you don't have to clean it every time.

FIG. 15 The finished Tea Boxes. Red oak and purpleheart, $3^7/_8$x$3^7/_8$x$3^7/_8$" and 3x 3x$2^1/_2$".

FIG. 14 The Tea Boxes were finished with varnish sanding sealer and clear satin gel varnish.

Earth Boxes

These boxes will always be my sentimental favorite because they were the first band saw boxes I made. Although they are not the easiest

boxes, it is a forgiving design; the boxes look good even when not done perfectly. The design features all curves, from the oval plan to the curved top.

This is a real showcase for beautiful, dramatic woods. My first nested oval box was made out of lacewood, a wonderful wood that is shown best when it is cut on a curve. For the model, I used a wood that is very hard and attractively patterned. I believe that it is a piece of ziricote with mostly sapwood. It was perfect for these boxes. It reminds me of the earth's color and layered composition, so the boxes are called Earth Boxes.

Level of difficulty: Easy

MATERIALS

4¹/₄x2¹/₂x1⁷/₈" or larger hard wood*

¹/₈" band saw blade

Oval template

10° wedge

Tung oil and urethane topcoat, semigloss (I used Arm-R-Seal)

Nylon mesh pad, maroon

*A larger piece will make it easier to make more boxes.

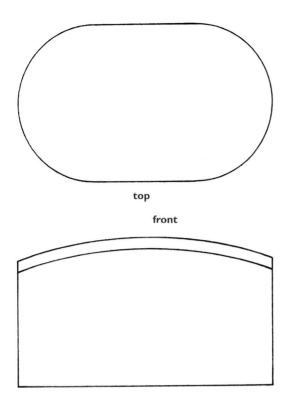

top

front

PLAN A Top and front views of the Earth Boxes.

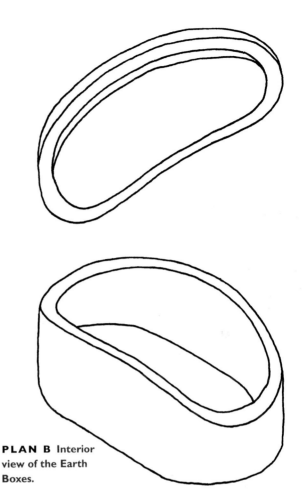

PLAN B Interior view of the Earth Boxes.

MAKING THE BOX

1 Plans A, B, and C show the basic configuration and assembly of the boxes.

2 After squaring and smoothing the block, draw centerlines on the top and one side of the block. Use these lines to help to keep the layout square and even (Fig. 1). Cut out the side profile first (Fig. 2), making the lid and base $^3/_{16}$" thick.

3 Then reassemble all four pieces, including the top scrap piece, with double-sided tape. Cut out the top view (Plan A) through all the layers (Fig. 3).

4 Disassemble the pieces, and cut out the interior core, leaving the sidewall $^3/_{16}$" thick. Use your fingers as a guide to make it easier to mark the body for cutting (Fig. 4).

top view

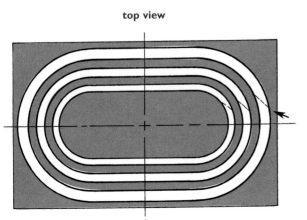

front view

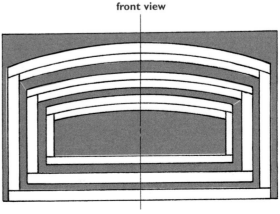

PLAN C Top and front plan cross-section views of the Earth Boxes, showing how three boxes can be cut out of one block and how they nest together. Dashed lines are entrance cut kerfs.

FIG. 1 Center lines drawn directly on the wood are a good way to keep your plan straight. Templates, like the circle and oval templates here, are handy when adapting the given pattern to different sizes of wood blanks.

FIG. 2 It will take three cuts to make the side profile for the box. Don't discard the scrap from the top of the block because you will need to double-tape the pieces back together and then cut the top profile.

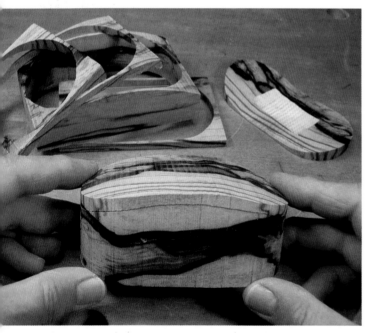

FIG. 3 After reassembling the pieces and cutting out the top view, you have a good idea of what the final box will look like.

FIG. 4 Use your fingers to space your cut-line mark in from the sanded outer edge of the body, or use a depth gauge or marking gauge.

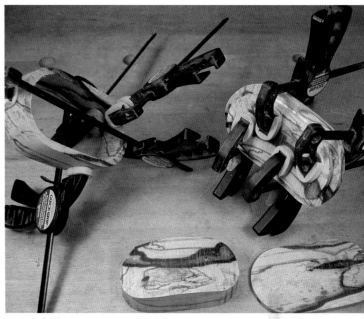

FIG. 5 Use a wedge-shaped piece of wood to carefully pry smaller pieces of wood from the stabilizing block.

FIG. 6 The body is glued and clamped together, and the lid liner is glued to lid. While you're waiting for the glue to set up, you can make another box from the core.

5 Attach the core to a stabilizing block, and cut $1/8$" off the core to make the lid liner. As the pieces get smaller, it becomes more difficult to remove them from the stabilizing block. Use a sharply angled (10°) wedge to pry the pieces apart (Fig. 5).

6 Glue the body together, and glue the lid liner to the lid (Fig. 6). Sand the interiors and bottom of the body and glue the body to the sanded base.

7 When you fit the lid to the body, it will not be very tight because so much wood was removed with the saw blade. Everything needs to stay in place during power sanding, however, so use a piece of paper towel to fill the gap (Fig. 7). Just place one or two layers of thick, soft paper towel between the lid and body, and press them together. Trim off any excess and proceed with sanding the exterior to 220-grit with the belt sander. The paper towel on the outside will just get sanded away, but the paper between the lid and body will stay in place until you open the box again.

8 Sand the remaining core to make it smooth and squared, and then proceed to make it into a box. If you are careful

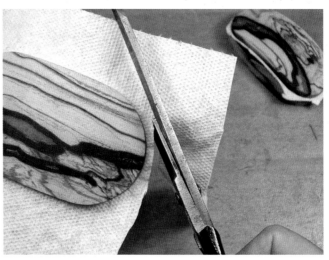

FIG. 7 Here's a trick to keep loose-fitting lids on firmly while sanding the contour: use a piece or two of paper toweling sandwiched between them to tighten up the fit.

(and lucky) you may even be able to get a third box out of your wood block; but you will have a better chance at three boxes if you start with a larger block.

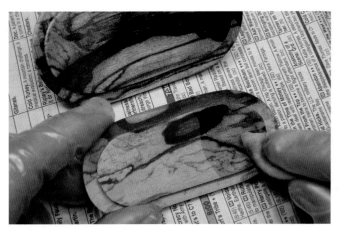

FIG. 8 What a thrill it is to apply the finish and see the wood come to life. This is a rub-on oil and polyurethane topcoat.

FIG. 9 The semigloss oil/urethane finish highlights and protects the unique grain pattern of the Earth Boxes.

FINISHING

1 For this box, I tried a different finish, one which doesn't need to be buffed with wax to have a nice, even shine. It is a semigloss tung oil and urethane topcoat (Arm-R-Seal, by General Finishes) that is easy to work with and leaves the box with a wonderful luster. Application is with a rag so there are no brushes to clean, and the odor is less offensive than other finishes (Fig. 8). Simply wipe on the liquid, ending with light strokes going with the grain, and let dry overnight. To make handling easier, I did the insides of all four pieces and let them dry before doing the exteriors.

2 I applied 3 or 4 coats, buffing the finish with a maroon scrubby between coats. Do not buff the final coat. This finish was so easy and successful that it may end up becoming my newest favorite finish (Fig. 9).

3 Figure 10 shows the finished Earth Boxes.

FIG. 10 The finished Earth Boxes. South American hardwood, $3^3/_4$x$2^1/_4$x$1^5/_8$" and $3^1/_2$x$1^5/_8$x1".

Bamboo Boxes

Here's a different angle on band saw boxes: a vertical format. Tall boxes have many possible uses. They are a bit difficult to reach into, but they

take up very little shelf space, so there are advantages and disadvantages to the design. You could even forget about making the lids and just make the body as a great vase for dried flower arrangements.

Because I started with a large piece of wood, I was able to make four boxes. The wood I used is ash, an inexpensive, though attractive, hard wood. There are distinct differences in the grain of this wood. The hard grain is like a rock, and the soft areas are quite porous. It looked like bamboo to me, so I wood-burned a bamboo design on all sides of each of the boxes. If you don't have a wood burner, you can paint the designs or draw them with a permanent marker. For a nice variation, you could make birch boxes with designs of birch trees.

Level of difficulty: Moderate

MATERIALS

5x3x7" ash

4x6x³/₈" ash (or contrasting wood) for the lid liners

Circle template

¹/₈" band saw blade

Drum or spindle sander

Carbon or graphite paper, or transfer tool

Copies of bamboo patterns sized to fit boxes

Wood burner with writing tip (or indelible marker or paint)

Gel varnish, satin

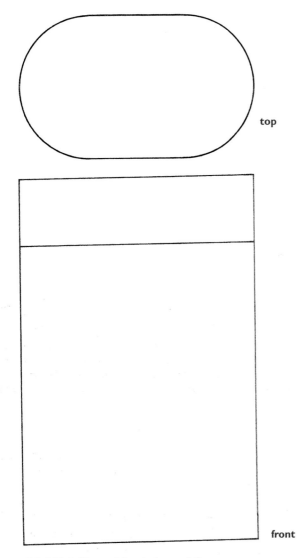

top

front

PLAN A Top and front views of the Bamboo Boxes.

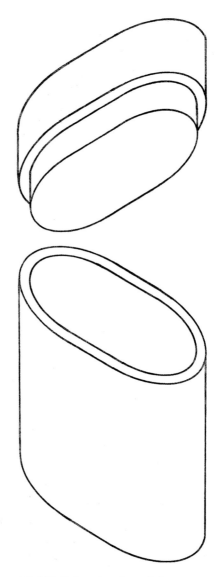

PLAN B Interior view of the Bamboo Boxes.

MAKING THE BOX

1 Plans A, B, and C show the basic configuration and assembly of the boxes.

2 How can you make a 7"-tall box with a 6"-capacity band saw? You can do it by first cutting 1 1/2" off for the lid and 1/2" off for the base, leaving a manageable 5"-tall block for the interior cut. The boxes won't nest back together

though, so if that is important, this is not the best plan for your project.

3 Square your block, finishing the top and bottom to 220-grit.

4 Cut the lid and base piece, and put them aside for now.

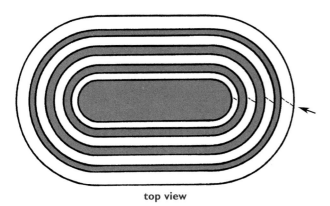

top view

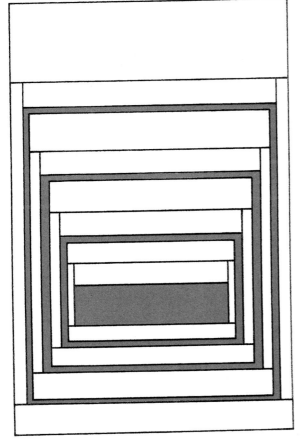

front view

PLAN C Top and front plan views, showing how the Bamboo Boxes are cut out of a single block of wood. Dashed lines are entrance cut kerfs.

5 Mark the top of the remainder of the block with the pattern for the outside of the largest box body, and then cut it out. Because of the long cut, it is especially important that the band saw blade and the block be perfectly square. Check them before making the cut.

FIG. 1 When making deep cuts with your band saw, be extra careful to position your fingers where they will be safe when the blade comes through the block of wood. Remember the safety zone, and use a push stick to control the piece instead of using your fingers.

6 Mark the interior body pattern on the top of the body piece, and cut it out carefully. The walls will be $^1/_4$" thick (Fig. 1).

7 If you are going to cut the lid liner from the core, cut it off now. If you do that, however, the fit will be sloppy. A tight-fitting lid requires a separately cut lid liner.

8 Glue the sides of the body together, sand the inside and outside, and then use it to trace the exterior outline on the lid and base pieces. Try to keep the same orientation by looking closely at the grain where they meet. Cut the lid and base out a little larger than the pattern. Leave about $^1/_{16}$" extra all around for later shaping.

9 Sand the inside of the top and base, and the top and bottom of the body, to 220-grit.

10 With the smaller boxes, the core will not be perfectly formed, so sand it to square the top and bottom. Mark the top with the pattern, or use drafting tools to make a new pattern right on the wood (Fig. 2). Use the belt sander to coarsely shape the block to the line (Fig 3). Make sure all marks from the band saw blade are gone before proceeding.

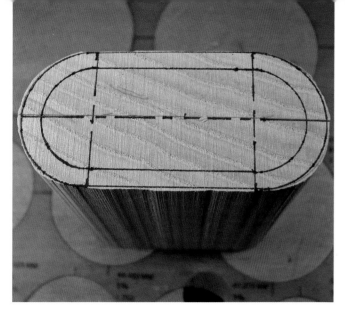

FIG. 2 To make the next box from the previous box's core, make a new plan right on the wood. That way you will be able to keep the piece symmetrical as you sand the sides to form.

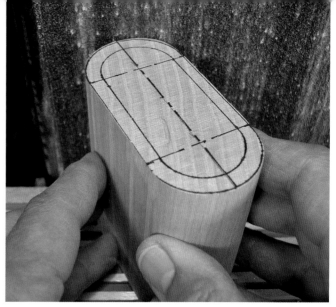

FIG. 3 Use a coarse grit sanding belt to sand to the line. Keep your fingers away from the moving belt. It gives a rough manicure.

11 For the second box, cut off the top at $^7/_8$" and the bottom at $^1/_2$", and make the sides $^3/_{16}$" thick. For the third box, cut them at $^5/_8$", $^3/_8$", and $^5/_{32}$", respectively. The smallest box has a $^1/_2$"-thick lid, $^1/_4$"-thick base, and $^1/_8$"–thick walls. The smaller boxes get more and more difficult to control, so use a stabilizing block to keep them vertical and steady as you make the interior cuts for the body (Fig. 4).

12 Glue the rest of the bodies together, and then sand their interiors to 220-grit.

13 You will now use the bodies to trace the patterns for the lid liners onto the ⅜"-thick piece of wood set aside for the lid liners. The lid liners have to be cut out of a different piece of wood for two reasons. First, the core cut from rounded forms is always going to be too small to make a tight-fitting lid. Second, we want the boxes to be as tall as possible, so we don't want to lose wood from the cores to make liners.

HELPFUL HINT: SAVING TIME

By doing all the machining, sanding, and gluing at the same time for all the boxes in a nested set, you will save setup time.

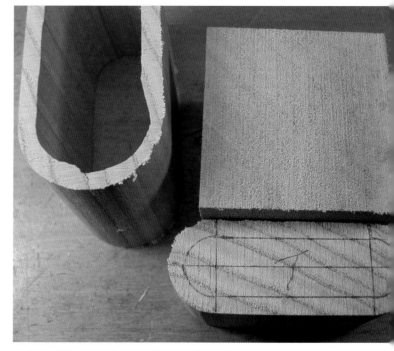

FIG. 4 When cutting out the core from the smaller blocks, you must use a stabilizing block. The irregular edge on the box at left was the result of tilting the block during the interior cut without a stabilizing block. On the right, the smallest box is ready to have its core cut out; the stabilizing block is attached.

FIG. 5 These four boxes are ready to be glued together. Making many boxes from one piece of wood is a good way to save on wood costs. It also saves setup time.

PLAN D The bamboo design used to decorate the boxes. Photocopy this design at the appropriate percentage for the size of box you make.

14 Make light registration marks on the liners and insides of the boxes. Draw with a sharp pencil, just inside the top end of the bodies, onto the wood. Then cut out the pieces, leaving the pencil mark. This way, you can power-sand the lid liners to make a perfect fit by trial-fitting the liners to the bodies. Put the lids on the bodies, and then mark through the bottom opening the position of the liners on the lids.

15 Sand all mating surfaces smooth before gluing. Glue the lid liners, in the correct orientation, onto the lids. Then glue the bodies onto the bases, matching the registration marks. In Fig. 5, the box bodies are ready to be glued to the bases.

16 When you first put the lids on the boxes, you probably will not have a perfect fit, so modify the mating pieces with a little hand-sanding until there is a firm but not tight fit. Remember to leave a little room for the finish.

17 Now you may use the belt sander with a very coarse belt to bring the assembled boxes into form. Then smooth them with progressively finer grit belts.

18 The boxes were too plain as they were, so they got some wood-burned bamboo decoration. Plan D shows the bamboo design used to decorate the boxes. The first step was to make the pattern fit the boxes. In this case, the larger boxes got the larger design; but I also could have used the same-sized pattern for all of the boxes. In that case, just a small portion of the design would be used on the smaller boxes. Another option would be to spread out the bamboo stalks, to make the burning job easier.

19 Next, transfer the pattern to the boxes. The best way is to use graphite transfer paper. Unlike carbon paper, the lines made with graphite transfer paper can be erased; they are made from the same material as pencils. Carbon paper is oily and the lines cannot be erased.

HELPFUL HINT: TRANSFER PAPER

You can make your own transfer paper by thoroughly covering the back of a thin piece of paper with pencil shading.

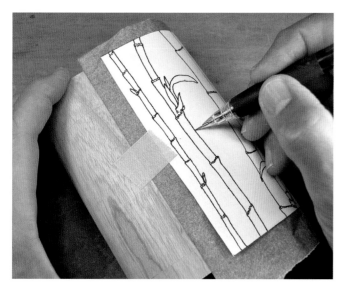

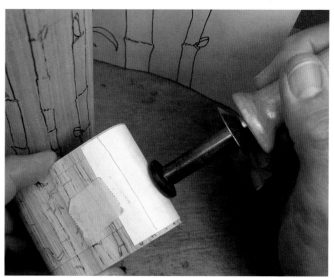

FIG. 6 Tape the transfer paper to the wood, and tape the pattern to the tracing paper and the wood. You don't want anything to move once you start tracing the pattern onto the wood.

FIG. 7 Using a transfer tool can save time, but the image is difficult to erase if you make a mistake because the pattern ink is wax-based.

20   Make as many copies of the pattern shown in Plan D as you will need to go around the box. Reusing the pattern is not recommended, because you cannot tell where you have traced the lines to transfer the pattern once you trace it the first time. Now tape the pattern and transfer paper to the block and transfer the lines (Fig. 6).

21   When you think you are done with a section, keep the pattern in place while you lift up one side of it to confirm that the lines are all there.

22   An easier way to transfer a pattern is to use a transfer tool (Fig. 7) and a pattern that has been made on a toner-based copy machine. When the tool gets hot and is rubbed on the back of the pattern, it melts the copier toner into the wood. This is quicker than laboriously hand-transferring every line. However, it has the same disadvantage as carbon paper: the lines produced are difficult to erase. Both types of permanent lines can be lightened with lacquer thinner and then removed with light sanding or scraping with a knife. The toner also will melt into the brown lines made with the burner, causing them to appear grayish, so you wouldn't want to use the transfer tool for a job where that would be distracting, like a portrait. In this case, it was not noticeable.

23   With a transfer tool, the design will be reversed. When you are transferring lettering or portraits, you would have to make a clear acetate photocopy first and then turn it over to make the copy you will use.

FIG. 8 Make a few practice burning strokes on the same type of wood as your boxes. The burn on the left is too light, the one on the right is too dark, and the middle one is just right to burn dark enough without creating smoke.

24   One way to make the pattern look different on the boxes is to start the pattern in different places on each of the boxes.

25   To do this kind of wood burning, it is helpful to have a burner with a temperature control. Some woods are hard and require more heat to burn correctly. Practice on a piece of the same type of wood as your project, and use similar designs (Fig. 8).

FIG. 9 Go over the lines lightly with the wood burner. These burned lines are much more permanent than the easily smudged transferred lines. After burning, erase the graphite lines. You may decide to leave the box with just this much detail.

FIG. 10 Build up the burn slowly to get the best result. Here, the top of the central bamboo shows just the outline. Lower down, the color deepens with more controlled burning, until the finished burn at the bottom.

26 Lightly burn over all the lines so you can erase the graphite marks (Fig. 9). Then, go over the design again, building up layers of burn until the bamboo looks rounded (Fig. 10).

27 Make the leaves darkest over the lightest parts of the bamboo and lightest over the darkest bamboo. This gives a sense of depth to the composition. As shown, the burning of all four boxes took about 10 hours.

FINISHING

1 The finish on these boxes was kept simple; clear satin gel varnish was applied and smoothed with a rag. Figure 11 shows the finished Bamboo Boxes.

FIG. 11 The Bamboo Boxes were finished with clear satin gel varnish. The wood is ash. Largest: $4^1/_2$x$2^3/_4$x$6^3/_4$". Second largest: 4x2x$4^3/_4$". Next to smallest: $3^1/_4$x$1^1/_2$x$3^1/_4$". Smallest: $2^3/_4$x1x2".

Puzzle and Sliding-Lid Boxes

Just like the jigsaw puzzles that you and Grandma spent fascinating hours putting together, boxes that include sliding and interlocking parts draw people to them. The key features of these boxes are sliding keyways for the lids and clever key locks, designed to lock the keyway so it doesn't slide. The Teacher's Pet Box and Poker Boxes are puzzle boxes, with lids that slide. The Bread Box is a sliding-lid box, although it's not a puzzle box.

One of the secrets to making successful sliding-lid boxes is making sure that the box block is held perfectly perpendicular to the cutting blade when cutting the keyway. If you do that, your lid will slide easily in both directions. Here are four projects that will introduce you to the wonderful art that can be created with this type of box.

OVERVIEW OF PUZZLE AND SLIDING-LID BOXES

You will need a $1/16$" band saw blade to cut the locking keys. If you used a $1/8$" blade, the fit would be too sloppy. Also, some of the cuts require tight radius cuts, for which the $1/16$" blade works much better. If the pieces are small and are cut individually, you also could use a scroll saw or coping saw. The next four projects use the following work plan:

1. Square the block and cut the outline if required.
2. Cut off the base.
3. Cut out the locking piece with a $1/16$" blade.
4. Cut the lid off with its sliding keyway, using a $1/16$" blade.
5. Cut out the interior of the box body.
6. Sand all interior surfaces.
7. Glue the body to the base.
8. Sand to shape, and smooth all surfaces.
9. Apply the finish.

Teacher's Pet Box

This apple box is so appetizing that people will want to take a bite out of it; but the worm will keep them away. Teachers always have a nice

assortment of apple items on their desks from their appreciative students, so it's the perfect gift for a favorite teacher. There are a lot of steps necessary to make this box look like an apple and still function as a box. It can be made much easier if you make it round instead of apple-shaped and don't concern yourself with tapered sides.

If you appreciate a challenge and want it to look like an apple, just follow the instructions and you will succeed. If the prospect of carving the worm is daunting to you, substitute a pencil, and make the hole the right size for the pencil.

Level of difficulty: Challenging

MATERIALS

$3^1/2$x$3^1/2$x$3^1/4$" cedar or other red-colored wood, such as redwood*

$^3/8$x$^3/4$x3" scrap of figured maple for worm and stem, or darker wood (e.g. walnut)

Thin cardboard or stiff paper, 4x6"

Protractor

Drill, with $^3/8$" and $^1/8$" drill bits, preferably brad-point

$^1/4$" thick scrap wood for spacer

Depth gauge, or thin stick

$^1/8$" band saw blade

$^1/16$" band saw blade or coping saw

Masking tape

Drum or spindle sander

Rasp or power-carving tool with sanding drum

Wood burner with writing tip (or indelible marker or paint)

Green dye or thinned green paint

Danish oil, clear and cherry

Brushing lacquer, gloss

Spray lacquer, gloss

*You could make the apple out of a white wood and dye or stain it red after sanding.

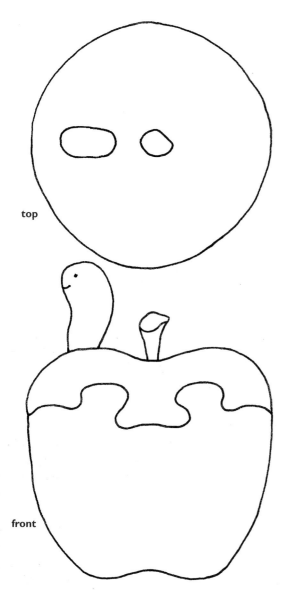

PLAN A Top and front views of the Teacher's Pet Box.

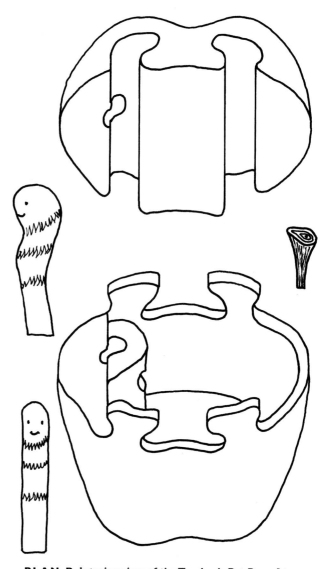

PLAN B Interior view of the Teacher's Pet Box. At left, worm.

MAKING THE BOX

The cedar used for this box was gleaned from the scrap pile of a nearby cedar timber-framing company. Many of the scrap pieces are cut-offs from trimming rafters, too small for them to use, but perfect for boxes. When the lumber is out in the open, it loses its color and develops cracks, or end checks, so it is difficult to find good pieces. I thought this pieces would work for a box because the end checks did not extend too far into the wood (Fig. 1).

1 Plans A, B, and C show the basic configuration and assembly of the box.

2 Square and smooth the block, as usual.

3 Draw the location of the wormhole from the cross-section drawing (Plan C). Note: The top of the box where the wormhole is located should be on the end grain.

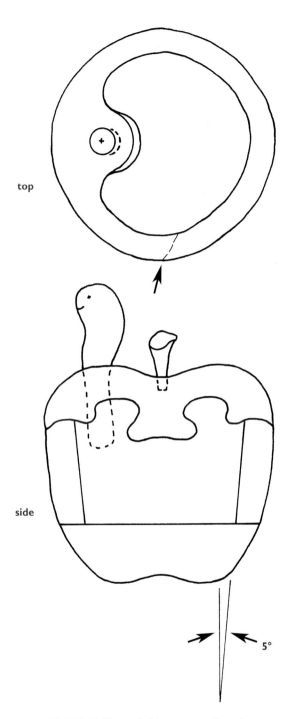

top

side

5°

PLAN C Top and side cross-section views of the Teacher's Pet Box. Dashed line in top drawing is entrance cut kerf. Note 5° angle of offset for blade in lower drawing.

FIG. 1 The depth of surface cracks in found wood determines whether the wood is good enough for making boxes. Notice the difference in color between the top (exposed) surface and the newly cut vertical grain.

4 To make it easier and safer, the hole for the worm needs to be made while the block is still square. Make a template out of a piece of stiff paper or light cardboard (Fig. 2). Draw a line perpendicular to the edge of the paper. Then, use a protractor to mark 5° to the left, and draw another line. Now, by placing the template on a tilted surface, it is easy to align the drill bit or band saw blade to the correct angle (Fig. 3). In this case, a ¼" spacer generated the required 5° angle when placed under the same side of the block as the hole (Fig. 4). Make sure the point of the drill bit is angled toward the center of the block, and drill a ³/₈" hole, 1¼" deep, as indicated on Plan C. Check the depth with a depth gauge, or a small stick and a ruler (Fig. 5).

HELPFUL HINT: DRILL MARKER

Use a piece of masking tape wrapped around your drill bit to indicate the proper depth of the hole. It is quicker and easier than using the settings on the drill press. It's also a good way to drill a hole to a certain depth with a portable drill.

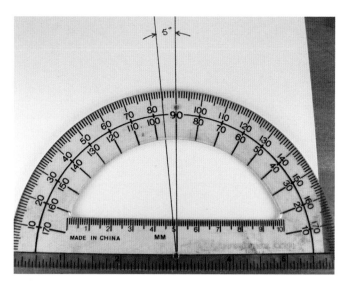

FIG. 2 Making a template now will help you to set a 5° angle for both the drill press and band saw. You could use a compass, but the template is much easier to see, and your tool setups will be more accurate.

FIG. 3 By setting the angle template on the $\frac{1}{4}$" spacer you can make adjustments with the spacer so the drill will make an accurate 5°-angled hole. Make sure the drill bit is aimed toward the center of the block.

FIG. 4 Place the block on the spacer just as the template was, and the angle will be correct. Hold the block firmly, and drill the hole, using a piece of masking tape on the bit as a depth stop.

FIG. 5 Double-check the wormhole (key) depth and angle with a depth gauge.

5   On the same side or opposite side of the block to the one where you drilled the wormhole, trace the side outline pattern without the keyway. Keep the pattern $\frac{1}{8}$" down from the top of the block. On an adjacent side, draw the pattern with the keyway, the same distance from the top (Fig. 6).

6   Make the keyway cut first, and then tape the top and bottom sections back together with masking tape.

7   Cut out the outline of the apple on that same side (Fig. 7). Keep the cut-off pieces together on the block, and tape them back into place. Use the location of the first taping

FIG. 6 In marking the block for the first cuts, notice that two of the sides have no keyways cut into them, just the apple outline. Be sure that you plan to cut the keyway side on a side that does not contain the key lock hole (wormhole).

FIG. 7 After cutting out the keyway, reassemble the block and tape it together securely before cutting out the outline on the keyway side.

to align the pieces correctly. Then cut out the second outline, without the keyway (Fig. 8). To make it easier to cut the bottom off at 3/4", leave the scrap pieces on one side so the rounded apple form will remain level during the cut (Fig. 9). It doesn't look much like an apple yet, but it has potential (Fig. 10).

8 Put aside the lid and base pieces, and trace the top view (Plan C, top view) outline onto the top of the body piece. The keyway will make it difficult, but if you sight down from the top, you will be close enough (Fig. 11). It is an irregular circle anyhow, so it will more closely resemble a real apple.

9 Use the template you made earlier to set up the band saw to cut at a 5° angle (Fig. 12). It is easy to adjust the angle of the table, and a spacer does not work when cutting out this concentric form. Double-check that you are getting the angle correct by placing the body next to the blade and confirming that it does cut toward the bottom center (Fig. 13). If you cut in the opposite direction, with the body on the other side of the blade, the blade will cut through the side of the box.

FIG. 8 After cutting the first outline, again reassemble the cut-off pieces and tape all back together again. Match up the cut ends of the old masking tape as a guide for the correct location for the new tape. Then make the second outline cut.

FIG. 9 Keep the cut-off pieces taped to one side of the box so the wood remains square and stable while you cut off the bottom.

FIG. 10 It's a funny-looking apple so far, but it will get better by the time we are done with it; trust me.

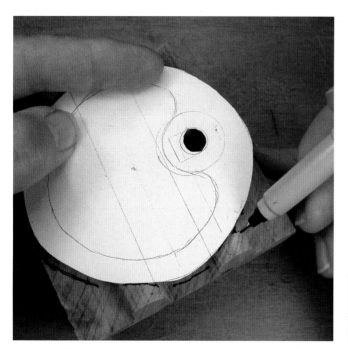

FIG. 11 Trace the pattern outline onto the top of the body. It has the cut-out top of the keyways on it so you need to be a little creative in drawing lines onto the block.

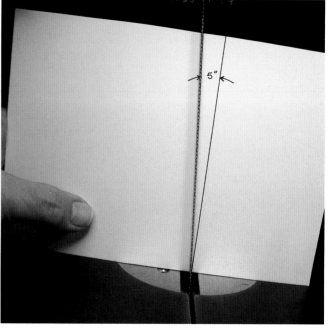

FIG. 12 Use the same template you made earlier to adjust the band saw table for a 5° cut.

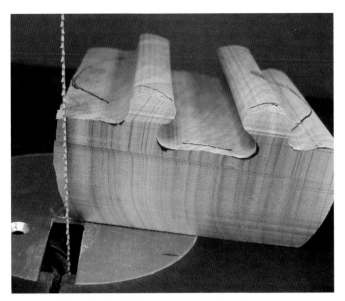

FIG. 13 Double-check that you are starting the cut on the correct side of the body. Put the body on the downside of the blade.

FIG. 14 After the body outline has been cut out, use it to mark the matching sides of the lid and base piece.

FIG. 15 When cutting the base, place it with the inside up and locate it downhill from the blade to insure that the angles will match those on the body. Repeat with the lid piece.

FIG. 16 Notice the location of my fingers while cutting the keyway lid outline. Keep away from the danger zone as you cut the lid piece. Your cut will move slower where the wood is thick, but speed up where it is thinner.

10 After cutting the outline on the body, reassemble the box pieces and trace around the body outline onto the lid and then onto the base piece (Fig. 14). Cut the outline on both the lid and base, keeping the outside of each piece on the table, and start the cuts with the pieces to the right of the angled blade (Figs. 15 and 16).

11 Mark and cut out the core from the body, keeping the same orientation to the blade as you did for the previous cuts. Of course, you will cut around the hole for the key lock (worm). Glue the body together.

FIG. 17 That's more like it! The block looks a lot like an apple now, even before we refine its shape.

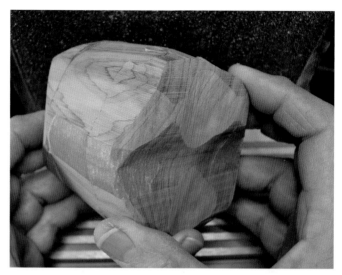

FIG. 18 Tape the keyway lid securely on two sides while you power-sand the other sides. Then tape the sanded sides so you can finish-sand the rest of the box. Aim for an apple shape, but don't worry about the details yet. Watch your fingers and hold on tight!

12 Sand the interior of body and base, except where it will be glued. Then glue the base to the body. Now the piece is really starting to look like an apple, and you can see that it won't take too much work to complete the shape (Fig. 17).

13 Use the belt sander with a 60- or 80-grit belt to make quick work of those sharp edges, and smooth the transition areas between sections. Don't try to get too detailed at this point (Fig. 18). Use tape to hold the lid in place, and then move the tape to a completed side to finish sanding.

14 Use a small drum sander or a rasp to smooth out the last of the bumps and lumps to get to the final apple shape (Fig. 19).

15 Drill a ⅛"-diameter hole, ¼" deep, in the center of the top of the lid, for the stem.

16 If you are going to make a worm for the lock, draw the pattern (Plan B) on the side of a scrap of ⅜" wood (Fig. 20). Keep the body of the worm longer than necessary so you will have something to hold onto while you shape it. Make the stem in a similar fashion, using the pattern shown on Plan B. A smart idea would be to use a piece of wood about 5" long and put the worm at one end and the stem

FIG. 19 This is where you get to sand all the imperfections away until what it left is a perfect apple form. Here I'm using a flexible-shaft sanding attachment.

at the other end. That way you would have a handle in the middle that you could use to hold the pieces through the finishing process. Then cut the pieces off of each end. I wasn't that smart, but I will be the next time I have to hold onto such small pieces.

FIG. 21 The Teacher's Pet Box was finished with cherry-colored Danish oil. The worm and stem were colored with green dye. They were top-coated with brushing lacquer and then spray lacquer.

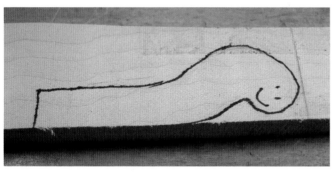

FIG. 20 This little worm is just begging to come out of this piece of figured maple scrap.

FINISHING

1 The stem and worm were wood-burned to add some detail and then dyed a light, bright green.

2 Topcoat the stem and worm with clear Danish oil; follow later with two coats of gloss brushing lacquer.

3 The apple was finished with cherry-colored Danish oil and two coats of gloss brushing lacquer, but there were too many runs in the finish. The apple was sanded lightly with 220-grit sandpaper to remove the runs, and then with 320-grit to remove the 220-grit scratches.

4 After cleaning the apple well, two coats of gloss spray lacquer were applied to the well-sealed wood (Fig 21).

5 Figure 22 shows the finished Teacher's Pet Box.

FIG. 22 Teacher's Pet Box. Cedar and figured maple, 3¹⁄₄" diameter x 3".

Poker Boxes

Each of these four boxes holds exactly 100 pennies. With four interlocking boxes on hand, there will always be enough stakes for the group

to ante up for some penny-ante poker. The design is complex, and this isn't the easiest project; but the challenge is rewarded by a neat-looking set of boxes.

The shape does not have to be square; it could be almost any shape. It could be the shape of an elephant, with the legs, head, and body as interlocking puzzle pieces. For

some designs you may want to make a tray to hold the pieces together.

The wood of the model was mahogany, picked out of a manufacturer's scrap heap, a cut-off from a larger project. It was perfect for our purposes, but it needed to be cleaned up a bit.

Level of difficulty: Challenging

MATERIALS

5x5x2$^{1}/_{2}$" mahogany

$^{1}/_{16}$" band saw blade, or coping saw or scroll saw

Drum or spindle sander

Wood burner with writing tip (or indelible marker or paint)

Colored oil pencils or paint

Heavy-bodied table-top varnish

Mineral spirits

PLAN A Top and front views of the Poker Boxes.

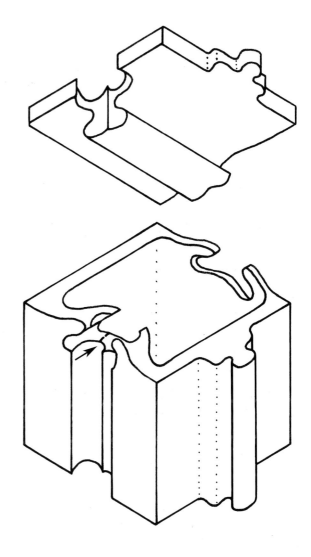

PLAN B Interior view of one section of the Poker Boxes. Dashed line is entrance cut kerf.

MAKING THE BOX

1 Plans A and B show the basic configuration and assembly of the boxes.

2 My first job with this project was to prepare the rough wood for use. I started with a 2x10" piece of scrap lumber, and the edges need to be cleaned up, or dressed. I drew two lines on the wood, with the first set, the interior lines, indicating the finished size for the block. The second set of lines, $^1/_8$" outside the first set, are where the first cuts were made using the band saw with a heavy-duty $^1/_2$" or $^3/_4$" blade. I made sure the lines met at a right angle (Fig. 1), and

I then cut along the outside lines, freeing the block from the board.

3 Placing each of these freshly cut sides against the fence and cutting off the extra $^1/_8$" resulted in a square block with clean sides.

4 Transfer the playing-card suit pattern (Plan A, top view) to the top of the sanded block, and then trace over the cutting lines only with a dark pen. The playing card symbols are made into keys that hold everything together (Fig. 2). Transfer the pattern for the keyways (Plan A, side

FIG. 1 Double lines will help you to get a clean, square block from a larger piece of lumber. Cut the block first on the outside lines; then, with the newly cut clean sides on the fence, cut off the rough edges.

FIG. 2 After tracing the suit pattern onto the block, darken the actual cutting lines with a pen so you do not cut into the box areas by mistake.

view) to the right-hand sections of each side of the block.

5 Cut along the lines on the top of the block using the $^1/_{16}$" blade, or equivalent. Cut across the block, making detours for the playing card symbols, and then cut the resulting two pieces in the same way. When completed, the blocks should look like a very thick jigsaw puzzle (Fig. 3).

6 Turn the blocks so their flat cut-out sides are on the table, and cut out the horizontal keyways on all four blocks. This also will generate the box lids. Be careful that the edges of the boxes don't get caught in the band saw's table insert. Hold the pieces firmly so they don't rock, and use a stabilizer. In this box, one of the keyways was cut at an angle because it rocked to one side during the cut (Fig. 4). Fortunately, the keyway still works, but that lid can be removed in only one direction.

7 Cut $^1/_4$" off each box for their bases.

8 Cut out the interiors by making each entrance cut at the center of each symbol keyway. That way when the sides are glued together, the fit will be tighter and the cut will be hidden.

FIG. 3 At this point it looks like an overgrown jigsaw puzzle for the fumble-fingered. Each piece has a key and a void for the key in the adjoining block.

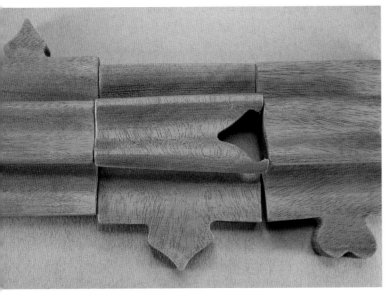

FIG. 4 The lid piece in the center is much wider at one end than the other. This is what happens if the block is not kept flat on the band saw table at all times. The result is a one-way keyway.

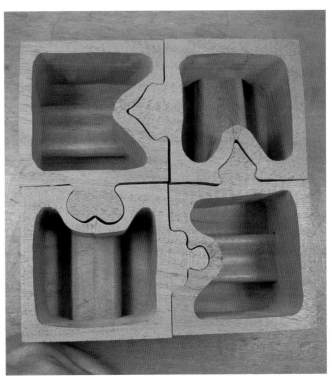

FIG. 5 This bottom view of the boxes with their interiors cut out and lids in place makes it look very complex, and it is. Follow the instructions carefully and you'll be successful.

9 Glue the sides of the bodies back together. When you are done, if you reassemble the boxes without the bases and turn it all upside down, it will look like a labyrinth (Fig. 5).

10 Sand the interior surfaces, especially the glue line, unless the saw blade left a smooth finish or you are planning to flock the interiors of the boxes.

11 Glue the bases to the bodies, keeping the symbols in alignment from the base to the lids. Keep the lids on during glue-up to distribute pressure from the clamps.

12 Make any necessary adjustments to the meeting surfaces on the four boxes so they form a compact unit.

13 Now, sand the exterior surfaces to correct any irregularities. This is a bit tricky because you are dealing with four separate boxes that are only lightly connected but that need to be sanded together. Sand the sides first, with the bases on the sanding table (Fig. 6). Then, flipping the boxes over like a pancake on the griddle, sand with the grain (Fig. 7). Finally, sand the top and bottom of the box by holding all four boxes against the belt (Fig. 8).

14 Sand by hand to slightly round all edges and correct any imperfections.

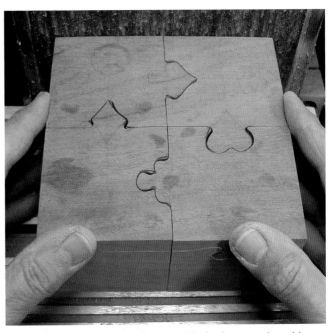

FIG. 6 Sand the sides of the box with the base on the table first. Careful positioning of your hands will hold all the pieces together.

FIG. 7 Hold the boxes together while you sand with the grain on the sides. Don't let your fingertips stray into the sanding belt.

15 Redraw the pattern for the symbols onto the finish-sanded box. Go over the outlines with a wood burner, using a ball-point tip. Go around the whole symbol, darkening the edges of the cut-out areas as well. If you don't have a wood burner, a permanent marker will do the job. You also could carve the outline of the symbols lightly into the wood.

16 Because this is a box representing a deck of cards, I used the traditional card colors of black and red. You can apply the color by any convenient means, but for this box I used colored oil pencils. Colored pencils are a forgiving medium. They are easy to erase, you can mix colors to create different hues, and they are inexpensive. Use artist-grade oil pencils if possible. Inexpensive pencils do not contain much actual pigment, or color, and they are harder, so you will end up having to press very hard to get enough color onto the wood. Let the grain show through your application of color for a subtle effect (Fig. 9). Rub the color with your finger to smooth the lines made by the pencils.

FIG. 8 Sanding four boxes at once is difficult and a little dangerous, but necessary for all the boxes to look like one box when they are done. If you position your hands carefully to hold everything together firmly and evenly, as this photo shows, when sanding the bottoms, you will do all right. It would be too dangerous to try to round the edges on the power sander, so that should be done by hand.

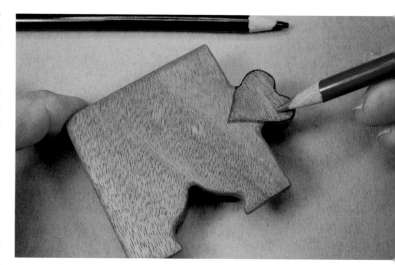

FIG. 9 Colored oil pencils do a good job of adding color without the mess of paints; no brushes to clean, no fuss, no bother. It is a good way to add small amounts of controlled color.

FIG. 10 Here are the completed Poker Boxes, with one section lifted out from its interlocking keys and the lid slid back on its keyway.

FINISHING

1 This box was finished with tabletop varnish. The first coat was thinned 50/50 with solvent, applied with a glue brush to reach into all the tight corners, and wiped off with a rag.

2 After 24 hours, the second 50/50 coat was done the same way.

3 The final coat was a 75/25 mixture (75% varnish). By wiping the varnish off with a rag, the coating is thinner and takes less time to dry. This cuts down on the possibility of dust settling into the finish. It is still a good idea to cover the pieces while they are drying.

4 Figures 10 and 11 show the completed Poker Boxes.

FIG. 11 The finished Poker Boxes. Mahogany, $4^3/_4$ x $4^1/_4$ x $2^1/_4$".

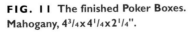

Bread Box

The Bread Box is not a puzzle box, but it does have a sliding lid. There are no keyways in this box; however, you could say that the entire box forms one big keyway. This box is not cut out all at once out of one block of wood. A couple of slices are taken off the block of wood first to make the ends/legs, and then the body is cut out from the remainder. Viewed from the end, the box looks like a loaf of bread. If you don't want the effect of legs on your box, follow the cross-section view pattern (Plan C) and cut off the ends at $3/8$" thick. If you don't want a box this long, you can slice the ends off the block as usual instead of making them from a separate piece.

There is a lot of fine-tuning necessary to make this box fit well, so I don't recommend making it from a very hard wood. The model is made in butternut, which is soft enough to make hand-sanding easy, but heavy enough to feel substantial in the hand.

Level of difficulty: Very challenging.

MATERIALS

$5^{1}/2$x4x4" butternut

$1/16$" band saw blade

Soft wood scraps to fit box opening

Large parallel-jawed clamp

Micro-rasps or other rasps or very coarse sandpaper

Hand profile sanders

Varnish sanding sealer

Nylon mesh pad, maroon

Gel varnish, satin

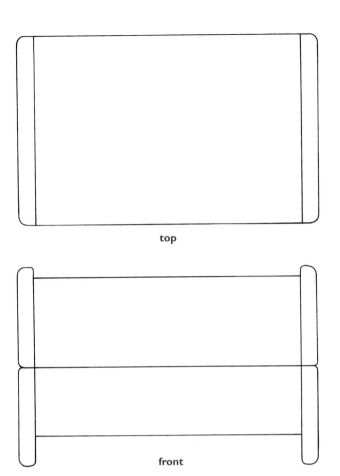

top

front

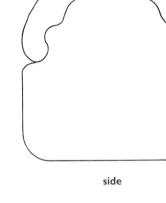

side

PLAN A Top, front, and side views of the Bread Box.

MAKING THE BOX

1 Plans A, B, and C show the basic configuration and assembly of the box.

2 Cut two $^3/_8$"-thick slices from one of the 4" sides to use later for the end pieces.

3 Draw the profile for the interior plan (Plan C) onto the end of the remaining block, and cut it out through the $5^1/_2$"-high block with a $^1/_{16}$" blade (Fig. 1). Go slowly, and be careful. Make the first cut around the outside of the body and the inside of the lid (Fig. 2). Then cut the outside of the lid, followed by the inside of the body. When all the cuts have been made, it should look like a sliding puzzle (Fig. 3).

4 Keep the two body pieces together as you sand their exteriors smooth (Fig. 4).

5 Take the pieces apart and sand the interiors smooth.

6 Sand the two flat end pieces that were cut off the block earlier. Join them with tape, transfer Plan A, the side view pattern, to them, and cut them out. If the pattern is significantly different from the actual lid and body because of some variation in cutting those pieces, use the outline of the actual lid and body to trace the shape of the sliding areas onto the end pieces.

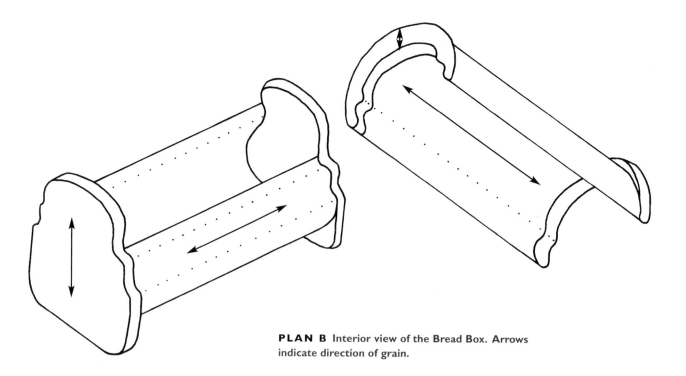

PLAN B Interior view of the Bread Box. Arrows indicate direction of grain.

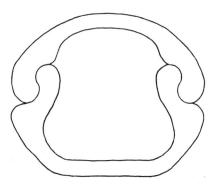

PLAN C Interior cross-section view of the Bread Box.

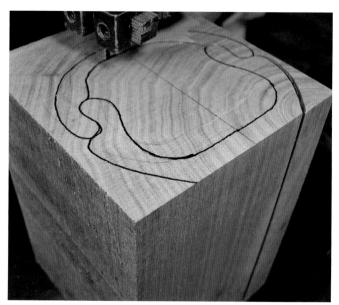

FIG. 1 Make your first cut on the outside of the body and the inside of the lid, keeping a smooth, uninterrupted line. Be sure your fingers are out of the way as the blade emerges from the wood. Note: in this photo the ³⁄₈" slabs have not yet been cut off from the block. They should have been cut off first. Live and learn.

FIG. 2 The results of the first cut show there are still two well-supported pieces ready for their second cuts. Don't worry if you stray a little off the line while cutting. It is more important that the contour is smooth and even.

FIG. 4 It is safer and easier to sand the body and lid on the belt sander table while the two pieces are held together vertically. If you were to try to do this job with the piece held horizontally, the force of the belt could cause the wood to spin out of your hands.

FIG. 3 How interesting is this? Putting the block back together is a lot of fun. Seeing how the mechanism works should give you ideas for other boxes that you could design and make.

7 Because this box needs a good, tight fit, and the wood removed in the kerf will result in a loose fit, we can use a little magic to remedy the problem. Cut two blocks of softwood, such as pine, basswood, or tupelo, $1/32$" larger than the opening in the box body. Gently force the blocks between the sides of the body so the sides are expanded evenly.

8 It would be difficult, if not impossible, to accurately align both ends at once, so glue the body to one of the end pieces, taking care that the ends of the body slide areas are completely covered by the end pieces (Fig. 5). Using a heavy-duty, parallel-jaws clamp ensures that the joint will be secure. After it is dry, glue the other end in place in the same manner.

FIG. 5 The spacer between the sides of the body is a piece of tupelo made to force the sides out just ¹/₃₂". Use two spacers to keep the sides parallel. The large clamp guarantees a good glue joint, and the sides will stay a little apart, causing the lid to fit better.

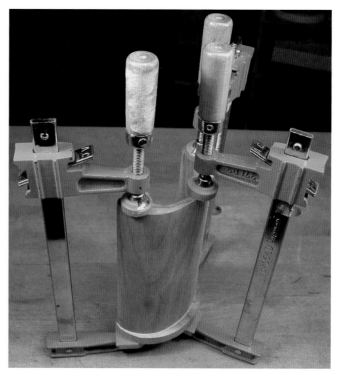

FIG. 6 Glue one end at a time when putting the lid together with its ends. Make sure the ends cover the edges of the lid. They always can be sanded back to ensure a good fit.

FIG. 7 The box looks almost done after the clamps are removed, but there is still a lot of work to be done. First, the sliding mechanism needs to function smoothly, and then the box can be sanded to a beautiful finish.

9   Check the fit between the body and lid. If it is snug, glue the lid to the lid ends. If it is still loose, use light-duty clamps to compress the lid ¹/₃₂" in two places so the sides are even. Then, glue on the lid ends, one at a time (Fig. 6).

10   The box will be very rough-looking after gluing, with many edges not meeting (Figs. 7 and 8). Don't worry; this is where finesse comes into play. The aim is to make the lid slide easily on the body. Everything that is in the way needs to be removed from both the lid and body. If you have to remove a lot of wood, it will save time to use rasps (Fig. 9). Micro-rasps are very sharp and leave a planed surface, so they are the ideal tool for this job. Don't take off more wood than is necessary to allow the two pieces to slide

FIG. 8 You can see in this closeup of the box corner that there are a lot of mismatched ends that need to be fixed before the lid will slide on the body.

FIG. 9 The quickest way to remove excess wood is with a rasp. This small planing rasp, or micro-rasp, does a great job in these coved areas. Do not go too far. It is safer to carefully sand the last of the wood away. Hold the box in a vise or with clamps for safety. These rasps are very sharp.

FIG. 10 Using rubbery profile sanders saves your fingertips and results in a nicely rounded, smooth finish in the coved areas.

FIG. 11 Once one end of the lid is fitted to the box body, you can use the profile of the end piece to mark where the wood needs to be removed. Be careful to keep the same orientation throughout the process. Because the ends probably are not identical, don't make the mistake of turning the lid around and tracing the wrong profile.

together smoothly. Finish the last fine-tuning with sandpaper. Hand profile sanders are a great help when sanding the coves of the sliding areas (Fig. 10).

11 You can achieve a better fit on the ends if you mark where the wood needs to be removed and then gradually reduce the wood until the fit is perfect (Fig. 11). Check your progress often to make sure you don't remove too much wood.

FIG. 12 Now that there is a good fit, round over the edges as needed, and sand the whole box to a smooth, flawless finish. Be sure to sand all traces of glue off the wood, or your finish will be splotchy.

FIG. 13 After the sanding sealer has dried, and before putting on the final coat, you will need to rough up the gloss and smooth down the surface of the finish. The best tool for this job is a maroon nylon scrubby. The left half of this end has not been scrubbed; the right half has been.

12 When the lid slides smoothly and the ends look balanced, it is time to round the edges and sand all surfaces smooth (Fig. 12).

FINISHING

1 The first coat of finish was a varnish sanding sealer, applied full strength, with a rag.

2 When the first coat was dry, the box was sanded with a maroon nylon scrubby and the dust removed (Fig. 13).

3 Then a coat of gel varnish was applied with a rag.

4 Figure 14 shows the finished Bread Box.

FIG. 14 The Bread Box was finished with varnish sanding sealer and gel varnish. Butternut, 6x3¹/₂x4".

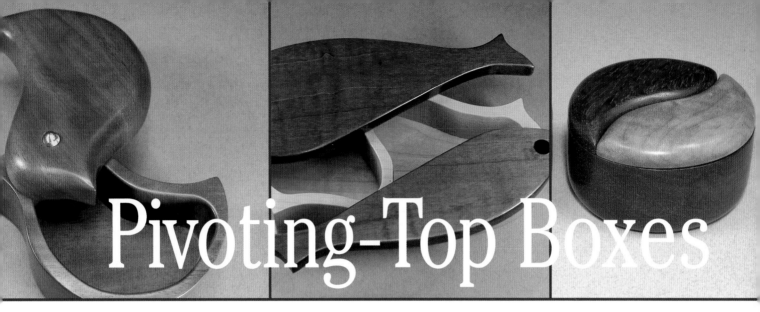

Pivoting-Top Boxes

Simple, clever, decorative, fun. These and other adjectives describe the boxes in this section. Using simple hinge pins made of dowel or metal rods, these boxes pivot open at the flick of a wrist. You can make the design simple like the Chickie Box or more complex like the Guppy Box. Either way, these boxes are not difficult to make.

OVERVIEW OF PIVOTING-TOP BOXES

Two of the secrets of creating pivoting-top boxes: Make sure the pin holes align between the lid and body and make sure the pin is perpendicular to the lid surface when you glue it in place. Follow the basic construction procedures listed below, and the next three projects will come together quickly and easily:

1. Square the block of wood.
2. Transfer the pattern onto the block and cut off the base.
3. Drill a hole for the hinge pin/eye, either through the lid area and into the body or through the body into the lid area. Either procedure will assure that the hinge pin holes align perfectly.
4. Cut off the lid.
5. Reassemble the pieces with cloth-backed, double-sided tape.
6. Cut out the top profile.
7. Cut out the interior of the body only.
8. Glue the body together.
9. Sand all interior surfaces.
10. Glue the hinge pin into the lid hole, making sure it is perpendicular to the lid.
11. Assemble and sand the exterior to shape with power-sanding tools.
12. Hand-sand to prepare for the finish.

Chickie Box

The Chickie Box is one of the easiest projects in this book. It is easy to cut out, easy to glue, and easy to finish. It has a simple elegance that

would make it a great present. You can make it in an afternoon. The model box was made out of koa wood from Hawaii. Koa sometimes has fantastic chatoyancy, but this piece was not figured. It is still a nicely colored, dense piece of wood that

feels great in your hands. Use a piece of brass rod for the hinge pin/eye to add a touch of class. You also could use a length of hard wood dowel.

Level of difficulty: Very easy

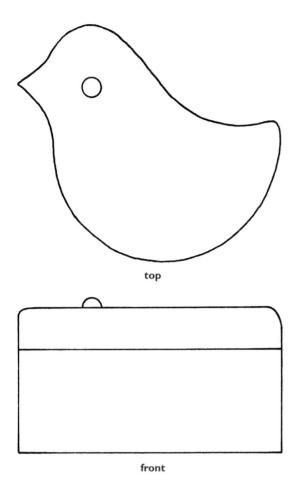

top

front

PLAN A Top and front views of the Chickie Box.

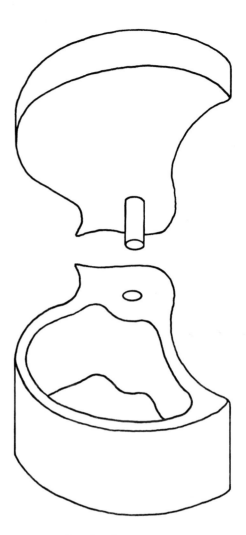

PLAN B Interior view of the Chickie Box.

PLAN C Interior plan view of the Chickie Box. Dashed line with arrow indicates entrance cut kerf.

MAKING THE BOX

1 Plans A, B, and C show the basic configuration and assembly of the box.

2 Mark the location of the hinge pin/eye on the squared and smoothed block, and then drill a $^1/_4$" diameter hole on the top of the block, $1\,^1/_2$" deep.

3 The shape of this box allows you to either cut off the lid and base of the box first, or cut the outline first. For expensive pieces of wood, such as koa, cutting the outline first wastes less wood. Then you can place the head and tail of the bird on the band saw table, and you have a stable support for cutting $^1/_2$" off the top for the lid and $^1/_4$" off the

FIG. 1 Use a feather board and push stick to be safe. Keeping the head and tail on the table creates a fairly stable arrangement, but keep some pressure on the piece to hold it to the table as it is being cut.

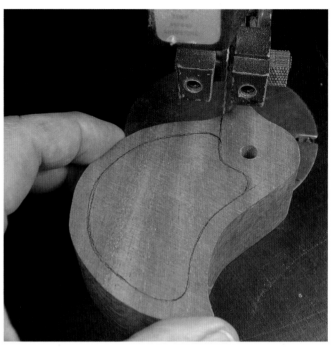

FIG. 2 Make the entrance kerf cut just under the bird's chin. That way it will be with the grain and invisible when the box is finished.

bottom for the base. The piece is fairly small, so use a feather board and push stick (Fig. 1) or two push sticks, to keep your fingers out of the danger zone.

4 Mark the body for ¹/₄" thick walls, with the entrance cut just under the bird's chin, and then cut out the core (Fig. 2). You will, of course, need to keep ¹/₄" away from the eye hole with this interior cut.

5 Glue the body together, cross-clamping as necessary (Fig. 3) to close up the entrance kerf.

6 Sand all the interior surfaces (Fig. 4).

7 I had a problem with the body-base joint on this project, and further hand-sanding was necessary. Maybe the pieces were not held correctly on the sanding belt, or perhaps the sanding belts were too old and warped out of flat. In any case, the belts were replaced, and this box needed serious damage control. Sanding boards were the best way to fix this problem. I used 120-grit until the straight edge sat flat on the surface and regular sanding scratches replaced the

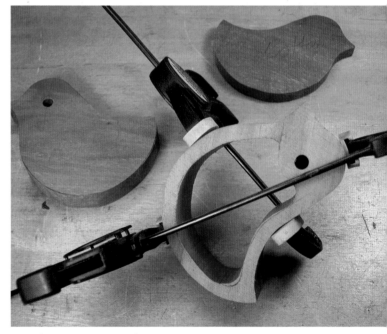

FIG. 3 Cross-clamping will hold the edges together while the glue dries, and it will keep the edges from sliding into the wrong position.

FIG. 4 Sand the interior of the body with coarse sanding sleeves to get the band saw blade's marks out of the wood and to make the sides evenly thick. Switch to finer grit sleeves to smooth the surface as much as possible. A little hand-sanding with 320-grit paper will finish the job. Here I'm using the oscillating spindle sander with a ¼"-diameter sleeve to get into the tight curve.

FIG. 5 A small problem with the sanding belt resulted in a big hand-sanding job using sanding boards. The pile of sanding dust on the paper towel will be saved for use in filling gaps in other boxes made of koa.

irregular shiny surface (Fig. 5). Then I used 220-grit to smooth out the wood. When this was done on the interior of the base and the bottom of the body, there was no longer a gap, and the final product was seamless.

8 Glue the body and base together.

9 The box was sized to use a ¼" brass rod for the hinge pin, creating the effect of the chick's eye. If you are making a larger box, you may need to size the hinge pin/eye accordingly. It's also possible to use a hard wood dowel for the hinge pin/eye.

10 Cut the hinge pin/eye with a hacksaw from a length of solid brass rod (Fig. 6). If you don't have a hacksaw, you can score the rod deeply all the way around with a metal file, and break the piece off. Use a metal file to flatten, and then

FIG. 6 A metal vise is useful to keep the brass rod steady for cutting with the hacksaw. Use slow, firm strokes and press down only on the push stroke for effective metal cutting.

FIG. 7 Use a metal file to first flatten and then round the eye end of the brass rod. Use both hands for better control with the file. Work with slow, firm strokes, and apply pressure only on the push stroke.

FIG. 8 Roll a section of sandpaper into a rod shape that can be used to make the holes in the lid and body a little larger, if necessary. You want the fit to be firm, but loose enough to allow the lid to pivot in the body, and to allow the pin to be epoxied into the lid.

round, the end of the pin that will function as the chick's eye (Fig. 7). Then use sandpaper to smooth and polish the rod, finishing with 600-grit. The rest of the pin should be sanded just to roughen the surface so the epoxy will adhere better.

11 Fit the hinge pin/eye to the hinge-pin/eye hole, but do not glue it yet. We need to have it in place for sanding the exterior, but need to be able to remove it for sanding the top of the lid. The hole may be a little small and require sanding with a rolled-up piece of 220-grit sandpaper (Fig. 8). Do not force the pin into either hole, or you may crack the short, cross-grained pieces of the box. Aim for a snug fit, and keep in mind that the eye will protrude $1/8$" above the top surface of the box.

12 Round the top edge of the lid with a rasp or sander (Fig. 9). If you are using a rasp, be sure to cut with the grain.

13 Power-sand the assembled box, except for the top of the lid, to shape, and smooth it. Sand the lid separately, with the pin removed, and then hand-sand for the rounded edges.

14 Because this box will be finished with wax polished with a buffing wheel and buffing the brass rod will discolor the buffing wheels, the pin cannot be installed until the box is completely finished. If you are using a different finish, the pin may be glued in place, with epoxy, at this time.

HELPFUL HINT: MAKING A DOWEL

If prepared dowel is not available in the wood species you want to use, you can make your own dowel stock using an impromptu lathe. First, cut a piece of wood $9/32$" x $9/32$" that is $2^1/2$" long. Then, chuck the piece into a portable drill, and sand it with 80-grit sandpaper while the drill is spinning at a moderate rate.

FIG. 9 Be careful when using these rasps. The teeth are as sharp as razor blades and, although they are designed to cut wood easily, they cut skin just as well. Hold the wood securely with clamps or in a vise so you can keep both hands behind the cutting edges.

FINISHING

1 Danish oil, clear, was used for the first finish coat.

2 That coat was followed with the Beall Wood Buff System (Fig. 10). You could also use wax, applied and buffed by hand.

3 After the wood was finished, the interior of the hinge-pin/eye hole was swabbed with epoxy, and the pin was inserted from the bottom side of the lid until the eye was $1/8$" above the top surface of the lid. Clean off any excess epoxy before it sets up. The waxy finish will keep it from being absorbed by the wood. Give it a final polish with a clean rag to make certain you have removed all traces of the epoxy from both sides of the lid and the eye.

4 Figure 11 shows the finished Chickie Box.

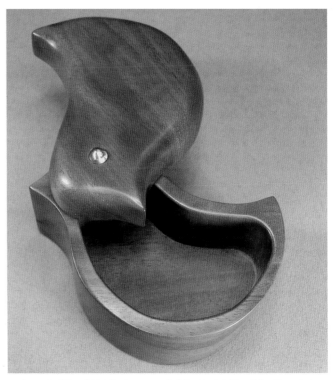

FIG. 10 The Chickie Box was finished with Danish oil and the Beall Wood Buff System.

FIG. 11 The finished Chickie Box. Koa wood, $3^3/4$x3x2".

Guppy Box

This pivoting hinge box uses wooden, instead of brass, hinge pins. Any hard wood dowel will work fine, but this one has redheart dowel pins

just because I happened to have some redheart dowel in my stock. When dyed green, redheart looks black like ebony. Birch dowel is easier to find, and the end could be colored black to produce the same effect. Construction of the box is similar to that used for the Chickie Box, but this one uses two hinge pins and has a divided compartment. The Guppy Box is partially dyed to bring out the figure in the maple and to provide contrast for the clear-coated body. It would make a neat box for holding special fishing lures or flies. You could change the design and make a dolphin- or whale-shaped box using these same techniques.

Level of difficulty: Easy

MATERIALS

$8^3/_4$x$4^1/_4$x$1^5/_8$" figured maple

$^3/_8$" diameter, 2" long hard wood dowel

$^1/_8$" band saw blade

Drill and $^3/_8$" drill bit, preferably brad-point

Drum or spindle sander

Blue dye, or thinned blue paint

Yellow dye, or thinned yellow paint

Tung oil and urethane topcoat, semigloss (I used Arm-R-Seal)

Nylon mesh pad, gray

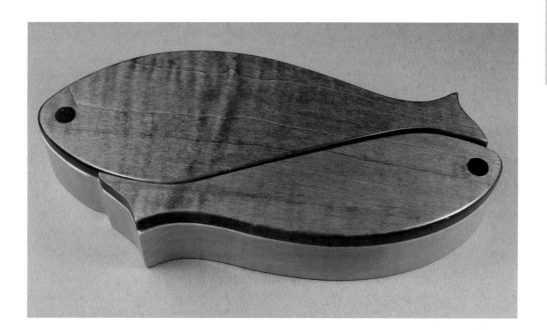

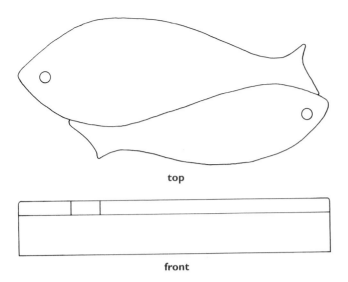

top

front

PLAN A Top and front views of the **Guppy Box**.

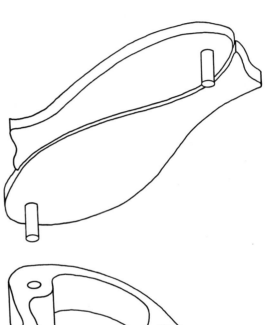

MAKING THE BOX

1 Plans A, B, and C show the basic configuration and assembly of the box.

2 Trace the plan outline onto your wood, using Plan A, top view. Drill 1" deep holes for the wooden hinge pins (at the fish's eyes) using a $^3/_8$" brad-point bit.

3 Then cut the block off at $^1/_2$" for the lid and $^1/_4$" for the base.

4 Reassemble the pieces with double-sided tape, and cut out the outline of the box, using Plan A, top view.

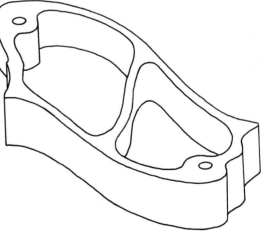

PLAN B Interior view of the **Guppy Box**.

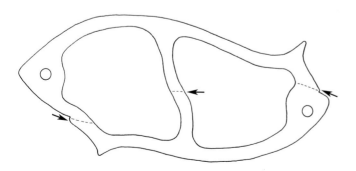

PLAN C Interior plan view of the **Guppy Box**. Dashed lines indicate entrance cut kerfs.

FIG. 1 Mark the interior plan on the body, after the lid and base have been cut off. Don't forget that a kerf will have to be cut through the divider for the sides to fit back together correctly.

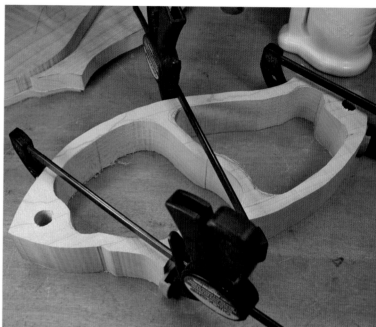

FIG. 2 Clamp at each of the glue joints, making sure that the edges are even and have not slipped out of place.

5 Remove the tape, and trace and cut out the interior sections of the box body, using Plan C (Fig. 1). Cut a kerf across the divider so the sides will meet. Make all entrance cuts with the grain, and they will practically disappear when the box is finished.

6 Glue the body together (Fig. 2).

7 Cut the lid into two sections, using Plan A, top view.

8 Sand all interior surfaces to 220-grit. Be especially careful with the fish form so it doesn't spin out of your hands. Keep the fish in "diving" mode, and it will be balanced (Fig. 3).

9 Glue the base to the body.

10 While getting ready to glue the dowels in place, I discovered that the dowel was a little small for the holes (Fig. 4). This happens when the dowel was dimensioned in metric units, and the drill in inches; or, in this case, one end of the dowel rod was smaller than the other. Next time I'll check the fit before cutting the dowel to length. I filled the area

FIG. 3 To keep the fish from taking off in undesired directions at the belt sander, keep it nose down and be sure to touch the bottom side of the piece of wood to the moving belt first. Hands were removed for clarity in this photograph, but both hands should be used to keep consistent pressure on the wood.

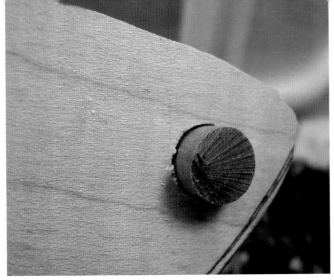

FIG. 4 The fit of this hinge pin was not good enough to secure with just glue. I mixed some fine sanding dust with glue to make a paste to put into the hole and around the dowel. Use a square to keep the dowel perpendicular to the lid as the glue sets up.

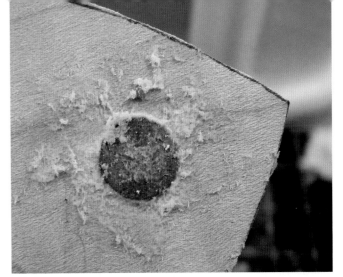

FIG. 5 The result of the dowel fix is messy, but power-sanding will fix the exterior quickly. The interior, where the dowel sticks out, will require some scraping before sanding by hand. All the glue must be removed or the dye will not be absorbed into the wood and the finish will be uneven.

between the dowel and lid with a thick mixture of fine sanding dust and glue (Fig. 5). I cleaned up the extra glue and sawdust from the exterior and interior.

11 I removed most of the glue residue by scraping with a knife before sanding. Scraping makes it easier to see that the glue has been completely removed. Then I smoothed the surface with sandpaper.

12 Hand-sand the edges of the lid where the two fish meet. Try to remove as little wood as possible, just enough so the saw marks are gone.

13 Now assemble the box, and sand the exterior edges to form and to finish-ready smoothness.

FINISHING

1 I wanted this box to look like the deep blue-green of the sea, so I mixed up a dye solution using mostly blue, with a little yellow (Fig. 6).

2 Don't paint with the dye; float the dye onto the lids using a generous amount of liquid. This dye was mixed with water, and only a few drops of dye were used, so it is not an expensive mixture. Work fast, cover the surface completely, and then wipe off any excess. Using this technique will result in an even distribution of dye over the surface (Fig. 7). The figure in the wood is not vibrant after dying, but when the coats of clear finish are applied it will come alive.

FIG. 6 Be generous when applying dye. If you try to paint it on, the result will be streaky and irregular. Try out the mixture on a piece of scrap figured maple to see how it will look before using it on the box lid. At first the color was too green; a couple more drops of blue made it just right.

FIG. 7 Don't be too worried if the dried dye does not show off the chatoyancy in the piece of wood. The clear finish will act like a magnifying lens to bring out the wood's figure.

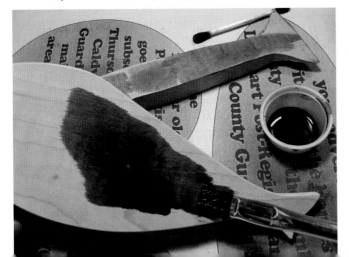

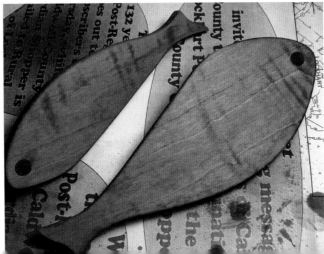

3   Three coats of a tung oil and urethane topcoat were used for the finish; I sanded with a gray nylon scrubby between coats (Fig. 8).

4   Figure 9 shows the finished box.

FIG. 8 With the tung oil and urethane finish applied, the grain of the figured maple now jumps out of the finished **Guppy Box.**

FIG. 9 The finished **Guppy Box.** Figured maple and redheart, 8$^1/_2$x4x1$^1/_2$".

Yin Yang Boxes

The yin yang design is an ancient Chinese symbol representing the opposing cycles and forces of nature that, when in balance, result in

harmony and peace. The dark form is yin: feminine, cool, dark, and negative. The light form, either white or red, is yang: masculine, warm, light, and positive. The dot of opposing color in each form stands for the element of opposing forces that exists in each extreme. Day and night, hot and cold, pleasure and pain, male and female; each is related to the other and unable to exist without its opposite. Together the two shapes form a circle without beginning or end.

These boxes are constructed together. Each gives a part of itself to the other to make them complete, like true friends.

Level of difficulty: Moderate

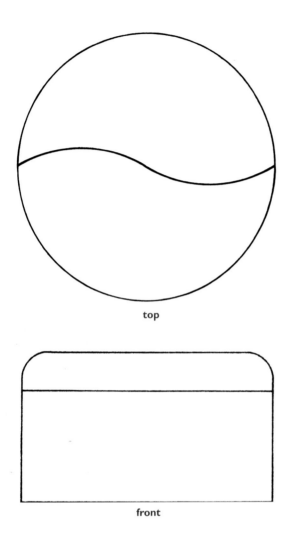

top

front

PLAN A Top and front views of the Yin Yang Box.

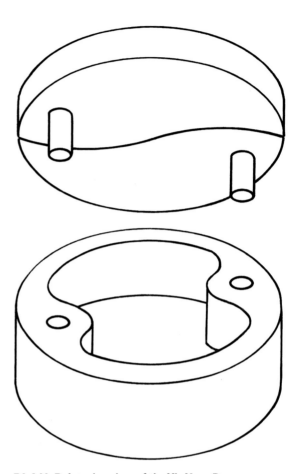

PLAN B Interior view of the Yin Yang Box.

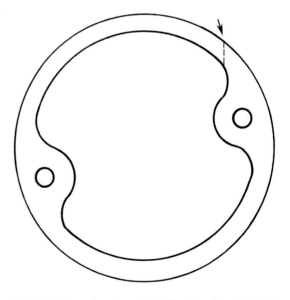

PLAN C Interior plan of the Yin Yang Box. Dashed line is entrance cut kerf.

MAKING THE BOXES

1 Plans A, B, and C show the basic configuration and assembly of the boxes. Plan D is the yin yang symbol.

2 We'll start with two equal blocks of hard wood in contrasting colors. Padauk's deep, rich red color and pronounced grain makes a good contrast to the light, tight-grained, and highly figured maple.

3 Choose the best faces, orient the grain of both blocks in the same direction, and tape the best faces of the blocks together with double-sided tape. The faces that are taped together will become the tops of the boxes. Draw a 3¹/₂"-diameter circle on the lighter colored maple block so it will be easier to see during cutting.

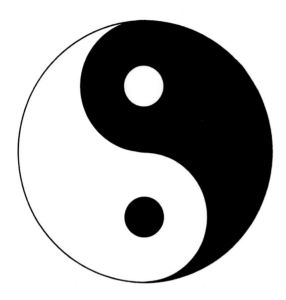

PLAN D The Chinese yin yang symbol represents the opposing cycles and forces of nature in balance.

FIG. 1 Cutting through 4" of hard wood is difficult for a ¹/₈" blade, so go slowly. For such a large circle, a ¹/₄" blade could be used, but then you would have to change blades for the interior cuts.

4 Cut out the circle, staying to the outside of the line, and leaving the pencil mark on the wood (Fig. 1). Place the cylinder on the belt sander's table, and use the sander with its miter gauge to square the ends (Fig. 2). Then redraw the circle on the light end.

5 Set one end of the block on the table, and remove the band saw blade marks by sanding to the center of the pencil line.

6 Draw a large V from one end of the assembly to the other (Fig. 3). This registration mark will help you to keep the pieces in their proper orientation after the wood is cut into components for the two boxes. The boxes will look better if their grain is consistent.

7 Mark ¹/₂" on either side of where the two blocks join for the lids; mark ¹/₄" on each end of the cylinder for the bases. Attach a stabilizing block to one end of the cylinder, and with that end against the fence, cut off the first base, first body, both lids together, and then the second body.

8 Keep the two tops taped together, and mark the lighter side with the lid plan (Plan A, top view). Then you can cut through both pieces at once (Fig. 4). Split the pieces apart by twisting or by using a smooth wooden wedge.

9 Position the lids that have registration marks on the bodies with the registration marks aligned. Position the other

FIG. 2 Use the miter gauge and table when sanding the ends square. If you don't have this arrangement, use a square to check the ends; then mark irregularities with a pencil, and sand to the lines by eye.

lid pieces upside down so they match the pieces on the bodies. Mark these four pieces with their designation as TOP, and draw new registration marks for the new arrangement.

Yin Yang Boxes **155**

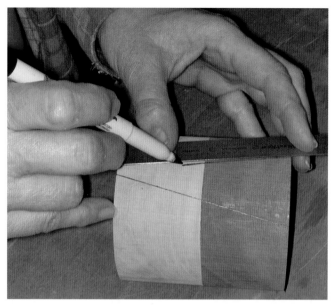

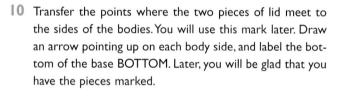

FIG. 3 Registration marks are particularly necessary with this box. There are a lot of parts, and the box will look best if these parts stay in the same relative position.

FIG. 4 Cut through both lids at the same time, and they are guaranteed to match.

10 Transfer the points where the two pieces of lid meet to the sides of the bodies. You will use this mark later. Draw an arrow pointing up on each body side, and label the bottom of the base BOTTOM. Later, you will be glad that you have the pieces marked.

11 Sand the meeting edges of the lids so they match up and are smooth. Sand the bottom side of each lid piece and the topside of the body pieces. Tape the lid pieces together and to the box body, being careful to align the registration marks. Turn the assembly over, mark the location of the hinge-pin holes, and then drill through the body and $^5/_{16}$" into the lids.

12 If you are going to make the variation of this box with inlaid dots, drill the holes in the lids and cut the contrasting plugs now (Fig. 5). When cutting the plugs, either for plugging holes or in this case for decorative buttons, you can break them off with a screwdriver or similar tool (Fig. 6).

13 Spread the holes and plugs with glue and insert the plugs into the holes, leaving a little of the plug above the surface of the lid to be sanded smooth later (Fig. 7).

14 On the top surface of each body piece, transfer the interior pattern (Plan C), aligned with the holes. Make sure you have $^1/_4$" of wood around each of the holes. The hinge pin hole needs to be located on the fatter end of the lid, so you will have to flip the pattern over for one of the boxes. Remember the marks you made in Step 10? Use them to check the position of the pattern relative to the lids.

15 Cut out the interior of the box bodies (Fig. 8). Place a chip of wood or a toothpick in the kerf to keep the space open while you finish the circle cut.

16 Glue the bodies together. Sand the interiors and bottoms of the box bodies and the tops of the base pieces.

17 Put the tops in place to distribute the pressure of the clamps, and glue the bodies to the bases. The base pieces will be bigger than the body pieces, so center them.

18 Trial-fit the hinge pins into the holes. Do not force the pin, or you may break the wood. If necessary, file and sand the metal so the pin fits firmly in the hole. Rough up the metal on the lid end of each pin using 80-grit sandpaper or a file. Epoxy the pins into the $^5/_{16}$" holes in the lids. Use a square to make sure the pins remain square to the lids. When the epoxy has set, smooth the exposed metal with sandpaper or a file.

FIG. 5 A plug cutter is used with a drill press on the face of the wood to cut out the required diameter inlay plugs.

FIG. 6 A screwdriver works well to break off the plugs.

FIG. 7 Leave a little of the plugs sticking out from the lids. They will be sanded smooth when the lids are sanded.

FIG. 8 Cut out the interior of the body, being careful to leave enough wood around the holes. Remember, the boxes are mirror images of one another so one interior pattern will be the reverse of the other.

19 You are now ready to assemble the box top to the base and see how well the tops swing open. Do not be disappointed if the exterior looks rough; we'll take care of that next with some serious sanding.

20 Start by power-sanding the sides smooth using 60- or 80-grit sandpaper on the belt sander with the table set to 90° (Fig. 9). Then sand the lids until they are even with one another. Hold them in the closed position with your fingers, or tape them shut along the sides of the box.

21 Contour the boxes' outer edges by drawing a line 1/8" in from the top and bottom edges, and then use the sander's table at a 45° angle to sand to the lines (Fig. 10). The sanding also can be done freehand (Fig. 11).

FIG. 9 It will take a lot of careful sanding to make the exterior of the box smooth and even. Take off only as much as is necessary so the sides of the box don't get too thin.

FIG. 10 If you have a tilting belt-sander table, it will be easy to make an even chamfer around the top and bottom edges of your box.

FIG. 11 The edges also can be rounded freehand on the belt sander if you have good eye/hand coordination and you check your progress frequently.

FIG. 12 Sanding the top of the lids' meeting edges is made easier with an oscillating spindle sander, but it can also be done with a drum sander in a drill or with a power rotary tool. Do not round over more than halfway through the thickness of the lids.

22 Sand by hand to round the edges.

23 Remove the top pieces, and mark ¼" on either side of their meeting surfaces on the top side only. Sand these center edges to round them, using a spindle sander and belt sander (Fig. 13). Do not go past that ¼" line in the

rounding process, or your tops won't meet. After machine-sanding to 220-grit, finish by hand-sanding with 220-, 320-, 400-, and 600-grits before applying the finish. Clean off all sanding dust and grit before finishing.

FIG. 13 Applying the first coat of finish is the best part of making boxes. Oil brings out the full beauty of the color, grain, pattern, and chatoyancy in the wood.

FIG. 14 One of the matching pair of Yin Yang Boxes. It's finished with Danish oil and buffed with the Beall Wood Buff System.

FINISHING

1 The boxes were finished with Danish oil and buffed wax; I used the Beall Wood Buff System (Figs. 13 and 14).

2 Because it is not possible to power-buff the interior of the boxes, you may choose to finish the interior first with a surface finish and then finish the exterior.

3 Figure 15 shows the finished box. Figure 16 shows a pair of boxes with inlaid dots.

FIG. 15 Yin Yang Box. Padauk and figured maple, 3¹/₂x3¹/₂x1³/₄".

FIG. 16 These Yin Yang Boxes, with their distinctive inlaid dots, were one of the first fine woodworking projects made by my brother, Mike. He did a mighty fine job.

Hinged Boxes

There's one advantage that hinged boxes have over most of the other boxes we've learned to build so far: you aren't going to lose the lids. Small hinges can lend a decorative touch to your boxes. We'll learn how to use and install three types of hinges in this section: barrel hinges, mortised butt hinges, and a hidden pivot hinge.

OVERVIEW OF HINGED BOXES

Barrel-Hinged Boxes

The Sea Shell Box, the Butterfly Box, and the Celtic Knot Box use barrel hinges. It's critical to make sure the holes for the hinges align between the lid and the body, and to assure that the pivot pin of the barrel hinge is located precisely where the lid meets the body.

Construction steps for barrel-hinged boxes can be outlined as follows:

1. Square and smooth the block of wood.
2. Cut off the lid and the base.
3. Cut off a piece for the lid lip if there is a recessed lid. Reassemble the pieces and cut the outline of the box.
4. Drill 5 mm holes from the bottom of body into the lid, or from the top of lid lip into the body if there is a recessed lid.
5. Drill ¼" holes for the magnet closure if you are using magnets.
6. Cut out the interior and glue the box body together.
7. Sand 45° chamfers on the outside of the hinge area edges.
8. Sand all interior surfaces.
9. Glue the body to the base, and glue the lid lip to the lid if there is a recessed lid.
10. Epoxy half of each hinge into the lid and then epoxy the other half into the body.
11. Sand the exterior to shape and smooth all surfaces.
12. Apply the finish.

Mortised-Hinge Boxes

The Flower Box and the Double-Cross Box use mortised hinges. Here the success of creating a smoothly opening lid depends on aligning the hinge holes in the lid and the body, but more important to a professional-looking job is making precise and neat mortises in which to seat the hinges. The two projects follow these basic construction steps:

1. Square and smooth the block of wood.
2. Cut off the lid and the base.
3. Cut off a piece for the lid lip if there is a recessed lid. Reassemble the pieces and cut the outline of the box.
4. Drill pilot holes for the hinge screws through the body bottom into the lid or from top of the lid lip into the body if there is a recessed lid.
5. Drill ¼" holes for the magnet closure if using magnets.
6. Cut out the interior and glue the box body together.
7. Sand all interior surfaces.
8. Glue the body to base and the lid lip to lid; then re-drill the hinge pilot holes deeper into lid.
9. Attach the hinges with screws, mark the hinge mortise locations, and then remove the hinges.
10. Cut the mortises for the hinges, and then reinstall the hinges.
11. Sand the exterior to shape and smooth all surfaces. (Remove the hinges to sand the hinge side of the box.)
12. Apply the finish.
13. Reinstall the hinges.

Hidden-Hinge Boxes

The last project in this section, the Ambrosia Box, uses pivot pins as we did on the pivoting-lid boxes. But in this case the pins are set into the side and lid of the box, creating a completely hidden hinge. Construction steps for the Ambrosia Box are listed below:

1. Square and smooth the block of wood.
2. Cut off the ends of the box.
3. Drill the holes for the hinge pins in the ends and in the lid.
4. Cut out the exterior shape of the box.
5. Cut off the lid.
6. Cut out the core.
7. Sand the interior and ends of the box body and the inside of the end pieces.
8. Fit the hinge pins into the holes in the body and lid.
9. Trial-fit the lid to the box and ends, sanding where needed so the lid opens easily. Epoxy the hinge pins into the lid holes.
10. Glue the box together.
11. Finish-sand the exterior and interior.
12. Apply the finish.

Sea Shell Box

The Sea Shell Box is one of the easiest projects in this book, if you don't carve the lid. The box would look fine using the plan provided and just rounding over the edges. Making a fully relief-carved lid adds to the beauty of the piece and gives adventurous woodworkers a real challenge. The 5 mm barrel hinges used in this project are inexpensive and effective if installed correctly. By following the instructions carefully, you'll succeed in making a fully functioning hinged box without having to cut mortises. You'll need a 5 mm brad-point drill bit and some careful workmanship, but good results are practically guaranteed.

The walnut wood used to make this box came out of a scrap pile; it was a leftover from someone's project. There is no such thing as scrap when it comes to such a nice piece of hard wood. One person's trash is another person's treasure.

Level of difficulty: Easy to challenging

MATERIALS

5^1/$_2$x4^1/$_2$x2^3/$_4$" walnut

5 mm mini-barrel hinges, two

^{1}/$_8$" band saw blade

Drill and 5 mm drill bit, preferably brad-point

Carving chisel, 1", full-sized, or modified carpenter's chisel

Carving gouge, #11, ^{5}/$_{16}$" wide

Mallet

10° wedge

Drum or spindle sander

5-minute epoxy

Heavy-bodied tabletop varnish

Mineral spirits

Spray lacquer, satin

Beall Wood Buff System, or wax applied and buffed by hand

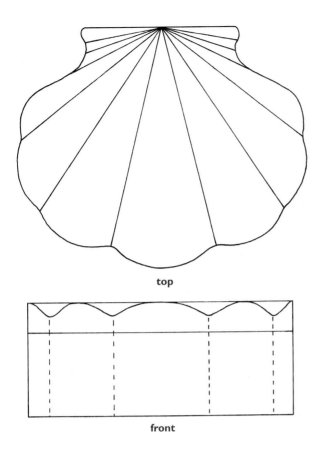

top

front

PLAN A Top and front views of the Sea Shell Box.

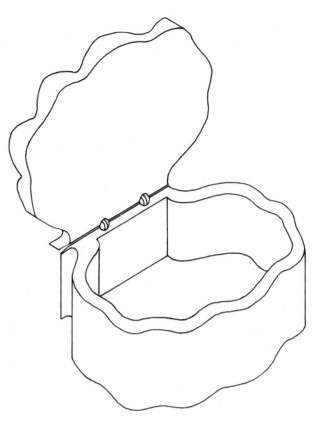

PLAN B Interior view of the Sea Shell Box.

MAKING THE BOX

1 Plans A, B, and C show the basic configuration and assembly of the box.

2 When you find a piece of laminated wood like this (Fig. 1), check that the laminations were done correctly. In this case, the end grain showed that the direction of the growth rings alternated with each layer, as it should. Because the block was so irregular, I first marked the block for minimum waste (Fig. 1). After making the cuts, I had a square block ready to become a sea shell and three pieces of wood that I set aside for making smaller boxes (Fig. 2).

3 Cut off the top at $^5/_8$" for the lid and cut $^3/_8$" off the bottom for the base.

4 Then tape the lid and body pieces together. Place the interior body pattern (Plan C) on the bottom of this assembly

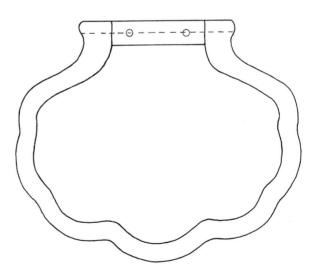

PLAN C Interior plan view of the Sea Shell Box.

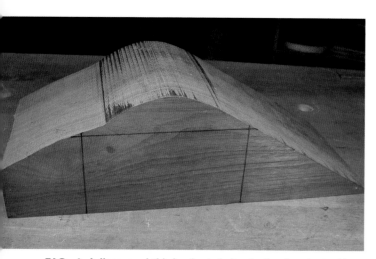

FIG. 1 I discovered this laminated chunk of walnut by looking through a trash bin at a woodshop. It was too nice to relegate to the burn pile.

FIG. 2 After a little pruning, I have a squared piece of wood for this box, plus a few smaller pieces, for which I will find other projects.

FIG. 3 By laying the hinge in place on the box, you can double-check that the drilling depth will be sufficient. Mark the depth with a piece of tape on the drill bit to easily see where to stop.

with the hinge side of the pattern along one of the end grain edges. Mark where to drill the hinge holes.

5 After removing the pattern, check that the marks for the holes are equidistant from the back edge. Drill two 5 mm holes that go through the body and $^3/_8$" into the lid (Fig. 3).

6 Tape the base back onto the assembly, and cut the perime-

ter of the box. Note: If you are not going to carve the box, skip the information on carving in Steps 7-14, and move on to Step 15.

7 If you are going to carve the lid, keep the pieces taped together. By keeping the base, body, and lid pieces securely taped together, it will be easier to hold onto the block using a wood vise or other device while carving the lid. See

FIG. 4 The box has been marked for carving, with the solid lines marking the lowest areas, where you will make the stop cuts. The broken lines are the centerlines of the scallops and should remain until all the carving is finished. Do not use ink markers, as I did here for the model, because the ink will be absorbed into the pores of the wood and will be difficult to sand away.

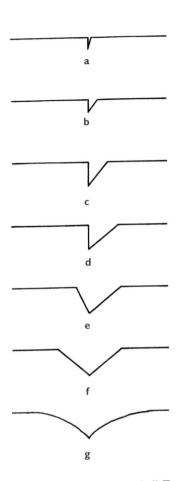

FIG. 5 Sequence of cuts for carving the shell. Top to bottom: a. Make the first stop cut. b. Make a shallow cut into the stop cut. c. Make a deeper stop cut followed by a deeper slice down to it. d. Broaden the cut. e. Work on the other side to make the sides equal. f. Broaden both sides to the halfway point between the grooves. g. Gently round the curves to make a seamless arc.

the Star Box project for more information on chisels and carving.

8 Transfer the top view pattern (Plan A, top view) to the top of the lid (Fig. 4).

9 The first carving cuts are stop cuts, made with a sharp chisel or #1 carving gouge, $3/4$" to $1^{1}/8$" wide. Tap the tool with a mallet straight into the wood along the solid lines, tapering the depth from near the surface at the point where the lines converge on the shell to deeper at the scalloped edges. Work on one side of a line only, so the line remains clear until you have reached the final depth (Fig. 5). If you work both sides at the same time, you will carve away the line, and then will not know where to cut (Fig. 6).

FIG. 6 Don't make your cuts on both sides of the line at the same time, as I did here. Your line will disappear, and you will have to redraw it. Work one side at a time for best results.

FIG. 7 At this point the cuts have been completed to halfway between the lines. If you don't trust your eyes to keep your cutting straight, draw in these halfway lines.

FIG. 8 Keep your chisel sharp enough to slice through the wood cleanly with just hand pressure. You'll get a better finish that will require less sanding. Notice how the edge of the blade is cutting with the grain. If the chisel digs into the grain, you're going in the wrong direction.

FIG. 9 Continue rounding the curves until you have a smooth, tapering arc at each division. You may want to draw an arc at the end of the division as an aid to keeping the curves consistent.

FIG. 10 To make the round-bottomed groove at the hinge end of the box, you will need a carving gouge. Here, I'm using a ⁵⁄₁₆" #11 gouge.

FIG. 11 Your final shaping should be done with sandpaper. The right side of the box top has been finish-carved, and the left side has been sanded smooth.

FIG. 12 With the lid carving complete, the lid and base can be cut off. Then the interior can be cut out of the body, and it can be glued together. Clamping is easy on this box.

10 Make gradually deeper and wider cuts, as shown in Figure 7, until you reach the halfway point between the centerline and the groove of a scallop.

11 Then work on the opposite side of the groove line, using a slicing cut, cutting with the grain (Fig. 8).

12 Finally, round over the edge to achieve a smooth transition and a graceful arc (Fig. 9).

13 The hinge side of the top of the lid requires a carving gouge or lots of sanding to make the rounded groove (Fig. 10). Don't use the chisel or gouge to round the tops of the hinge side detail, however; it is easier and safer to sand them to shape.

14 I wouldn't trust a power sander to sand the top of this box. It is all handwork, and there is a lot of it. Start with 120-grit paper to remove all roughness, and work up to 220-grit to smooth it. Make the last strokes for each grit with the grain (Fig. 11).

15 Take the block apart, mark the interior pattern on the body, and cut out the core. Sand only the interior side of the flat, back piece, and then glue the body together. Clamping is easy because it is just necessary to clamp straight across the back (Fig. 12).

16 Sand all the interior surfaces.

17 Mark the back side of the lid and body 1/4" from their meeting edges (Fig. 13), which should be halfway through the hinge holes. Set the table or fence on your belt sander to 45°. Place the meeting edges of the lid and base on the table/fence, and sand the hinge areas of both the lid and body to halfway through the holes (Fig. 14). Check frequently as you sand to be sure you don't take off too much wood.

18 Now trial-fit the hinges into the holes, and see how well they work. The hinge pin needs to be positioned on the meeting point of lid and body (Fig. 15) and in line with the back of the box.

Sea Shell Box **167**

FIG. 13 Mark the lid and body for the centerline of the hinges. The hinge chamfer must end at the center of the holes.

FIG. 14 As you chamfer the edges with the belt sander, check your progress frequently. Keep the pressure even, steady and light until you reach the center of the holes. Done correctly, the chamfers will be straight, flat, and will neatly bisect the holes.

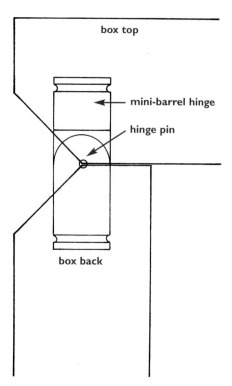

box top

mini-barrel hinge

hinge pin

box back

FIG. 15 For the barrel hinges to work properly, the hinge pin must be positioned at the meeting point of the lid and body, as shown in this hinge detail.

FIG. 16 The best technique for installing the hinges is to epoxy them into the lid first. That way you can easily check that they are oriented perpendicular to the box and that their depth is set correctly.

19 After you're satisfied with the fit of the hinges, epoxy one end of each of the hinges into the lid holes. Don't use too much epoxy or the excess may get into the mechanism. Make certain that the hinge pin is aligned with the back of the box, and that it is at the proper depth (Fig. 16). Then epoxy the other ends of the hinges into the body holes, and your box is ready for finishing.

FIG. 17 The Sea Shell Box was finished with varnish, lacquer, and wax to bring out the beauty of the walnut.

FIG. 18 The finished Sea Shell Box. Walnut, 5¹/₄x4¹/₄x2¹/₂".

FINISHING

1 This box was finished with two coats of 50/50 varnish and thinner. There were too many runs, so I sanded the whole box down to the wood.

2 Then I applied spray lacquer.

3 Finally, the finish was rubbed out with the Beall Wood Buff System (Fig. 17).

4 Figure 18 shows the completed Sea Shell Box.

Butterfly Box

This box gets a rating of 10 out of 10 for difficulty. Don't make it for your first band saw box. There are challenges in cutting the parts just right,

getting the locking body to fit snugly, and in making the eye key fit and function correctly. If you are willing to spend hours fine-tuning the details, and you want to make one of the prettiest boxes in this book, go for it! This design could be modified to make a dragonfly box or ladybug box.

I've already made every possible mistake with this box, and I've had to start over twice, so I hope my learning curve experience will make it easier for you. Read the instructions carefully, and then follow them precisely to save yourself unnecessary trouble. If that didn't scare you off, let's get to it.

Level of difficulty: Very challenging

MATERIALS

$7^5/8$x$4^1/4$x2" figured maple

$3^1/4$x$1^1/8$x$3/4$" purple-heart

$3/8$" diameter x $1/4$" ebony plugs, two

$1/8$" diameter x 1" long and $1/8$" x $1/2$" long brass rods

5 mm mini-barrel hinges, four

$1/8$" band saw blade

Double-sided adhesive tape

10° wedge

Drum or spindle sander

Drill, 5 mm and $1/8$" drill bits, preferably brad-point

Pliers

5-minute epoxy

Tung oil + resin + linseed oil compound (I used Waterlox Original Sealer and Finish)

Salad bowl finish

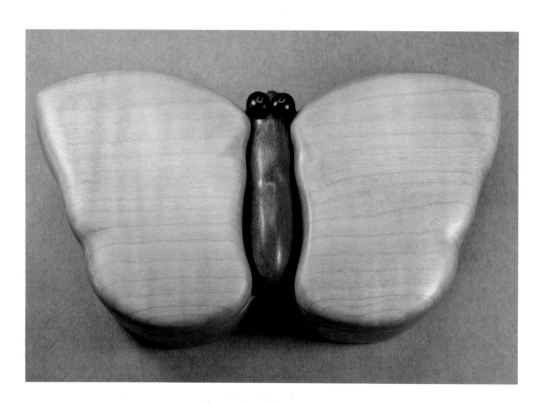

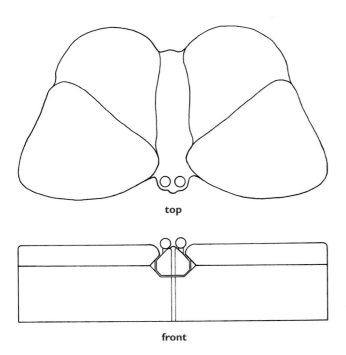

top

front

PLAN A Top and front views of the Butterfly Box. Note: Plan A shows a division on the wings, which wasn't used for the present box. You could wood-burn these lines as a detail if desired.

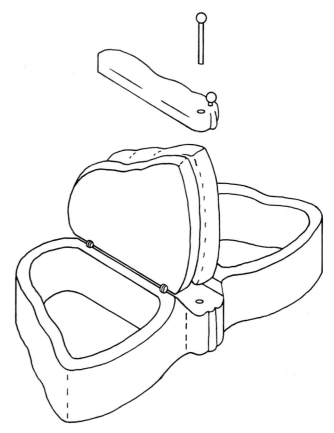

PLAN B Interior view of the Butterfly Box.

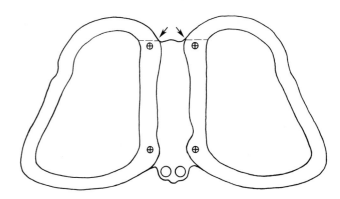

PLAN C Interior plan view of the Butterfly Box. Dashed lines are entrance cut kerfs.

MAKING THE BOX

1 Plans A, B, and C show the basic configuration and assembly of the box.

2 Start with a block of figured maple that has two parallel faces, and cut out the outline using the top view plan (Plan A, top view).

3 Place the head side of the box on the table, and rip off $1/2$" for the lid and $1/4$" for the base. Sand the four newly cut faces to 220-grit. It is easier and safer to hold the lid and base for sanding on the belt sander if you stick the outsides of the two pieces together with double-sided tape. After sanding, take them apart.

4 Place the lid section on the body section in the correct orientation, and use masking tape to hold the two pieces together. Turn the assembly over and mark the location of

FIG. I The centerline of the butterfly body must be perpendicular to the front edges of the wings. If the line is not square, adjust the front edge of the wings until it is square.

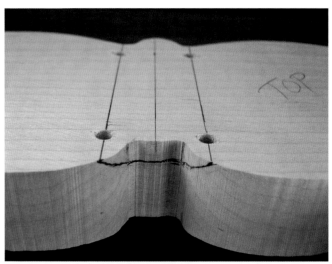

FIG. 2 After drawing lines through the centers of the wing hinge holes, extend the lines around the front edge of the box at 45° to meet the ends of the ⁵/₈" line.

Step I

Step 2

Step 3

FIG. 3 This is the best cutting order for making the body groove (from top down): Step I: Make the first two cuts from the topside to points A and B at 45°, and then back out of the cut. Step 2: Go back to the entrance cut to point A; halfway down to A, turn towards point B in a gentle curve. Most of the piece is now cut out. Step 3: For the last cut, start at the baseline at B and continue in a straight cut to the opposite corner, A.

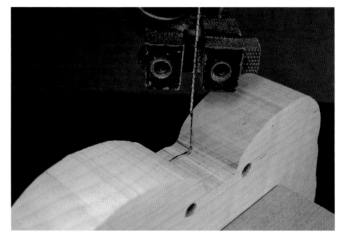

FIG. 4 Making the cuts through the body. Notice the stabilizing block attached to the back of the box to steady the tall block for an accurate cut.

the hinge holes on the bottom of the body, using the interior plan (Plan C).

5 Drill four 5 mm holes through the body and ³/₈" into the lid. Remove the lid piece, and put it aside for now.

6 On the top side of the body, draw a centerline midway between the two sets of wing hinge holes. Check that this centerline is perpendicular to the front edge of the wings (Fig. I). Draw two more lines through the centers of the holes, parallel to the centerline. At the back end of the box, make a centered line ⁵/₈" long, parallel to and ¹/₄" down from the top of the body. Connect the ends of this line to each of the lines extending from the hinge holes to mark the body groove for cutting (Fig. 2).

7 Attach a stabilizing block to the backside of the body block, and cut out the body groove. Do not try to make the cut in one pass; to make a neat job of it follow the cutting sequence outlined in Figure 3 and shown in Figure 4.

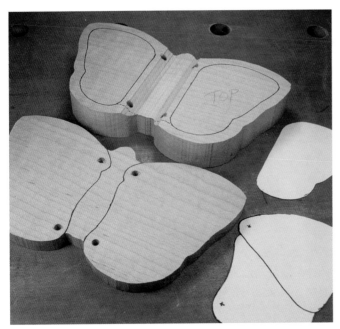

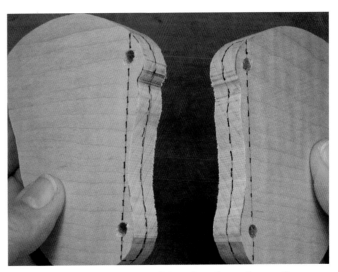

FIG. 6 Mark the underside of the wing pieces for sanding chamfers for the hinge clearance. Make sure the chamfer ends in the center of the holes.

FIG. 5 Mark the topside of the body piece and the body side of the lid/wings. Be sure to leave at least ¹/8" of wood around each of the hinge holes, and then cut out the interior and wings.

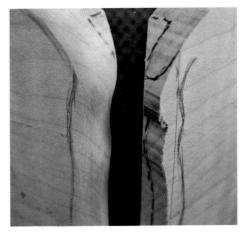

FIG. 7 The wing center on the right has been marked for rounding with the sander, and the wing on the left has been sanded round.

8   Mark the lid piece with the wing pattern (Plan A, top view), and mark the body with the interior pattern, Plan C (Fig. 5). Modify the plan, if necessary, to make sure there is at least ¹/8" of wood around the hinge holes. Cut the wings out, and cut out the interior spaces of the box body. If the exterior of the body is irregular and will require extra sanding, you should make the sides a little thicker when you cut out the interior so there will be some wood remaining when you have finished sanding.

9   Glue the body together, sand the interiors, and smooth any irregularities on the top and bottom of the body resulting from glue-up. Glue the sanded body to the sanded base.

10   Mark the center edge of each wing ¹/4" up from the bottom edge. This should equal the distance from the center of the hinge holes to the inner edges of the wings. If it doesn't, then modify the pattern accordingly and relocate the line on the side of the wing to match the distance on the bottom of the wing (Fig. 6).

11   Set your belt sander's table/fence to 45°, place the wing's bottom on the table, and sand a chamfer up to the line on the inside edge of each wing. Pick up the piece frequently

as you get closer to the line to check the holes. It is critical that the chamfer terminates at the centerline of the holes, and that the line is straight.

12   Use a drum sander or rasp to round over the top and inner edges of the wing to match the front view profile (see Plan A, front view). Try to remove as little wood as necessary from the inside edges. Sand just enough to smooth out the marks from the band saw blade. Do not sand at all on the hinge chamfer (Fig. 7). Sand the body groove just enough to remove any gross imperfections.

13   Now you can trial-fit the hinges and modify the wings and body groove as necessary so both sides open completely.

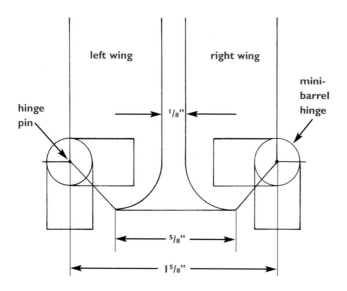

FIG. 8 The two wings should come within ¹/₈" of touching when they are completely opened, as shown here in this detail. You will have to do some modification with sandpaper to adjust the wing edges and the body groove. Maintain the given dimensions, and your wings will fly.

FIG. 9 Watch your fingers when sanding small and difficult-to-hold pieces of wood, such as the butterfly body shown here. It would be safer, easier, and result in a better job if you attached such small pieces to a block of scrap to give yourself more holding power.

FIG. 10 The body must fit snugly between and under the wings. You don't want a hammer-force fit, but remember that after you shape and sand the body, the fit will be looser so keep it as tight as possible at this point.

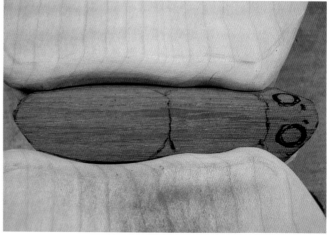

FIG. 11 Mark on the top of the body where to shape the head, thorax, and abdomen as shown here. Don't remove wood where the wings touch the body, or the body will not serve as a locking mechanism.

The hinges are a snug fit, and you may want to use pliers to insert and remove them. When the hinge action is just right, epoxy the hinges into place (Fig. 8).

14 When inserted between the wings, in the body groove, the body of the butterfly acts as a lock to keep the box closed. It needs to fit precisely in the body groove and snug up against the chamfer on the wings. Sand the body to shape using the belt sander set at 45°. First, draw lines on the sides of the body block ¹/₄" from the top and bottom edges. Sand to these guidelines on all four corners (Fig. 9). Next, sand away ¹/₈" of the points you've generated on the sides of the lock body to make clearance for the barrel

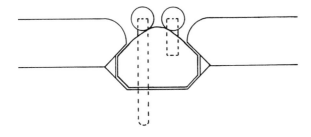

FIG. 12 The eye on the left functions as a key to hold the body lock in place. The eye on the right is just an eye. Try to make them look identical and the uninitiated person will not be able to open the box.

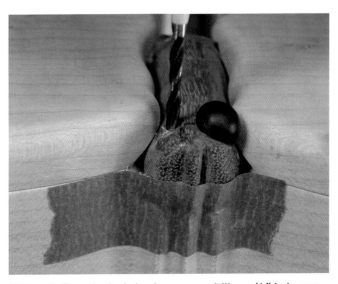

FIG. 13 Tape the body in place as you drill one ¹/₈" hole completely through the butterfly body and into the box body for the key lock. The second hole does not need to be more than ¹/₂" deep. Note that the ebony eye for this box is fitted to the curve of the body. This is difficult to do, and it doesn't function as well as if the eyes were round. Make the eyes spherical and let ¹/₁₆" of brass rod show on each eye.

hinges. Then, round the top side of the lock body using the sander. Trial-fit the butterfly lock body into the body groove, and remove whatever material is in the way until it slides in smoothly (Fig. 10).

15 Mark the lock body to indicate the head, thorax, and abdomen of the butterfly (Fig. 11). Use a small drum sander to gently round just the top of the piece at these lines. Do not sand any on the bottom or in the area of the chamfers; otherwise the piece will get too small to be an effective lock. Round the front of the head and back of the tail areas, and sand the body smooth.

16 Sand the exterior of the box to form, and finish. Position the body lock, and tape it in place.

17 You will need to make two eyes out of hard wood. One of the eyes will be the key that allows access to the box. That eye will be attached to a piece of ¹/₈" brass rod that goes through the head and into the box body. The other eye will be attached to the body with a short length of brass rod.

18 I made these eyes out of plugs of ebony; they would look fine in any dark hard wood. Drill ¹/₈" holes ¹/₈" deep in the wood before cutting them to shape or using the plug cutter. Epoxy the rods into the holes to give you something to hold onto while you shape the eyes into spheres. Use a pair of pliers to hold the rod while you sand the wood to shape.

19 Drill two holes into the head, where indicated on the plans (Figs. 12 and 13). Epoxy the static eye into place (Fig. 14). Work to get the eye key to fit smoothly into the hole

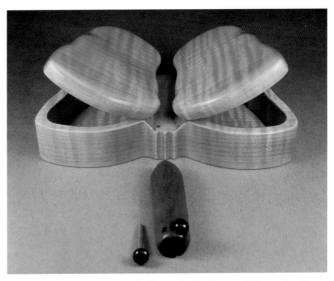

FIG. 14 The tung oil-resin-linseed oil mixture, followed with a salad bowl finish, impart a rich luster to the figured maple of the Butterfly Box. The eye key is on the table.

made for it. You may need to file or sand the rod to achieve a good fit. Make both eyes even in relation to the head.

20 Final-sand all surface to 320-grit on the figured maple and to 600-grit on the purpleheart and ebony.

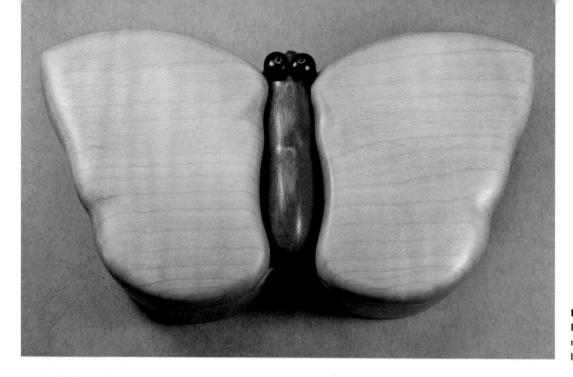

FIG. 15 The finished Butterfly Box. Figured maple and purpleheart, $7^{1}/_{4} \times 4^{1}/_{8} \times 1^{7}/_{8}$".

FINISHING

1 I used a tung oil + resin + linseed oil mixture for the first two coats on the Butterfly Box. I didn't want too heavy a finish to insure that the moving parts would retain their smooth movement. It did, however, have too much body, so I gently sanded it smooth with 400-grit sandpaper.

2 Then I applied a final coat of salad bowl finish.

3 Figures 15 and 16 show the finished butterfly.

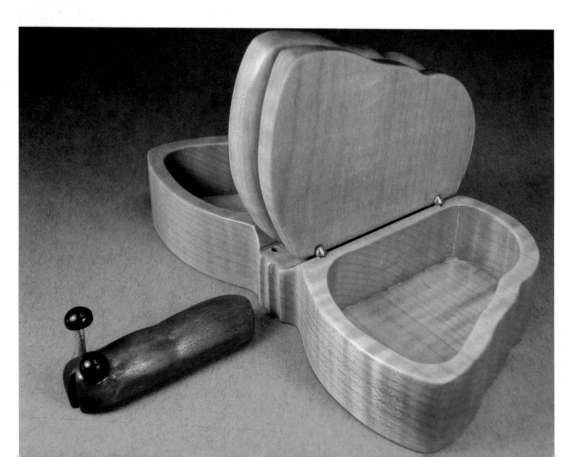

FIG. 16 The Butterfly Box, with the body key and key lock eye outside.

Celtic Knot Box

Complex ribbonlike patterns like the one used on this box are found in ancient civilizations from India to Arabia and Europe. The patterns

may have been an expression of people's desire to illustrate the complexities of life and the interweaving of different influences in their lives.

The Celts were an ancient people who lived in Ireland and Scotland. They used these designs in their embellishment of everyday objects and jewelry. Favorite Celtic designs were complicated lines that formed unending knots, sometimes with animal imagery worked into the design.

You can make this box with a carved lid or with the design drawn and woodburned onto the surface. Hinging for this box is the same as for the previous two boxes, but this box has a recessed lid and a hidden magnetic closure.

Level of difficulty: Moderate

MATERIALS

4¹/₈x4¹/₈x2" basswood

5 mm mini-barrel hinges, two

6 mm x 3 mm rare earth magnets, two

¹/₈" band saw blade

Drill, 5 mm and ¹/₄" drill bits, preferably brad-point

Drum or spindle sander

5-minute epoxy

¹/₄" plug cutter

Carbon or graphite paper, or transfer tool

Wood burner with writing tip, or indelible marker or paint

Colored oil pencils

Artists' acrylic paint, semigloss clear

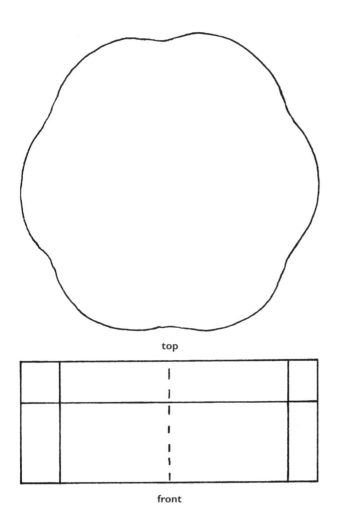

top

front

PLAN A Top and front views of the Celtic Knot Box.

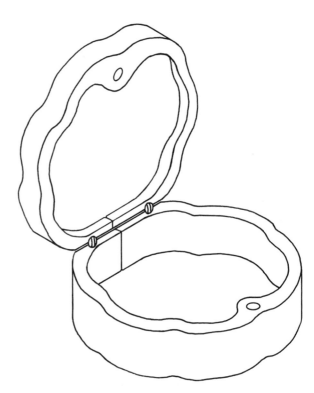

PLAN B Interior view of the Celtic Knot Box.

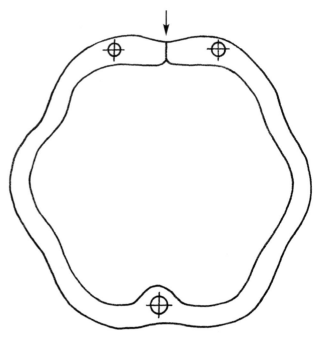

PLAN C Interior plan view of Celtic Knot Box.
(Arrow indicates entrance cut kerf.)

MAKING THE BOX

If you are going to carve the top of this box, do that after cutting the outline of the box but before cutting the block apart. That way it will be easier to hold the block in the vise.

1   Plans A, B, and C show the basic configuration and assembly of the box.

2   The first step, if you are not going to carve the lid, is to rip ¹/₄" off of both the top and bottom of the block. Then reassemble the block and cut the outside pattern (Fig. 1).

3   Mark the interior pattern for the holes on the top of the body only, using Plan C as a guide, and drill the two 5 mm

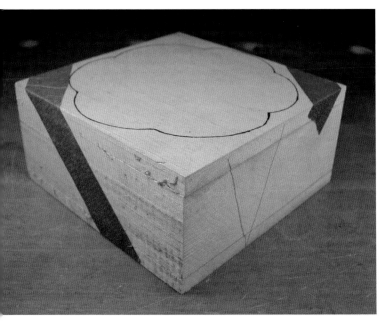

FIG. 1 Tape the box with blue painter's masking tape on the outside, and it will be easier to take apart for the next step. Use double-sided tape when you want the pieces to stay together for other processes, such as carving.

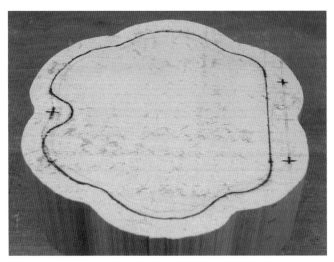

FIG. 2 Mark the centers for the hinge and magnet holes, and the interior is ready to be cut out. Use registration marks to remind you where everything belongs.

holes for the hinges and the $^{1}/_{4}$" hole for the magnets $^{3}/_{4}$" deep on the top surface (Fig. 2).

4 For an interior line, use Plan C to draw a line following the outline of the box, but about $^{1}/_{4}$" in from the outline and $^{1}/_{8}$" away from the holes. Cut out the interior. Notice that the entrance kerf, midway between the hinge attachments, is emphasized in this box and contributes to the overall design.

5 Glue the body together and sand smooth all surfaces. Then cut $^{3}/_{8}$" off the top side of the body to make the lip for the lid. Sand the interiors of the lid and base, and then glue the lid lip to the lid, forming the lid recess. Drill the hinge holes $^{3}/_{8}$" into the lid through the lid liner holes. Finally glue the body to the base. You can see the lid lip in Plan B.

6 Mark and sand chamfers for the hinge clearance (Fig. 3). Epoxy the hinges into the lid and then into the body, doing a dry-fit first to make sure everything works correctly. Use a toothpick to put the epoxy in the holes.

7 Rip two pieces of $^{1}/_{32}$" veneer from a scrap piece of the same wood used for the project. The veneer strips will

FIG. 3 The lid chamfer, on the left, is complete and ends halfway through the holes. The body chamfer, on the right, is marked for sanding with an X noting the wood to be removed.

conceal the magnets in the body and lid. Sand the veneers smooth, and test their thickness with two rare earth magnets (Fig. 4). The magnets should hold together strongly through the two pieces of wood. Use a $^{1}/_{4}$" plug cutter to cut two disks from the veneers, and epoxy the disks to the outside of the joined magnets (Fig. 5). Now, when the magnets are inserted into the holes, their orientation will be correct.

Celtic Knot Box **179**

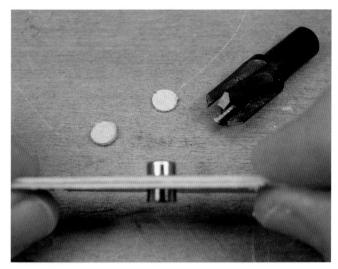

FIG. 4 With a rare earth magnet in the lid and one in the body, this box will close with a resounding snap. Make the veneer concealing strips thin enough so the magnets exert enough force through two layers. Cut circles of wood using plug cutters or a sharp knife.

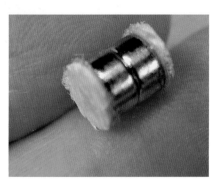

FIG. 5 Gluing matching wood veneer pieces to the magnets will disguise them and guarantee that they are correctly oriented in the holes.

FIG. 6 Use carbon paper or graphite transfer paper to transfer this Celtic knot design to the box lid.

8 Apply epoxy to the top ¼" of the walls of the holes for the magnets, and insert the magnets so the veneer fits into the holes. Orient the grain of the plug to match that of the surrounding wood. Allow a little of the plug to remain above the surrounding wood so you can sand it perfectly level after the epoxy sets up.

9 Sand the exterior of the box to shape and to ready it for finishing.

FINISHING

1 If you are going to draw, paint or otherwise color and wood-burn the Celtic knot design onto the box, you need to sand it to 320-grit to make a smooth surface. Transfer

FIG. 7 Wood-burning is a good way to make a permanent design on a wood surface. First go over the design lines lightly, and then erase the traced lines before darkening the burn lines.

FIG. 8 You can stipple the background to make it visually recede. Stippling means making a series of dots, evenly arranged, to darken and texture an area.

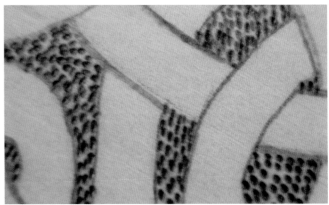

FIG. 9 Closeup of stippling.

FIG. 11 The same Celtic knot design, but carved in relief. This variation is not for the faint of heart or for the novice wood carver.

FIG. 10 This photo shows all three stages of burn and color. On upper right, the stippling is complete. On upper left, some shading has been done on the knot. At bottom, color has been applied in layers to the entire surface.

the pattern lightly to the wood and burn the image outline (Figs. 6 and 7). Then burn a matrix of dots, called stippling, to make the background dark (Fig. 8). You can see this in detail in Fig. 9.

2 The box was colored with oil pencils in mulberry, metallic green, silver, metallic gold, and white (Fig. 10). Use whatever colors you like.

3 I've made this design before with a carved lid (Fig. 11). Figure 12 is a comparison of the two designs.

FIG. 12 These boxes, one carved and one wood-burned and colored, are both attractive, so choose the method that appeals to you and is within your capabilities.

FIG. 13 This Celtic pattern can be used to jazz up the interior of a box. Or use it as a pattern for a triangular box.

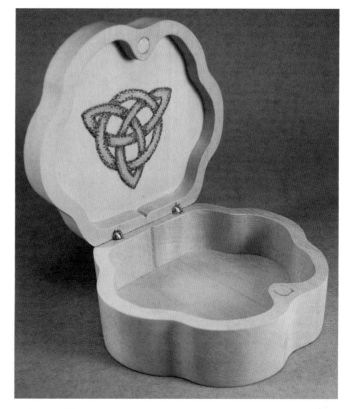

FIG. 14 The Celtic Knot Box was finished with clear satin acrylic.

FIG. 15 Here's an alternative, somewhat simpler, Celtic knot pattern.

FIG. 16 The finished Celtic Knot Box. Basswood, 4x4x1⁷/₈".

4 I burned a triangular Celtic pattern on the inside of the lid of our present box to add interest to an otherwise plain interior (Figs. 13 and 14). I colored it with colored pencils.

5 This box has vibrant color and detail, so I chose a water-based finish (artists' clear semigloss acrylic paint), which will not yellow over time. A solvent-based finish would have dissolved the oil pencil colors, so if you are using oil-based colored pencils, avoid a solvent-base finish.

6 Figure 15 is a simpler Celtic Knot pattern, which would make the box easier to do, in case you prefer it.

7 Figure 16 shows the finished wood-burned box.

Flower Box

This box has a flower growing on the lid. It was designed to show off the effects of appliqué: applying thin, shaped pieces of wood onto

a larger piece of wood. You can buy appliqués ready-made at woodworking and hobby supply stores and home outlets; they come in rosettes, letters, and other decorative forms, but only in certain sizes and types of wood. By learning how to make your own appliqués, there is no end to the beautiful, decorative effects you can achieve.

Bloodwood was used for the basic box because of its lovely red color. For the greatest contrast, yellowheart was used for the petals and ebony for the center of the flower. The entire box could have been made from one type of light-colored wood, and the petals and center could have been painted, stained, or dyed before attaching them to the box top.

We'll make the box using mortised hinges, but barrel hinges would work just as well.

Level of difficulty: Moderate

MATERIALS

4^1/$_8$x4^1/$_8$x2" bloodwood

^{1}/$_8$x1^1/$_2$x3^1/$_2$" yellowheart, two

^{3}/$_8$" diameter x ^{3}/$_16$" long ebony plug

^{3}/$_4$x^5/$_8$" solid brass, narrow hinges, two

Ruling compass

3" round beveled mirror

^{1}/$_8$" band saw blade

Drum or spindle sander

Drill and ^{1}/$_16$" drill bit, preferably brad-point

Chisel, ^{1}/$_2$" wide, more or less

Drum or spindle sander

Scrap of 2x4" wood to make sanding jig

10° wedge

Plug cutter, ^{3}/$_8$"

Tung oil and urethane topcoat, semigloss (I used Arm-R-Seal)

Adhesive caulk

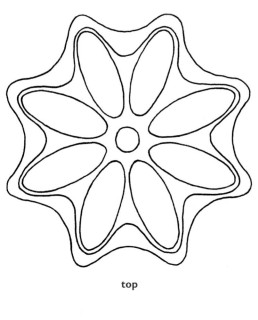

top

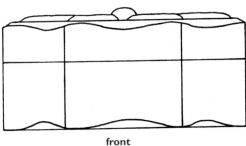

front

PLAN A Top and front views of the Flower Box.

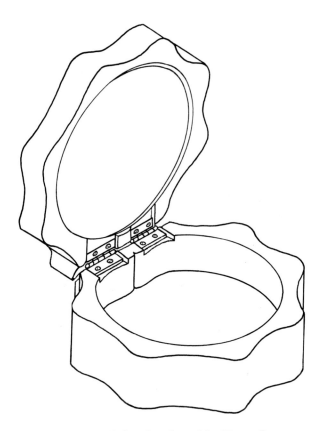

PLAN B Interior view of the Flower Box.

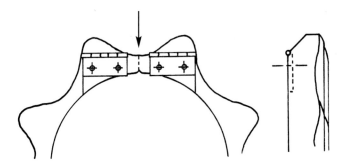

PLAN C Partial interior plan view of the Flower Box, showing the location of the hinges and depth of the hinge mortise. Entrance kerf cut is between hinges.

MAKING THE BOX

With so many curves on a box made of very hard wood, it is important to size the exterior curves of the box to the sanding drums you will be using. Modify the design as necessary to make it easier to sand the curves with the sander you own.

1 Plans A, B, and C show the basic configuration and assembly of the box.

2 Cut ¹/₄" off the bottom and ¹/₂" off the top for the base and lid, respectively. Then cut another ¹/₄" slice off the new body top for the lid lip. Reassemble the four pieces with double-sided tape, and cut the outside outline through all the layers.

3 Remove the lid and base, but keep the lid lip in place with the body. Draw the interior circle plan and hinge area onto the body. Then drill pilot holes for the hinge screws through the top of the lid lip and into the body piece (Fig. I). See Plan C for the location of the hinges.

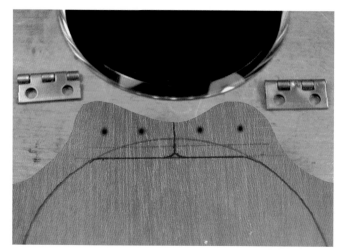

FIG. 1 Make sure that there is sufficient wood around the hinge holes even if that means altering the plan. There also needs to be clearance for the mirror to fit inside the lid.

FIG. 2 For the lid to fit and open properly, it is very important that the hinges are in alignment; check them with a straightedge.

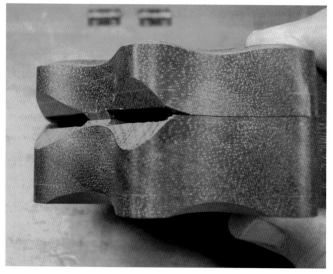

FIG. 3 The hinge mortises need to be deep enough to accommodate the hinges. Put the lid on the body, and check that the holes are even and that they line up. This photo also shows the material removed at the rear at a 45° angle to enable the box to open.

FIG. 4 If you have made your mortises correctly, the hinges should fit snugly into the recesses. Remember, you always can make a mortise larger, but it's difficult to make it smaller.

4 Cut out the interior of the box, using your judgment as to the thickness of the walls but making sure there is clearance for the hinges and mirror. Sand all interior and meeting surfaces, and glue the lid lip to the lid. Glue the body to the base. Drill holes in the lid, deep enough for the hinge screws.

5 Place the hinges over the drilled holes, and check that the hinges are in alignment (Fig. 2). Temporarily install the hinges, and mark the wood on the sides of the hinges with a sharp pencil or a marking knife. Mark the location of the hinge pin centers on the lid lip and the top of the box body. Remove the hinges. Sand at 45° to the lines marking

FIG. 5 By using this inexpensive shop-made jig (a cut-off 2x4" scrap), you can control the angle of your scallops on the top and bottom surfaces. Stop frequently to check your depth because it's easy to get the depressions uneven. Note that one hand has been removed in the photo setup for clarity, but this job requires both hands.

FIG. 6 In this top view of sanding the scallops on the base of the box, you can see that I'm holding the block and box together with both hands. Alternatively, the block could be clamped to the box section.

the hinge pin centers to create the clearance space for the lid to open.

6 Use a ¹/₂" chisel to make stop cuts on the inside of the pencil marks indicating the sides of the hinges. Mark the depth necessary to seat the hinges, and chisel down to that line (Fig. 3). Trial-fit the hinges in the mortises, and then install the hinges (Fig. 4).

7 Trial-fit the mirror, and make any adjustments necessary to allow it to fit easily into the lid recess. Do not install the mirror until the box has been completely finished.

8 Sand all exterior surfaces to shape and finish-sand. If you choose to make the shaped top and bottom edges, you will need to make a simple jig to help you to maintain a consistent angle at the spindle or drum sander. Cutting a scrap piece of 2x4" pine at a 70° angle was all that was necessary to make this tool. Just hold the two pieces (jig and box) together while sanding, or use small clamps if you prefer (Figs. 5 and 6).

9 Finish-sand all surfaces.

FIG. 7 Cut the pattern for the petals out of the same pattern that you used to mark the box perimeter. If you sandwich two layers of wood together, you only need to cut out four petal shapes. Note that this version of the pattern used a large center piece, but the final pattern has a smaller center.

10 To make the petals, sand both sides of the yellowheart pieces to flat and finish. Tape the two pieces together with double-sided tape, mark four petal patterns using Plan A (top view), and cut them out (Fig. 7).

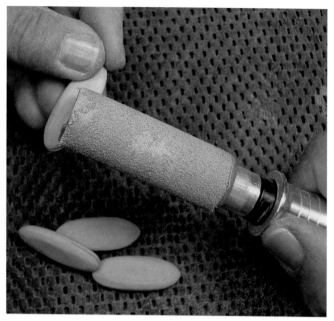

FIG. 8 If you keep the two petal layers taped together while you sand them to form, they will be easier to handle. Watch your fingers when you power-sand such small pieces.

FIG. 9 Position the petals evenly around and radiating out from the center. When they look pleasing to you, lightly draw around each one so you can glue them in the proper location.

11 Keep the pieces taped together as you round the edges to form the petal shapes with a power sander or by hand. Sand to 600-grit (Fig. 8).

12 For the center of the flower, cut a plug out of ebony or another dark wood. Round one surface and make the opposite side perfectly flat. Sand to 600-grit. Glue this piece to the box top at the center of the lid.

13 Position the eight petals around the center, keeping the spacing as even as possible. Mark their location lightly with pencil (Fig. 9). Glue on one petal (Fig. 10), and then glue the petal on the opposite side, followed by one halfway between them, etc., until they are all in place. Here's an easy way to do this: Spread a little glue on the bottom side of the petal, and then press it on a smooth piece of plastic sheeting to squeeze out any excess. Wipe the edges clean, and then press it into place on the box.

FIG. 10 Glue each petal in place with a thin layer of glue applied to the petal. Avoid any glue squeeze-out at this point, because it will be very difficult to sand away.

FIG. 11 The mirror had a label on the back, so I placed the adhesive caulk there. One good drop in the middle should hold it just fine.

FINISHING

1 This box was finished with a tung oil and urethane topcoat to bring out the luscious colors of the wood.

2 The mirror can be attached to the inside of the lid with adhesive caulk after the finish has cured (Figs. 11 and 12).

3 Figure 13 shows the finished box.

FIG. 12 The mirror is in place.

FIG. 13 The finished Flower Box. Bloodwood, yellowheart, and ebony woods, 4x4x1³/₄".

Double-Cross Box

This box is not as curvy as my usual boxes, but it gives me a good opportunity to demonstrate how to make normal mortised hinges. In

this project we will be making a divided, lift-out tray to give us two layers for storing small items. We'll also use the band saw to make basic, straight inlays. If you want to make the job easier, don't include the inlays in your design. You could appliqué the owner's initials on the top instead, for a personal touch. The box could be used to hold pencils, with a place in the lift-out tray for erasers and the like, or it could be a nice jewelry box for cuff links and bracelets.

Level of difficulty: Moderate to challenging

MATERIALS

$9^1/8$x$3^3/4$x$2^3/4$" mahogany

$^1/4$x$^1/4$x24" and $^1/4$x$^3/8$x6" maple for the inlay strips

$^3/4$x$^5/8$" narrow solid brass hinges, two

6 mm x 3 mm rare earth magnets, four

$^1/8$" band saw blade

Miter-gauge auxiliary fence

Drill, $^1/16$" and $^1/4$" drill bits, preferably brad-point

$^1/8$" band saw blade

Drum or spindle sander

Plug cutter, $^1/4$"

Chisel, $^1/2$" wide

5-minute epoxy

Tung oil

Mineral spirits

Nylon mesh scrubby pad, gray

Wax, applied and buffed by hand

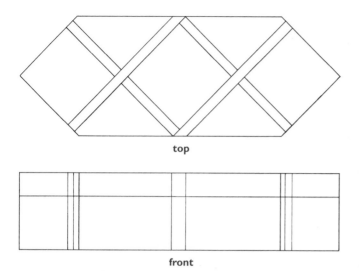

top

front

PLAN A Top and front views of the Double-Cross Box.

FIG. 1 To support the box block at the required 45° angle, use the scraps that you generated when you cut the ends off, or cut another piece of scrap to a 45° angle.

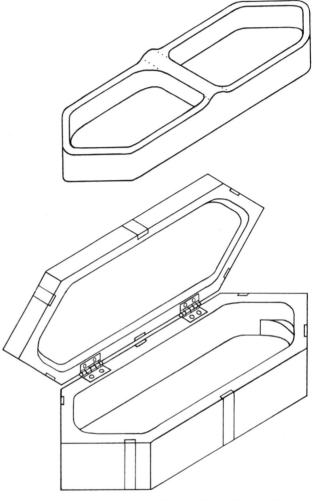

PLAN B Interior view of the Double-Cross Box and its lift-out tray.

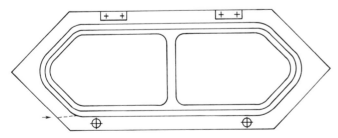

PLAN C Interior plan view of the Double-Cross Box, showing location of lift-out tray and the hinge and magnet closure holes.

MAKING THE BOX

1 Plans A, B, C, and D show the basic configuration and assembly of the box.

2 Make the 45° corner cuts to give the box its distinctive diamond shape. Save the cut-off pieces. Sand the cuts smooth and flat but maintain the 45° angles.

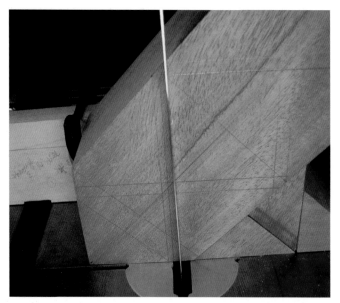

FIG. 2 Get around to the back of your band saw so you can see to line up the blade with your layout lines. Notice the small clamp to the left of the block. It is attached to the miter-gauge auxiliary fence and acts as the stop for that side of the inlay line.

FIG. 3 Fit all the lid inlay sections before gluing. Make the butt joints as snug as possible, and allow the edge pieces to extend over the sides by $^1/_8$". Glue these pieces in place before proceeding.

3 Mark the two cross patterns on your box top, using Plan A, top view. Tape the scrap cut-off pieces from Step 2 to hold the block at a 45° angle (Fig. 1).

4 You will need to attach an auxiliary fence to your miter gauge for this job unless you have the steady hands and eagle eyes of a surgeon. Use the auxiliary fence to keep the block square to the band saw blade, and look from behind the blade to line up the blade to one of the cross pattern lines for the inlay (Fig. 2). Attach a small clamp to the auxiliary fence to function as a stop. Slide the box block to the line on the other side of the inlay, and place another small clamp as a stop on the fence. Next, position a clamp on the band saw table to stop the wood when it is $^3/_{16}$" into the teeth of the blade.

5 Now you can start the band saw; advance the block with the fence at one extreme of the insert until the block hits the clamp on the table. Pull back, and then move the block to the other side of the insert area and make another cut. Make subsequent cuts between these two cuts until most of the wood in the area of the inlay has been removed, and then slide the block from one side to the other until the bottom of the inlay groove is smooth. Test-fit a section of your inlay strips to make sure your cuts are correct. You

FIG. 4 One option for this box is to leave the inlays above the surface of the box, either just on the lid or all over. It gives a nice pattern and texture to the overall box design. Notice that I cut my box apart before making the inlays—bad idea. Save time and effort by making the inlays first.

may want to test your skills with a scrap block before using your good wood. Repeat for all four inlay lines on the top of the lid.

6 The side cuts are much easier because the block will be

FIG. 5 There are many pieces to this box, so use lots of registration marks to keep them all in the correct order for gluing. For the grain to remain consistent, you need to glue the pieces back where they came from. This is not an easy thing to do. The foreground scrap piece has been marked for cutting to make tray supports.

FIG. 6 Be sure to use a backing of scrap wood when using a plug cutter to cut the thin pieces of wood to attach to the magnets.

sitting flat on the table. Continue the ends of the inlay lines around the corner and down to the bottom of the block. Cut these lines as you did the lid lines.

7 After you have the grooves cut, you may decide to leave the grooves as they are. The recessed grooves are attractive and have a nice feel to them.

8 If you decide to continue with the inlay, cut the top inlay pieces to length, allowing them to overlap the sides by ¹/₈" or so, test-fit, and glue them into place (Fig. 3). Then glue in the side pieces, butting them firmly up against the lid pieces. One possible arrangement is to leave the inlay pieces raised above the surface of the box (Fig. 4). You could give it a light sanding and be ready to go on making the box. If you want the inlay effect, however, power-sand the strips flush with the surface of the block.

9 Now you are ready to make the box. Rip ³/₈" off the top and ¹/₄" off the bottom for the lid and base, respectively. Mark the interior plan (Plan C), and drill the holes, where indicated, for the hinges and the magnet closures. The

holes for the magnets must be as deep as the depth of the magnets plus the mahogany veneer strips used to conceal the magnets (see Step 14).

10 Cut out the interior. Glue the body together, and then sand the interior.

11 Now, rip ¹/₄" off the top of the body to create the lid lip.

12 The interior tray will be made from the interior waste block. Sand the block to square and smooth, and then rip ¹/₈" off the bottom of the block for the base of the insert tray. Cut the side profile with the center handle (Plan D). Cut out the interior of the tray in two sections, glue the sides back together, and sand the insides. Then glue the insert to its sanded base. Cut the two ends off of the other piece of waste (Fig. 5) to use later inside the main body to hold the insert tray in place (Plan D). They may need some finessing to fit well.

13 Now sand all the pieces and the interior surfaces, and glue everything together.

14 Cut ¹/₄" plugs from ¹/₁₆" thin mahogany scraps (Fig. 6), and epoxy them to the sets of magnets. As we did with the magnets in the Celtic Box project, make sure the veneer

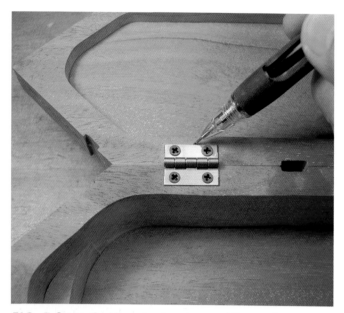

FIG. 7 Screw the hinges in place temporarily, and then trace around them with a fine line. Cut the mortises within these lines for a professional-looking, snug fit.

FIG. 8 Make clean stop cuts all around the hinge location for the mortises. Mark the depth to about $1/16$", and chisel to the stop cuts.

FIG. 9 The parts drying again after being finished with tung oil. It is easier to go through the entire finishing process without the hinges getting in the way. Reinstall the hinges after the finish is applied.

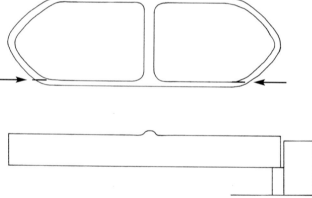

PLAN D Interior plan (top) and side view of the lift-out tray. Note the small block insert to support the tray. Dashed lines indicate entrance kerf cuts.

pieces are thin enough that the magnets hold together through a double thickness of the veneer. Keep the magnets in pairs to make them easier to handle and so their polarities remain in their correct orientation. Install the magnets, leaving a bit of wood above the surface for later sanding.

15 To install the hinges, you will first need to increase the depth of the pilot holes through the lid liner and into the lid, and then screw the hinges into place. Mark the location of the hinges (Fig. 7), including the inside edges. Remove the hinges, and chisel inside the pencil lines to make a good,

tight-fitting mortise for the hinges. Use stop cuts and shallow slicing cuts to cut the mortise to fit the hinges (Fig. 8).

16 Trial-fit the hinges, and then sand all the box surfaces except the back side where the hinges are located. Remove the hinges, tape the box together on the front and ends, and sand the back side.

17 Sand all surfaces to their finished state.

18 It will be easier to handle the box for finishing if you leave the hinges off for now (Fig. 9).

FINISHING

1 For this box I first applied a 50/50 mixture of tung oil and mineral spirits. I followed the first coat with a coat of 100% tung oil. You may decide to continue applying coats of oil for more protection, allowing each coat to dry thoroughly.

2 When you have built up a good finish, scuff the final coat with a gray nylon scrubby, and then apply wax for a lustrous finish. Finally, reinstall the hinges.

3 Figures 10, 11, and 12 show the completed Double-Cross Box and the lift-out tray.

FIG. 10 The finished Double-Cross Box. Mahogany, 9x3^1/$_2$x2^1/$_2$".

FIG. 11 Here's the completed Double-Cross Box, showing the position of the lift-out tray. It was finished with tung oil and wax.

FIG. 12 The space below the lift-out tray on the Double-Cross Box can provide storage for your treasured items.

Ambrosia Box

This box is named for the ambrosia maple wood from which it was made. The wood is named for the ambrosia beetle, which loves to

infest many species of trees and freshly cut logs. At first, the beetle trails were thought to render the timber useless because they made holes and stained the usually white wood in streaks of blue, green, pink, and gray. Then woodworkers noticed that the resulting colors and patterns were attractive and started to use this wood in more creative projects. Once the wood is dry, there is no further damage or change to the wood.

This project will show you how to make

a hidden hinge. If you want to make a box like this and don't care if your hinge pins show, the job will be easier. In that case, before cutting off the ends, drill from the outside of the block through the wood that will become the sides and into the wood that will make the lid. Continue making the box, and epoxy the brass rods to the side pieces before assembly. Making a hidden hinge takes more effort, but the finished product is worth it.

Level of difficulty: Challenging

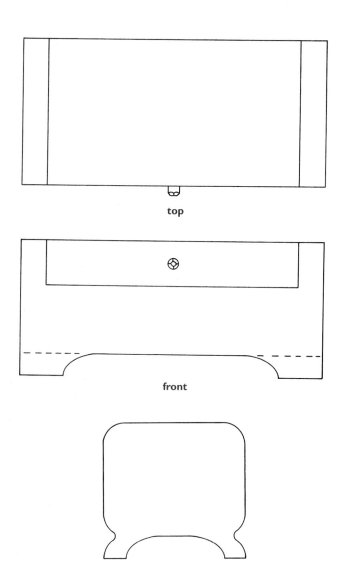

top

front

side

PLAN A Top, front, and side views of the Ambrosia Box.

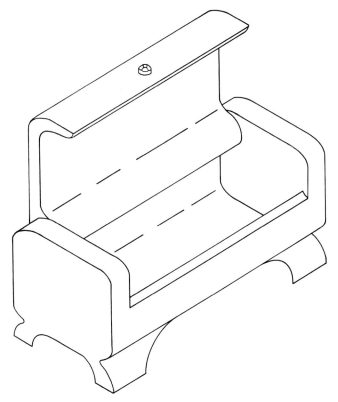

PLAN B Interior view of the Ambrosia Box.

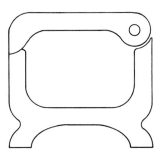

PLAN C Cross-section view of the end of the Ambrosia Box, showing the location of the pivot hinge hole.

MAKING THE BOX

1 Plans A, B, and C show the basic configuration and assembly of the box.

2 Cut ⁵/₈" off each end of the block to make the box's end pieces (Fig. 1).

3 Use Plan C to mark the location of the hinge pins on both ends of the body piece, and on the end pieces (Fig. 2).

FIG. 1 To make a 7"-long box with a 6"-capacity band saw, cut wood off of each end to leave a 6" box body block.

FIG. 2 Carefully mark the hinge hole position on both ends of the top back corner of the block, and then transfer those measurements to the matching end pieces.

FIG. 3 A simple corner jig like this can help you to keep your tall block upright.

FIG. 4 These are the pieces cut from the block after the interior cuts have been made. It is very important that the band saw blade be as vertical as possible, so the hinge shape is equal on both ends.

4 You can make a corner jig to stabilize the tall, narrow pieces for drilling (Fig. 3). To make a simple corner jig, glue two square, flat pine boards (or pieces of plywood) at right angles to one another, and then attach them perpendicular to a flat baseboard. (See materials list for dimensions of boards.) Then drill the hinge holes.

5 While you're at the drill press, use the front view drawing (Plan A, front view) to mark the location of the lid knob on

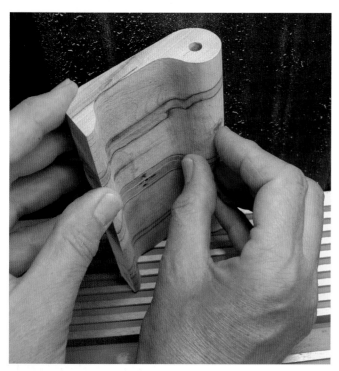

FIG. 5 If there is some deviation in the hinge, you will need to sand it to be as symmetrical as possible. Don't worry about the outside shape too much yet; just keep the hinge holes centered as best you can.

FIG. 6 The lid pivots on the hinge pins in the end pieces. When the sides are attached to the body, the lid will fall into place.

the front of the body block, and then drill a $1/4$" hole, $3/16$" deep for the knob.

6 Mark the body block and end pieces with the end profile pattern (Plan C), and then cut out the exterior outlines, cut the lid off, cut out the interior core, and finally, cut out the bottom area between the legs (Fig. 4).

7 Unless you are a better band saw operator than I am, you will need to refine the hinging part of the lid to make it work (Fig. 5). Rough-sand all interior and glue surfaces so you can get an idea of how it will all fit together with the hinges. You will have to make the lid two hairs smaller than the box interior width so it can open without binding.

8 Mark the leg cutout on the front profile (Plan A), and cut out the area between to make the legs.

9 Cut the two brass pins for the hinges, sanding or filing them to fit into the holes. Now assemble the box with the hinge pins in place but not glued (Fig. 6). Clamp the box together and observe how the hinge works. Something will

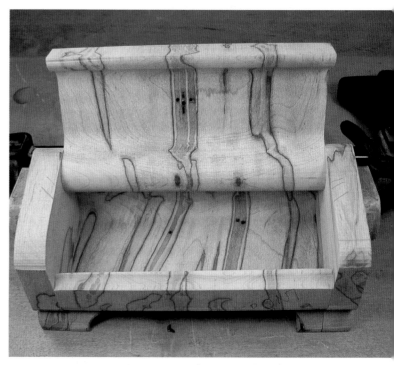

FIG. 7 Use a quick clamp for trial-fitting the pieces together. I usually have to assemble and disassemble the box a dozen times before I feel that the fit is as good as it can get.

FIG. 8 The big-boy clamps come out for this glue-up. This large parallel clamp makes an easy job of applying even pressure, but you could use three regular clamps instead.

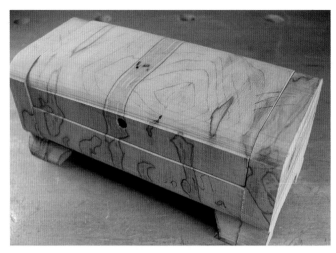

FIG. 9 The box looks terrible; the edges don't meet anywhere and the surface is a mess. Never fear, the belt sander is here, and it will take care of everything with little effort on our part.

FIG. 10 In places that the belt sander cannot reach, like the groove above the feet, you will need to use either a powered profile sander or lots of elbow grease to get the areas smooth.

bind—it always does. So look for shiny spots on the wood where it has rubbed against another piece, and sand the high spots until you have a smoothly functioning lid. Make the gap even between the sides of the lid and the sides of the box. It may take one or two, or ten, trials before the box is just right. A quick clamp works well for these test-fits (Fig. 7). Epoxy the hinge pins into the lid.

10 Round and polish one end of the short piece of brass rod, or other handle material, and fit it to the handle hole, but do not attach it yet. You can use it, if necessary, to open the lid if it gets stuck. The knob for this box was faceted with a file and then finished with progressively finer sanding grits up to 600-grit. Put the knob aside until all sanding is complete.

11 Use a larger, parallel-jawed clamp for glue-up. Avoid getting glue near the hinge area, and keep the lid open during gluing so you don't inadvertently glue it shut (Fig. 8).

12 The box will be uneven and ugly at this point, but we can fix that (Fig. 9). Take all the exterior surfaces down to their lowest points using the belt sander with 60- and 80-grit sanding belts. Use the miter gauge to keep it all square.

13 There will be many areas that cannot be sanded with the belt sander. Use contour sanding pads to get consistent results and save your fingertips (Fig. 10). Sand the entire box to 320-grit, by hand.

14 Epoxy the knob to the lid.

FINISHING

1 The model box was finished with three coats of a tung oil and urethane topcoat, applied with a rag (Fig. 11).

2 Figure 12 shows the completed Ambrosia Box.

FIG. 11 Where are the hinges? Finished with a tung oil and urethane topcoat, the Ambrosia Box opens without a hint of the pivoting hinges.

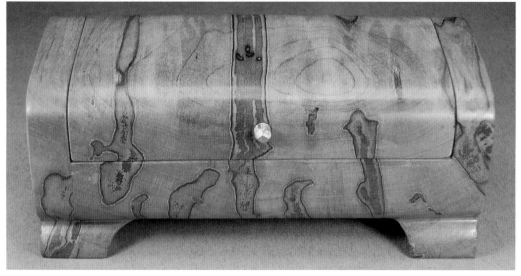

FIG. 12 The finished Ambrosia Box. Ambrosia maple, 7x3x2³/₄".

Drawered Boxes

Boxes made with drawers are not at all difficult to construct. They can also be among the most creative projects. When planning a drawer type box, make the depth of the drawers at least 3". If the drawers are too shallow, they will not function well.

OVERVIEW OF DRAWERED BOXES

It's critical to make sure your band saw blade is aligned squarely with your table and that you hold the block of wood absolutely square as you cut out the drawer section. Any misalignment will mean an ill-fitting drawer and lots of sanding.

The next three boxes, the Scroll Box, the Infinity Box, and the Ultimate Box, all follow the general construction sequence outlined below:

1. Square and smooth the block of wood.
2. Cut the front profile outline of the box.
3. Rip the back off the box block.
4. Cut out the drawer.
5. Cut the front and back off the drawer block.
6. Cut out the drawer's interior.
7. Sand the interiors of the drawer parts.
8. Glue the drawer parts together.
9. Sand the exterior of drawer, but as little as possible, otherwise it will fit too loosely in the drawer opening and you'll have to make modifications.

10. Adjust the fit of the box opening to the drawer, glue the box together, and then glue on the back piece.
11. Sand the front of the box with the drawer in place to make the front of the box and the drawer even with each other.
12. Finish-sand the rest of the exterior surfaces.
13. Apply the finish.

Scroll Box

The marvelous wood for this piece came from a big leaf maple burl.

Most of this wood comes from Canada. The totally erratic grain and

fantastic patterning make for a beautiful box in any design, but the smoothly curved surfaces of this box design show off the wood's features very well. Because of this wood, the Scroll Box is a jewelry box that is in itself a jewel. The design for the Scroll Box visually raises the box above the surface by incorporating legs in the exterior outline.

Level of difficulty: Easy to moderate

MATERIALS

6x4x3 $^{1}/_{2}$" big leaf maple burl

Brass knob, $^{5}/_{16}$x$^{5}/_{16}$"

3 mm x 6 mm rare earth magnets, two

Drill, $^{1}/_{4}$" drill bit, and bit sized for knob

$^{1}/_{8}$" band saw blade

Drum or spindle sander

5-minute epoxy

Danish oil, clear

Beall Wood Buff System, or wax applied and buffed by hand

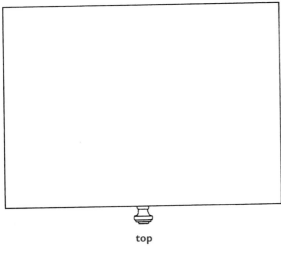

top

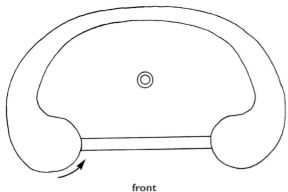

front

PLAN A Top and front views of the Scroll Box. Arrow indicates entrance kerf cut.

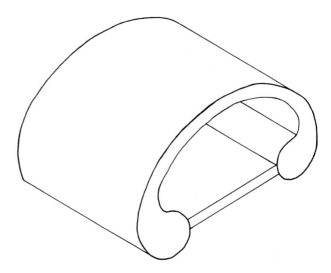

PLAN B Interior view of the Scroll Box.

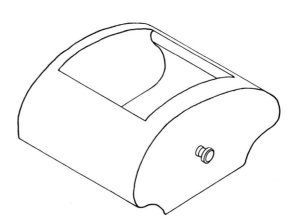

PLAN C Interior view of the drawer.

MAKING THE BOX

1 Plans A, B, C, and D show the basic configuration and assembly of the box. Big leaf maple burl wood is often coated with wax to slow the drying process and keep the block from developing cracks. This piece had been in my shop for at least three years, so I was certain it was dry enough. It was obvious that this would make a fine box.

2 The first step is to cut the front profile outline of the box, using the front pattern (Plan A).

3 Then slice 1/4" off the back of the box block for the back.

4 Cut out the interior core by starting your entrance kerf cut at one of the "legs" (round parts that the box will

sit on) and coming out at the other. See Fig. 1 for Steps 4 and 5.

5 Rip 1/4" off the bottom of the core to make the piece that will become the bottom of the box.

6 Glue the box bottom in place between the legs. Use some big, strong clamps for this job, because you will be compressing the sides of the box to compensate for the wood removed with the kerfs (Fig. 2).

7 Cut 1/2" off the front and 1/4" off the back of the drawer block. Cut out the interior of the drawer, using Plan D for a pattern.

FIG. 1 The back of the box is at the top, the body is in the middle, and the drawer/core is at the bottom. The base of the box has not yet been glued into place.

FIG. 2 You will need to bring out the heavy-duty clamps for gluing the base between the legs of the box. By forcing the two legs against the base, the box body will become smaller, which will result in a better drawer fit.

FIG. 3 Here the drawer pieces have been cut from the core. Notice that the band saw blade is beginning to burn the wood, a sign that the blade needs to be replaced. It broke while working on the next project.

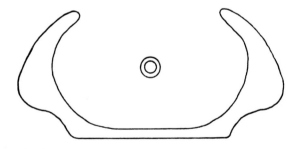

PLAN D Cross-section view of the drawer of the Scroll Box.

8 Sand the interior surfaces of the drawer, and then glue it together. You can see the parts in Fig. 3.

9 Sand the exterior of the drawer just enough so it looks smooth. Try to leave as much wood as possible so that the drawer will fit well.

10 If you are going to use magnets at the rear of the drawer and the back of the box to hold the drawer closed, drill the

FIG. 4 The drawer will be shorter than the box interior because of the two kerfs created when cutting off the front and back. Put the box front, with the drawer in place, against a 60-grit sanding belt, and bring the box body to the same level as the drawer.

FIG. 5 The Scroll Box was finished with Danish oil and the Beall Wood Buff System.

holes and epoxy the magnets in place now. (See the Infinity Box project for a good way to align the holes for the magnets.) Glue the back of the box to the box body.

11 The drawer will be shorter than the depth of the box interior (Fig. 4). Fix this by power-sanding the front of the box with the drawer in place. Use the coarsest sanding belt you have, and check the front edge frequently so you don't remove more wood than necessary. If you want rounded edges, sand them to shape now, and then sand the rest of the outside of the box with progressively finer grits until it is smooth.

12 Drill a hole for the drawer knob, but don't epoxy the knob in place yet. A well-polished short length of $1/4$" brass rod would make a nice handle, and the price is right. Don't epoxy the knob in place until the finish has been applied to the box, but you will need it for removing the drawer now.

FIG. 6 The finished Scroll Box. Big leaf maple burl, $5^1/2$x$3^3/4$x$3^1/4$".

FINISHING

1 Danish oil and wax were used to bring out the maximum grain definition in this maple burl.

2 The oil coat was wet-sanded with 400-grit wet/dry sandpaper to smooth out any imperfections.

3 Finally, the surface was buffed with the Beall Wood Buff System to give it a lovely sheen. Then the knob was epoxied into place (Fig. 5). Figure 6 shows the completed box.

Infinity Box

The infinity symbol has been used for thousands of years. It is found in Greek culture as an *ouroboros*, or two snakes consuming each other,

indicating the cyclical nature of life. In mathematics, this symbol is referred to as a lemniscate; it is used to indicate a extremely large number. Another example is the Möbius strip, a ribbon with one simple twist, which results in a three-dimensional object that has only two dimensions. It reminds me of a band saw blade in the process of being twisted into a circle for storage. In any case, it makes an excellent design for our boxes.

This box was made from native Texas cedar wood, a form of juniper. Since is available to me without cost, and in large pieces, it was a good choice for making the largest box in this book.

Level of difficulty: Easy to moderate

MATERIALS

12x5$\frac{1}{4}$x4$\frac{1}{2}$" cedar

3 mm x 6 mm rare earth magnets, four

$\frac{1}{8}$" band saw blade

Drum or spindle sander

Drill, $\frac{1}{4}$" and $\frac{1}{8}$" drill bits

Dowel/tenon pins, $\frac{1}{4}$", or short length of $\frac{1}{4}$" dowel

5-minute epoxy

Carving chisel, $\frac{1}{2}$" wide, more or less

$\frac{1}{8}$" dowel, $\frac{1}{2}$" long, two

Brushing lacquer, gloss

Acetone/lacquer thinner

Oil and urethane topcoat, semigloss (I used Arm-R-Seal)

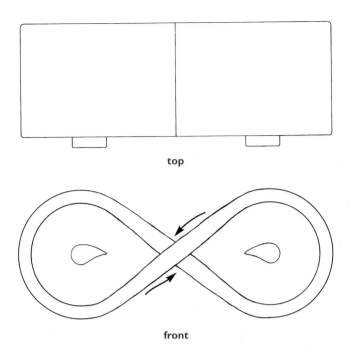

top

front

PLAN A Top and front views of the Infinity Box. Arrows indicate entrance kerf cuts.

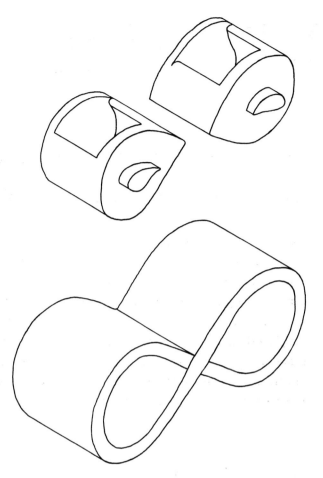

PLAN B Interior view of the Infinity Box and drawers.

PLAN C Cross-section view of the Infinity Box drawer.

MAKING THE BOX

1 Plans A, B, and C show the basic configuration and assembly of the box.

2 The block for this project was very rough because it came from a timber framer's construction scrap pile (Fig. 1). Once you get your wood, decide how you want to lay out your plan, and trim away any excess wood before squaring the block (Fig. 2). This design is more dynamic if the grain goes diagonally across the block.

3 Cut out the front view exterior outline of the box (see Plan A). Start by making relief cuts towards the center from both the top and bottom of your initial blank (Fig. 3), and then cut along the outline.

4 Cut $1/2$" off the back of the box block for the back.

5 Cut out the two interior drawer sections as smoothly as possible. If you make your entrance cuts at the crossing and in the direction of the diagonal center, the cuts will be invisible in the finished box. There will be two entrance kerfs, which will reduce the size of the drawer openings and make a better fit.

6 Glue the box closed using strong clamps to hold the wood in place, four around each loop of the infinity shape.

7 Cut $5/8$" off the fronts and $3/8$" off the backs of the drawers. Be sure to use a stabilizing block because these are curved pieces. Then cut the interiors out of the drawers, using the drawer plan (Plan C). You will have to flip one

FIG. 1 It takes imagination to visualize this rough hunk of wood as a beautiful finished box. With experience you will be able to "see" boxes in rough wood. In this case, the lines look best running diagonally across the box. Do not locate the box pattern with the grain running vertically, or the box will be weak at the center area.

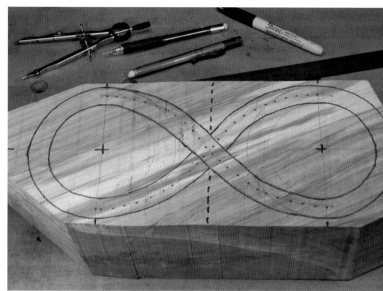

FIG. 2 Size the plans to fit the block of wood available. There is no need to keep to the size of the plans in this book. Just proportionally shrink, or enlarge, all of the drawings and dimensions. Dashed lines indicate relief cuts. Notice that this model was made with the opposite crossing to that of the plans. Oops!

copy of the plan so you have mirror images for the drawers.

8   Sand the drawer parts' interiors, and then glue the drawer parts back together. Sand them only as much as necessary to make them look smooth.

9   Place the drawers into their box openings to see how they fit. Adjust either the box body or the drawers until you have a good fit.

10 One good way to mark the location of the holes for the magnet closures is to use dowel/tenon pins. First drill a hole ¼" deep in the center back of each drawer. Place one end of each pin in its hole, and then line the back up with the box body (Fig. 4). Once the back is in position, carefully turn the unit over, with the back held in place, and tap the drawer firmly to make a mark on the inside of the back piece (Fig. 5). If you don't have dowel/tenon pins, you can sharpen one end of a short length of ¼" brass rod to use instead. Another technique is to cut pieces of ¼" dowel and coat one end with lipstick to mark the matching location. Once marked, drill matching ¼" holes in the back piece.

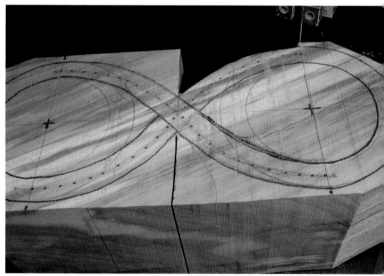

FIG. 3 When cutting the exterior outline, make relief cuts to the center of the block to allow the scraps to fall away. Without relief cuts, it would be difficult to make such a sharp turn, and backing out of the cut would be dangerous.

11 To install the magnets to hold the drawer closed, epoxy the magnets in place in the drawers first. After the epoxy has set, attach the second magnets to the ones in the drawer and put indelible marks on the visible ends. Now

FIG. 4 Using dowel/tenon pins will make it easier to locate matching holes from the back of the drawers on the inside of the back piece. You could make your own tools by sharpening one end of a short length of $^1/_4$" brass rod, but these manufactured pins are not very expensive and come in a convenient set with four different sizes.

FIG. 5 When the marking pins are in place on the drawers and the back piece is in alignment, tap on the front of the drawer to transfer the magnet location to the back piece.

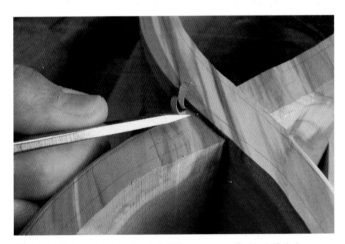

FIG. 6 To emphasize the twisting concept of the infinity or Möbius symbol, I carved a separation at the crossing. Use a simple gouge with stop cuts and slicing cuts to make about a $^1/_6$"-deep relief carving that tapers to the surface. This maneuver also effectively disguises the entrance cuts.

you know for sure which ends of the magnets go into the holes in the back: the ends with the markings. Epoxy the magnets into the holes in the back.

12 Glue the back to the box body.

13 The drawers will be shorter than the front of the box, so sand the unit with the drawers in place to make them even.

14 Do any shaping of the edges now. This box was sanded on the belt sander to generate a small chamfer around all the edges of both the box body and the drawer fronts before hand-sanding. To emphasize the ribbon effect of the infinity symbol, I carved the crossing at the front center of the box using just a carving chisel (Fig. 6).

15 Sand the outside of the box, including the drawer fronts, to 220-grit.

16 Make handles for the drawers out of scraps of the same, or contrasting, wood. This box looks great with turned knobs or even fake turned knobs. Just cut out small cylin-

ders of wood, and sand them round to get almost the same effect. The handles for these drawers are more sculptural; they were cut from the cores from inside the drawers. Drill $^1/_8$" holes in the center of the handles and the drawers. Shape the handles as desired, sand, and then glue them in place with a section of $^1/_8$" dowel extending into both the holes in the drawer and the handle.

FINISHING

1 The first application of finish was a 1:1 mixture of lacquer and lacquer thinner.

2 Then I applied a coat of 3:1 lacquer to thinner. Then I noticed there were scratches showing through the finish (Fig. 7). Since succeeding coats of finish would have emphasized these scratches even more, the only solution was to sand completely through the layers of finish and down to the grit that had created the scratches. In this case that was to 120-grit. Then the box was sanded back up through 150-, 180-, 220-, and finally, 320-grit.

3 The final finish coat was done with three coats of an oil and urethane topcoat. Figures 8 and 9 show how that finish brought out the beauty of the many colors in the cedar.

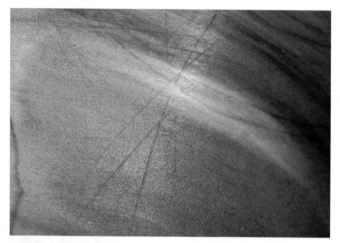

FIG. 7 Oh misery! After the first coat of lacquer, a mess of scratches became visible. I must have skipped a step in the sanding procedure. No help for it but to sand it down through the finish and back to the grit that created the scratches, and then work carefully back through the finer grits to 320-grit.

FIG. 8 The beauty of the cedar Infinity Box was enhanced with a finish of lacquer (which was subsequently sanded off) and then multiple coats of an oil and urethane topcoat.

FIG. 9 The finished Infinity Box. Cedar, 11x5x4".

Ultimate Box

This box has it all: hidden hinges, a drawer, a divided compartment, and legs. It is one of the most difficult boxes to make, so we've saved it for last. Get some experience with easier boxes before tackling this one. The wood used here is from a piece of walnut log that was given to me. Advantage: free wood of a good size. Disadvantage: hours spent filling cracks in the wood and sanding until the cows came home. I could have laminated walnut boards to get the required thickness, and there would have been much less repair work. It is interesting, though, to look at the sides of the box and see heartwood end grain. It is the first piece of spalted walnut I've ever seen.

There are a lot of tricks to making a box like this work. I've worked out all the bugs so that you'll have smooth sailing with the project. Good luck!

Level of difficulty: Very challenging

MATERIALS

7x5x5" walnut

$1/4$" diameter x 1" long brass rod, two

$1/4$" diameter x $3/8$" long brass rod

6 mm x 3 mm rare earth magnets, optional

Drill and $1/4$" drill bit

$1/8$" band saw blade

Drum or spindle sander

5-minute epoxy

Large parallel-jawed clamps

Disposable glue brush

Tung oil and urethane topcoat, semigloss (I used Arm-R-Seal)

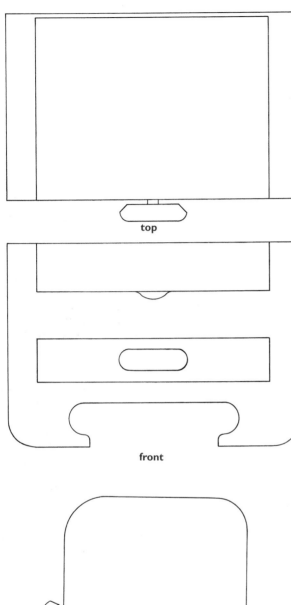

top

front

side

PLAN A Top, front, and side views of the Ultimate Box.

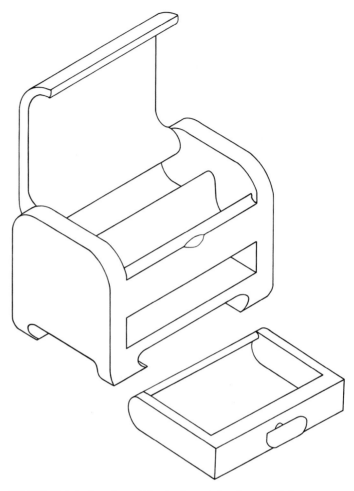

PLAN B Interior view of the body and the drawer of the Ultimate Box.

MAKING THE BOX

1 Plans A, B, and C show the basic configuration and assembly of the box.

2 Cut ³/₄" off each end of the squared block of wood to make the end pieces.

3 Mark the interior pattern (Plan C) on one end of the body block, and also use the plan to mark the hinge-pin hole locations on the body and on the end pieces (Fig. I) as we did with the Ambrosia Box (pages 198–199).

4 Using the same jig and procedures as used for the Ambrosia Box, drill ¹/₄" holes for the hinge pins ³/₄" deep on both ends of the body block and ³/₈" deep into each of the end pieces.

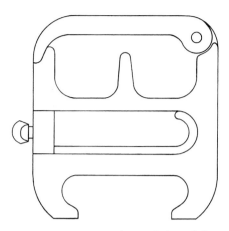

PLAN C Cross-section end view of the Ultimate Box.

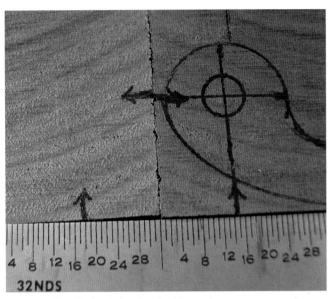

FIG. 1 To drill the holes for the hinge pins, you can transfer the location from the cross-section illustration (Plan C), or make coordinating markings on the matching pieces of the box.

5 Cut the exterior outline of the box body end profile (from Plan A), and then trace that exterior body outline to the insides of the corresponding end pieces. Cut the exterior outline on the end pieces.

6 Cut out the interior of the body as carefully as possible. Any wiggles during cutting will result in either a sloppy fit or a lot of repair work (Fig. 2).

7 Now you can assemble the lid onto the ends using the two prepared hinge pins; you can then place this assembly on the box body to see how it all fits together (Fig. 3). Do a little rough sanding in the hinge area and clamp the ends to the body to judge the lid function. The lid and body hinge groove probably will need some adjustment to work smoothly.

8 When you have the hinge working well, sand the interior of the box and lid to 220-grit.

9 Sand the drawer block only as much as is necessary to remove the saw marks. Rip ⁵/₈" off the front of the block, and then rip ³/₈" off each of the ends.

10 Mark the interior plan of the drawer (see Plan C) on one of the drawer body ends, attach the drawer block to a stabilizing block, and then cut out the drawer interior. Sand the interior of the drawer pieces to 220-grit, and glue them together (Fig. 4). Afterward, sand the outside of the drawer, as needed (Fig. 5).

FIG. 2 Be careful when cutting out the body interior. Any misalignments of the block and the band saw blade will result in a badly fitting drawer and require lots of sanding.

Ultimate Box **215**

FIG. 3 Assemble the box to trial-fit the hinge, but do not epoxy the hinge pins in place until the final sanding has been completed. Notice that a stabilizing block has been attached to the drawer body (lower left) to prepare it for interior cutting.

FIG. 4 Clamp the drawer in two directions to hold the front and sides to the body. Use plenty of clamps to keep the sides square. There will be some overlap, but that can be sanded away later.

11 When you put the drawer in place in the body piece, you'll notice the difference between the front of the drawer and the front of the body (Fig. 6). The drawer doesn't extend as far. If the difference is less than $1/8$", you can adjust that with sanding. If the back gap is greater than $1/8$", you may want to place a spacer at the back of the drawer opening. The core that was cut out of the box interior is a convenient source of matching wood. Cut $1/4$" off of the back of the core to get a piece that is just the correct length and nearly the right shape (Fig. 7). Sand it as necessary to get it to fit the back of the drawer opening.

12 The previous adjustment provides a good way to attach a magnet to the back of the drawer opening for a secure closure for the drawer. First drill a $1/4$" diameter hole in the fitted spacer. You may either drill all the way through the piece, or drill from the curved side to $1/32$" from the front, leaving a thin skin of wood in place on the front. You could also drill all the way through the piece and then glue a thin plug of wood to the magnet before gluing it in place. Transfer the hole location to the back of the drawer, and drill a $1/8$" deep hole there. If you are going to hide the magnet in the drawer, you will need to leave the back of the drawer a bit thicker and drill the hole deep enough to accommodate the wood plug and the magnet (Fig. 8).

FIG. 5 With the drawer assembled and sanded, you can trial-fit the assembly. Use quick clamps for holding the sides to the box body to make it easier to make the trials necessary to get a good fit. (The drawer exterior in this photo still needs to be sanded.)

13 If you are not using a spacer behind the drawer but want to use magnet closures, epoxy the magnets to the outside of the sides of the drawer, toward the back, and then glue matching magnets to the interior of the box's sides.

FIG. 6 The drawer will be smaller than the opening due to wood lost in cutting and sanding to remove saw tooth marks. You'll need to make a few adjustments to make a tight-fitting lid and drawer.

FIG. 7 The core that you cut from the box interior will be close in width and length to the filler block needed to bring the drawer even with the front of the box. Use the belt sander to shape it to fit in the back of the drawer opening.

14 The drawer will also be narrower than the body (Fig. 6), so the next fix is to power-sand the body's ends until they nearly match the width of the drawer. Leave a hair or two of clearance so the drawer will slide in smoothly.

15 The lid also will need to be sanded down to this new width, and then $1/32$" more, for clearance. Make sure to keep the ends of the lid parallel while it is being sanded. Also finish-sand the insides of the box's end pieces.

16 Cut a piece from your scrap to make a handle for the drawer. In this case, there was a little of the spalted walnut left over, so I used it to form the handle. Shape the handle with the belt sander. Drill a $1/4$" hole $1/8$" deep for the brass rod centered in the front of the drawer and in the handle, but epoxy it into the handle only. You can use the handle to open the drawer during the fitting stages.

FIG. 8 It is easy to line up the holes for the magnet closures in both the filler block (bottom) and the drawer (top, with rear at the top) before the filler block has been glued into place. You may want to disguise the magnets with thin wood veneer plugs.

17 The last adjustment is to the vertical clearance between the drawer and box body (Fig. 9). If the gap is too large, or if the wood is too brittle or hard to squeeze, glue a thin sheet of matching wood to the bottom of the drawer opening. When fitted well and carefully sanded, this repair is almost unnoticeable with most types of wood.

18 Squeeze the top part of the body down to the top of the drawer, and make marks on the end pieces to indicate where that top part needs to be during glue-up (Fig. 10). Before glue-up, do one final test with the ends clamped to

the body. See to it that the lid and drawer work well. After glue-up it will difficult to adjust the fit of either the lid or the drawer. Epoxy the brass hinge pins $11/16$" into the lid holes.

19 Lay the body of the box on its back between the jaws of parallel-jawed clamps. Have one for the bottom and one for the top of the box. Apply glue to both ends of the body, position the end pieces, and tighten the two clamps just enough to hold everything together. Check the legs to

FIG. 9 There will be a gap above the drawer no matter how careful you are. You may fill the gap with a thin sheet of wood glued to the bottom of the interior of the drawer opening and carefully sanded.

FIG. 10 An easier way to close that vertical void is to squeeze the box body until it fits the drawer, and then glue the box together. A smaller box, made with a harder wood, may not allow this much movement. In that case, use the previous fill technique.

FIG. 11 This cut was stopped just before completing the cut on the legs to show how exposed the blade is. This is dangerous, so pay attention to your hand positioning at all times.

FIG. 12 Sanding between the lid and box sides is difficult after the box is glued together. Use just one layer of sandpaper and slide it between the surfaces so you can round the hinge area reveal to match the rest of the lid.

20 After the glue dries, power-sand the exterior of the box with the drawer in place, with 60- or 80-grit to smooth all surfaces except the bottom.

21 Mark the front profile for the legs on the box using Plan A (front view). You will have to accommodate the other curve of the legs. Cut out the legs while keeping an eye focused on the location of the blade. You want the blade to run along the same plane as the previous leg cut (Fig. 11).

22 Sand the bottom and legs of the box to form. Add the finger groove with a drum sander to the front of the box to make lifting the lid easier. Sand all parts of the box to 220–grit (Fig. 12).

make sure the ends and body are aligned, and tighten that clamp to hold them in position. Squeeze the top part of the body down to the marks you made earlier with the drawer and tighten that clamp. Double-check the mating surfaces, and then fully tighten the clamps.

FINISHING

1 A tung oil and urethane topcoat was used for this box. It has become my finish of choice for most boxes. It is easy to use and leaves a nice finish. I apply it with a rag. Whenever I don't need to clean a brush, I'm happy.

2 For the far corners of the interior, I used a disposable glue brush and then wiped the surface smooth.

3 Walnut changes dramatically when finish is applied and the dusty sanded surface is replaced with the rich colors and depth in the wood. The interiors were finished first and allowed to dry (Fig. 13), providing a place to grasp the box while finishing the outside.

4 Epoxy the handle in place on the drawer, and you are done. Figure 14 shows the completed Ultimate Box.

Congratulations, you have graduated to super-advanced band saw box making!

FIG. 13 The Ultimate Box was finished with a tung oil and urethane topcoat.

FIG. 14 The finished Ultimate Box. Spalted walnut, $6^1/_2$x$4^1/_2$x$4^3/_4$".

Gallery

Now that you know how to use the tools to construct band saw boxes, you should be able to make any box you can imagine. To spur your imagination, here is a gallery of unusual and beautiful boxes, made by craftspeople from many places. Study their work to help you to get inspired to make your own variations.

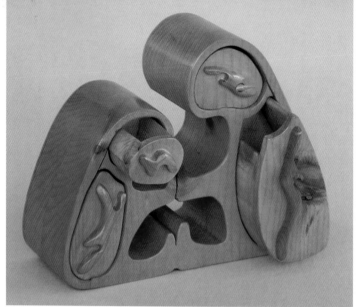

Leah and Boo Box. White pine, 9x3x7". Finished in Danish oil, followed by wax buffing. By Kathy Sawada, Kathy and Jim Sawada Wood Art, Scarborough, Ontario, Canada. Kathy's boxes have a playful bent, like this abstract interpretation of patty-cake. Her inspiration was her granddaughter, Leah, who was 3¹/₂ at the time and called her grandma "Boo."

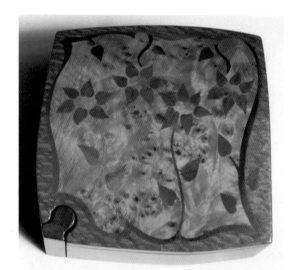

Secret Garden Box. Mahogany, with masur birch burl for the background, madrone burl petals, turtleback poplar leaves and stems, and lacewood veneer for the frame, 6x6x2³/₄". Finish is Danish oil and several coats of lacquer. By Jane Burke, Green Tree Creations, Duluth, Georgia.

Jane uses marquetry (cutting and applying veneers) to add interest to her box tops. She makes many interior compartments in her boxes.

Turned Band Saw Box. Spalted beech, 6¹/₂x3" in diameter. Finished with Watco oil under Krylon 1311 (fixative). By Tom Crabb, Richmond, Virginia. Tom wrote the original book on band saw boxes (*Making Wood Boxes with a Band Saw*, 1985, Sterling Publishing Co., Inc.), and now he has combined his passion for turning with box making to make turned band saw boxes.

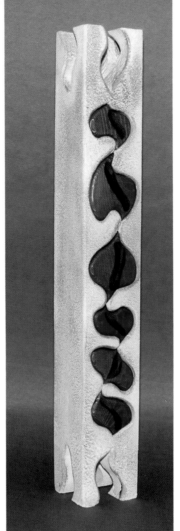

Tower Box. Cedar fence post, 4x4x20". Gel stain was used for the drawers, along with stone spray paint for the box body and clear lacquer spray finish. By Harold Engelke, St. Charles, Missouri. Harold was inspired to design and make tower boxes when he saw New York City's Twin Towers.

Cat Box. Made of four laminated redwood 1x6" fence boards. Final size: 4x3¹/₂x4". The cat intarsia was cut from western red cedar fence boards, redwood fence boards, and pine. By Keith Gudger, Soquel, California. Keith made the cat face as a separate intarsia project (sections of different woods cut and shaped then reassembled), and then added it to the front of the box. The finish was Danish oil on the box and polyurethane varnish on the intarsia.

Jensen's Jewelry Box. Cherry, 10x5x6", finished with hand-rubbed tung oil. By Chris and Donna Jensen, Wildwood Crafters, Columbia, Kentucky. Chris and Donna have created some wonderful designs. The knobs were turned on a lathe.

Tree of Life Box. Pine, 13x5x14". Finished with an alcohol stain and lacquer. By Jeff Trag, Jeff Trag Boxes, Jalisco, Mexico.

Metric Equivalents Chart

(to the nearest mm and 0.1 cm)

inches	mm	cm	inches	mm	cm
$^1/_8$	3	0.3	14	356	35.6
$^1/_4$	6	0.6	15	381	38.1
$^3/_8$	10	1.0	16	406	40.6
$^1/_2$	13	1.3	17	432	43.2
$^5/_8$	16	1.6	18	457	45.7
$^3/_4$	19	1.9	19	483	48.3
$^7/_8$	22	2.2	20	508	50.8
1	25	2.5	21	533	53.3
$1^1/_4$	32	3.2	22	559	55.9
$1^1/_2$	38	3.8	23	584	58.4
$1^3/_4$	44	4.4	24	610	61.0
2	51	5.1	25	635	63.5
$2^1/_2$	64	6.4	26	660	66.0
3	76	7.6	27	686	68.6
$3^1/_2$	89	8.9	28	711	71.1
4	102	10.2	29	737	73.7
$4^1/_2$	114	11.4	30	762	76.2
5	127	12.7	31	787	78.7
6	152	15.2	32	813	81.3
7	178	17.8	33	838	83.8
8	203	20.3	34	864	86.4
9	229	22.9	35	889	88.9
10	254	25.4	36	914	91.4
11	279	27.9	37	940	94.0
12	305	30.5	38	965	96.5
13	330	33.0	39	991	99.1

Index